New Top Technologies Every Librarian Needs to Know

NOTE THE W P LIBRARY
EMPLOYEE'S ARTICLE
PAGE 107 & 260

ALA Neal-Schuman purchases fund advocacy, awareness, and accreditation programs for library professionals worldwide.

New Top Technologies Every Librarian Needs to Know

A LITA Guide

Edited by
Kenneth J. Varnum

CHICAGO 2019

KENNETH J. VARNUM is the senior program manager at the University of Michigan Library. In this role, Ken is responsible for the library's discovery systems, document delivery and link resolver interfaces, and the library's evolving and emerging analytics infrastructure. He received his master's degrees from the University of Michigan's School of Information and Center for Russian and East European Studies and his bachelor of arts from Grinnell College. Over his two decades working with public-facing technology in academic, corporate, and special libraries, he has gained a deep appreciation and understanding of the need to tailor systems and interfaces to the local user base. A frequent speaker and author, Ken presents and writes about discovery systems, library analytics, and technology. In addition to numerous articles and chapters, he wrote *Drupal in Libraries* (2012), compiled the *LITA Guide The Top Technologies Every Librarian Needs to Know* and *Exploring Discovery: The Front Door to Your Library's Licensed and Digitized Content* (2016), and edited Lorcan Dempsey's *The Network Reshapes the Library* (2014). Contact Ken through his website at www.varnum.org or on Twitter at @varnum.

© 2019 by the American Library Association.

Extensive effort has gone into ensuring the reliability of the information in this book; however, the publisher makes no warranty, express or implied, with respect to the material contained herein.

ISBNs
978-0-8389-1782-4 (paper)
978-0-8389-1803-6 (PDF)
978-0-8389-1805-0 (ePub)
978-0-8389-1804-3 (Kindle)

Library of Congress Cataloging-in-Publication Data

Names: Varnum, Kenneth J., 1967– editor.
Title: New top technologies every librarian needs to know / edited by Kenneth J. Varnum.
Description: Chicago : ALA Neal-Schuman, An imprint of the American Library Association, 2019. | Series: A LITA guide | Includes index.
Identifiers: LCCN 2018043367 | ISBN 9780838917824 (print : alk. paper) | ISBN 9780838918036 (pdf) | ISBN 9780838918050 (epub) | ISBN 9780838918043 (kindle)
Subjects: LCSH: Libraries—Information technology. | Libraries and the Internet. | Digital libraries.
Classification: LCC Z678.9 .N455 2019 | DDC 027.00285—dc23 LC record available at https://lccn.loc.gov/2018043367

Book design in Berkeley and Avenir. Cover image © Adobe Stock.

♾ This paper meets the requirements of ANSI/NISO Z39.48-1992 (Permanence of Paper).

Printed in the United States of America

23 22 21 20 19   5 4 3 2 1

*I dedicate this book to Elliott and Milo,
who change even faster than the technologies
that they are growing up with.*

Contents

Preface xi

PART I
Data

1 Linked Open Data in Libraries   3
Cliff Landis

2 Everything Is Online
Libraries and the Internet of Things   17
Matthew Connolly

3 Link Rot, Reference Rot, and Link Resolvers   29
Justin M. White

4 Engaging Libraries with Web Archives   43
Todd Suomela

PART II
Services

5 Privacy-Protection Technology Tools
Libraries and Librarians as Users, Contributors,
and Advocates   59
Monica Maceli

6 Data for Discovery   75
Julia Bauder

Contents

7 Libraries and Information Visualization
Application and Value 89
Elizabeth Joan Kelly

8 Virtual Reality: Out of This World 107
Austin Olney

PART III
Repositories and Access

9 Digital Exhibits to Digital Humanities
Expanding the Digital Libraries Portfolio 123
Daniel Johnson and Mark Dehmlow

10 Digital Repositories
A Systems Perspective 137
Joshua A. Westgard, Kate Dohe, David Durden, and Joseph Koivisto

11 Digital Repositories 153
Jessica Wagner Webster

12 Maximizing Assets and Access through Digital Publishing
Opportunities and Implications for Special Collections 167
Ellen Engseth and Marguerite Ragnow

PART IV
Interoperability

13 Impact of International Image Interoperability Framework (IIIF) on Digital Repositories 181
Kelli Babcock and Rachel Di Cresce

14 Embracing Embeddedness with Learning Tools Interoperability (LTI) 197
Lauren Magnuson

15 Bots and the Library
Exploring New Possibilities for Automation
and Engagement *211*
Jeanette Claire Sewell

16 Machine Learning for Libraries *223*
Alan Darnell

17 Mobile Technology *241*
Gordon F. Xu and Jin Xiu Guo

About the Contributors   257

Index   263

Preface

The original *Top Technologies Every Librarian Needs to Know* was published in 2014. Similar to what this volume's authors were asked to do, the authors of the 2014 edition were tasked with thinking about technologies that were relatively new then (either new in general or perhaps somewhat well-established but still novel to libraries) and forecast what libraries would be like in three to five years when that technology had become part of the landscape. Now that we have reached that five-year horizon (2018) from when the first edition's authors were writing (in 2013), it seems a good time to review the predictions from the first set of chapters and, with a different group of authors, take a gaze into 2018's near-term future with a new set.

A LOOK BACK

The original book focused on these broad trends: content and technology convergence, augmented reality, cloud-based library systems, discovery systems, web services, text mining, large-scale digital libraries, and open hardware. Some of these technologies are still being adopted, whereas others have become firmly entrenched in the routine of libraries. For example, text mining, large-scale digital libraries, and cloud-based library systems have become core to what many institutions do. The race to the cloud for many back-end (and user-facing) services continues apace. Discovery layers on top of whatever suite of resources a library offers its clientele are still common; the desire to provide access to the breadth of a library's content is still strong—but with increasing recognition that one-size-fits-all discovery interfaces do not necessarily meet all the needs of all the users.

Other technologies are still on the rise, with potentials constantly being explored. Augmented and virtual reality technologies described in 2014 are now becoming technologically possible as the tools to support them become cheaper. Content and technology convergence, in which users bring their own desires for how they wish to consume the content they seek and libraries can offer multiple formats to meet those needs, is still actively developing. Open hardware and the Internet of Things are still tantalizingly at hand but not quite commonplace.

A LOOK AHEAD

Like the original volume, chapters in *New Top Technologies Every Librarian Needs to Know* are structured around a rough topical outline, but authors were free to adopt a style they wanted. In each of this book's chapters, you will find a description of a technology or trend as it exists in the world in early 2018; how it is being used in libraries, archives, or museums by its early adopters; and what the future will look like if, as the authors envision, the technology is widely adopted in the next three to five years.

The book is organized into four parts, each looking at a broad swathe of library activity: "Data," "Services," "Repositories and Access," and "Interoperability." Part 1 explores linked open data, the Internet of Things, and the criticality of web archiving for the medium- and long-term preservation of the scholarly record. Part 2 explores ways that libraries are beginning to enhance their offerings to their particular patron base. The chapters cover patron privacy protection, data and data visualization, and virtual reality.

Part 3 explores how the information age will continue to reshape the ways libraries support scholarship. The chapters discuss digital humanities, digital repositories, and digital publishing. Finally, part 4 covers standards (IIIF and LTI), interoperability of content and tools, and the ever-expanding functionality of mobile devices for access.

Kenneth J. Varnum
Ann Arbor, Michigan
January 2019

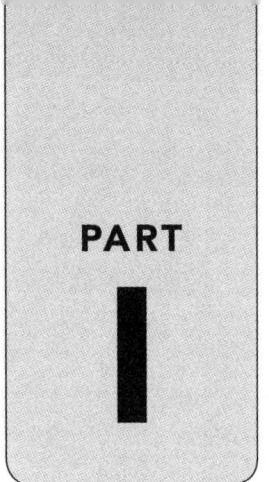

Data

Chapter One

Linked Open Data in Libraries

Cliff Landis

Most library users will interact with linked data about your library before they ever interact with the library itself. If a user does a web search on Google for your library's name, they will see a summary of the library's vital information displayed in a "knowledge panel" to the right of their search results. This box displays information pulled from Google's proprietary Knowledge Graph, a specialized database of aggregated facts.

If your user prefers Wikipedia as a starting point, a quick search for the library will pull up a Wikipedia page that includes an "infobox" that again is populated with linked data facts. These were initially pulled to Wikidata, the linked open-data knowledgebase used to tie together facts across Wikimedia projects and languages. Under the menu of every Wikipedia page is a link to the Wikidata item for that page. On that Wikidata page, you can add more details about your library or correct erroneous information (with proper secondary source citations, of course). Unlike

PART I: Data

Google's Knowledge Graph (linked proprietary data), Wikidata facts can be edited and reused under a Creative Commons license (linked *open* data).

But linked open data can do much more than display facts in handy little boxes. It also connects content across systems, opens up content for reuse, disambiguates similar concepts, creates relationships among data sets, and makes semantic searching possible. At its most basic, linked open data is a group of technologies and standards that enables

- writing factual statements in a machine-readable format,
- linking those factual statements to one another, and
- publishing those statements on the web with an open license for anyone to access.

For example, we know that *Harry Potter and the Deathly Hallows* is a fantasy book written by J. K. Rowling and published on July 21, 2007. That sentence can be broken up into simple three-part statements, or triples, consisting of a subject, predicate, and object:

Harry Potter and the Deathly Hallows -> has format -> book

Harry Potter and the Deathly Hallows -> has literary genre -> fantasy literature

Harry Potter and the Deathly Hallows -> was written by -> J. K. Rowling

Harry Potter and the Deathly Hallows -> has publication date -> July 21, 2007

Each fact triple describes how two concepts are connected by a relationship. Triples are stored in specialized databases variously called graphs, triplestores, or knowledge bases. But we don't need to limit these facts to bibliographic information; most information can be expressed in this three-part format:

J. K. Rowling -> has place of birth -> Yate

Yate -> has county -> Gloucestershire

Gloucestershire -> has country -> England

J. K. Rowling -> graduated college from -> University of Exeter

With these triples linked together, we can quickly answer very specific questions like "Which fantasy authors born in Gloucestershire County in England went to University of Exeter?" A semantic query like this uses the meaning of relationships between concepts to provide a results list. You can try out your own semantic searches like this one using examples on Wikidata's Query Service (https://query.wikidata.org).

Chapter One: Linked Open Data in Libraries

The example triples above are human readable, but for them to be machine readable, each part must be represented by a web address (a Uniform Resource Identifier, or URI)—in this case from DBpedia, one of the earliest large-scale triplestores.

Subject	Predicate	Object
Harry Potter and the Deathly Hallows	Has literary genre	Fantasy literature
http://dbpedia.org/page/Harry_Potter_and_the_Deathly_Hallows	http://dbpedia.org/ontology/literaryGenre	http://dbpedia.org/page/Fantasy_literature

The subject and object are both things or concepts (often called entities) represented by their own pages, whereas the predicate is stored in an ontology, a set of definitions for different types of relationships. Collections of these URIs (both entities and ontologies) are called vocabularies. Because each URI stands on its own, you can combine entities and relationships from vocabularies across the web to connect information—that's what puts the *linked* in linked open data and makes it possible to create meaning across different triple databases. It's easy to show that an entity in one database is the same as an entity in a different database using the "sameAs" predicate from the Web Ontology Language (OWL) vocabulary.

Subject	Predicate	Object
Harry Potter and the Deathly Hallows (in DBpedia)	Is the same as	Harry Potter and the Deathly Hallows (in Wikidata)
http://dbpedia.org/page/Harry_Potter_and_the_Deathly_Hallows	www.w3.org/2002/07/owl#sameAs	www.wikidata.org/wiki/Q46758

These equivalence connections can be made manually by humans (such as editing Wikidata) or matched in large batches automatically using data tools like OpenRefine (http://openrefine.org). Either way, connections must be validated by humans because we can differentiate nuances of meaning that are lost on computers. Making these "sameAs" connections between databases makes it possible to connect the same concept across multiple languages and across multiple sites, dissolving information silos among different systems. This decentralized approach to metadata management also means that openly publishing locally rich metadata records can potentially help users accessing completely different systems.

Of course, to break down these metadata silos, the information has to be accessible and free to use—this is why the *open* in linked open data is so important.

PART I: Data

By releasing metadata and datasets with open licenses, other users can transform and reuse the data, making new connections possible. Tim Berners-Lee suggests a five-star scheme for linked open data, and it begins with open licensing (http://5stardata.info/en/). This orientation toward openness and providing access aligns well with the ethos of libraries and archives.

But as librarians and archivists know, maintaining open access to information isn't a one-shot effort. Records that are enriched with linked open data must be maintained by metadata experts to ensure that the connections persist over time. This is one of the commitments that cultural heritage institutions make when they create persistent online resources of any kind; linked data URIs, just like digital object identifiers (DOIs), need to be maintained to ensure that connections among systems don't break.

One barrier to linked open data adoption by librarians is the alphabet soup of technologies and standards that make it all possible. There are free online glossaries describing the multitude of linked data and semantic web terms, but for the purpose of this chapter, only a few need to be defined. First is the Resource Description Framework (RDF), a set of specifications from the World Wide Web Consortium that explains what a triple is and how triples should be connected and queried. RDF was originally designed as a data model for metadata of web-based resources but has grown to encompass all types of metadata. It is paired with the Extensible Markup Language (XML) to create RDF/XML, the first standard format for writing linked data triples. XML is a versatile language for writing machine-readable content and is used widely in libraries and archives for publishing and exchanging metadata.

Although RDF/XML was the frontrunner for implementing linked data, other ways of expressing RDF triples have been created, including RDFa, N-Triples, N-Quads, Turtle, TriG, and JSON-LD (www.w3.org/TR/rdf11-primer/). Notably, JavaScript Object Notation for Linked Data (JSON-LD) has seen wider adoption in recent years because it is more concise and human readable than RDF/XML. Once linked data is published, it is accessed remotely using the SPARQL query language. (SPARQL is a recursive acronym that means "SPARQL Protocol and RDF Query Language" and is pronounced *sparkle*.) You can see SPARQL in action by using the Wikidata Query Service mentioned above.

Technical jargon aside, it is important to point out that linked data is fundamentally changing how people will access information in the future. To date, users have had to sift through dozens or hundreds of documents retrieved in keyword searches to find the nuggets of information that they need. However, users in

Chapter One: Linked Open Data in Libraries

the near future will have rich facets to search and additional context to discover and visualize information. For example, history students studying Renaissance dragomans (diplomatic interpreter-translators) can now browse by the dragomans' languages or professional titles thanks to the linked open data records in the Dragoman Renaissance Research Platform from the University of Toronto Scarborough (http://dragomans.digitalscholarship.utsc.utoronto.ca). This platform also provides visualizations of the geographic distributions of dragomans and a timeline of their careers, but because the data are openly accessible, users can access the database to create their own visualizations. Although coding visualizations from scratch is too difficult most users, tools are becoming available that allow users to explore linked open data and create their own visualizations with little technical knowledge. For example, RelFinder (www.visualdataweb.org/relfinder.php) shows connections between different linked open data points in DBpedia. A quick search of J. K. Rowling and Stephen King shows that both authors are influenced by author Michael J. Sullivan, while a search for gothic fiction and fantasy literature shows a cluster of books and authors that bridge those genera.

Linked data promises to unlock information from its container and break it down into interlinked facts, allowing users to discover and interact with resources in new ways. But like all new technologies, linked data will come with its own challenges and problems and will amplify older problems that librarians have always dealt with (e.g., verifiability, contextualization, interpretation, and politicization of information). However, even with these problems, linked data will reshape the landscape of information seeking and retrieval. Thankfully, librarians and archivists are hard at work staying abreast of this change and approaching these challenges head-on.

LARGE-SCALE LINKED DATA IN LIBRARYLAND

Large university libraries, national libraries, and library consortia have been the frontrunners in laying the groundwork for library linked data in two ways: by developing data models and schema for representing resource information as linked data and by publishing and aggregating resource metadata as linked data.

Library resource description is undergoing a dramatic transformation as new models, standards, and schemata are produced. As these tools are being tested in the field, they are evolving to meet the practical needs of the library community. For example, the Bibliographic Framework Initiative (BIBFRAME) from the Library of Congress aims to create a new alternative to the MARC 21 formats

PART I: Data

and, more broadly, to expand the way that resource description happens in the networked environment of linked data (www.loc.gov/bibframe/). After its initial pilot in 2015, experiments and community feedback led to further development, resulting in BIBFRAME 2.0 being released in 2016.[1] Experiments with both versions are available to explore, like BIBFRAME 1.0 implemented at the University of Illinois at Urbana–Champaign Library (http://sif.library.illinois.edu/bibframe/) and BIBFRAME 2.0 at the US Army Corps of Engineers Research and Development Center Library (http://engineerradcc.library.link/). BIBFRAME is building on the momentum created by Resource Description and Access (RDA), the international cataloging standard designed to replace AACR2 (www.rda-rsc.org).[2] RDA was created with linked data principles in mind and published in 2010, and in 2013 it was adopted by several national libraries. Support for both old and new tools will be needed for years to come, as transitions will happen slowly and carefully.

In both of the above BIBFRAME examples, bibliographic records are enriched with information from external RDF vocabularies. Some of these are smaller vocabularies, such as licenses from Creative Commons Rights Expression Language (http://creativecommons.org/ns) and metadata classes from DCMI Metadata Terms (http://purl.org/dc/terms). Larger vocabularies are now being provided by national and international organizations, such as authority data from the Virtual International Authority File (http://viaf.org) and Library of Congress Linked Data Service (www.dublincore.org/documents/dcmi-terms/). VIAF aims to provide linked data connections among authority records at national libraries, providing a global source for disambiguating person, organization, and place names. While most contributing members are national libraries, you can also find records from other linked data initiatives such as Wikidata and the International Standard Name Identifier International Agency (http://isni.org). The connections among these international metadata initiatives mean that a metadata expert can correct an error in one system (such as disambiguating the two Robert W. Woodruff Libraries in Atlanta, Georgia) and see that correction cascade to catalogs around the world as new linked open data connections are made. This type of "long-tail" effort can leverage local knowledge to enrich and repair records on a global scale.

The scope of the Library of Congress Linked Data Service is broader than VIAF, as it encompasses both general authority and subject terms as well as subject-specific terms for areas like children's literature, art, and music. Additionally, the Library of Congress provides vocabularies for preservation metadata, languages, and formats. This has been no small task, since building the infrastructure for

Chapter One: Linked Open Data in Libraries

linked open data requires publishing machine-readable metadata alongside the human-readable metadata that already exists for millions of records.

Linked open data is being leveraged to improve access and discovery at national and international scales. Europeana Collections (http://europeana.eu) is a search engine portal that aggregates more than fifty-four million metadata records from across Europe. Aggregating this number of records from a variety of sources creates challenges, as the metadata from different libraries needs to be mapped to a central data model (the Europeana Data Model, or EDM). A similar project in the United States, the Digital Public Library of America (https://dp.la/) has created its own Metadata Application Profile (MAP) modeled on Europeana's EDM. DPLA and Europeana have also collaborated to create RightsStatements.org, a linked data website with a set of twelve standardized rights statements that can be freely used to declare the copyright and reuse status of digital cultural heritage objects. By mapping these data models to an increasing number of metadata standards, combined with standardized rights statement, Europeana and DPLA are opening the door for a truly global search of cultural heritage resources. However, to take part in this opportunity for increased discovery and access, libraries have to dedicate time and energy to cleaning up resource metadata and making it ready for a global audience. As stated in DPLA's MAP (http://dp.la/info/map), "Consider how your data will work in a global context next to the data of thousands of other institutions in DPLA. Will John Brown in Australia understand that your geographic location 'Washington' is different than the State of Washington or Washington County in Wisconsin?" In practice, metadata experts at each institution will need to make sure that their local metadata records align to the larger metadata profile (i.e., the title field contains titles and not dates). Additionally, metadata experts will need to review linked open data URIs in their records (both manually created and automatically generated ones) to ensure that ambiguities are avoided. This extra work will pay off by making the library's records more globally findable, but it will also allow those records to be included in linked open data apps.

Because many users find library resources through public search engines, it is important for libraries and library consortia to create connections to the linked data efforts of large technology companies. Schema.org and the Open Graph protocol (http://ogp.me) are two examples of linked data projects initiated by tech giants that have since been released as open source schema. For consortial aggregation like Europeana Collections and DPLA, it is important to have resource metadata mapped to these larger efforts so that search engine results can point to library resources.³ Otherwise, there is a risk of libraries creating larger collective information silos rather than breaking those silos down.

Unfortunately, large general schemata like Schema.org often do not begin with the depth necessary to fully describe library resource metadata. The Online Computer Library Center (OCLC) addressed this problem by building on the work of Schema.org to create an extension, BiblioGraph.net. This extension included library-centric vocabulary terms such as *agent, microform, newspaper, publicationSeries*, and *thesis*—terms that are more descriptive than "schema:Person" or "schema:CreativeWork." Schema.org has since added a bibliographic extension into its schemata, which pairs well with OCLC's larger effort to include linked data on their bibliographic records in WorldCat. Since 2012, users have been able to view linked data in WorldCat by clicking on "Linked Data" at the bottom of each bibliographic record. Meanwhile, machine-readable linked data have been published at the same URI with different formats available at different extensions (i.e., http://worldcat.org/oclc/155131850.rdf, http://worldcat.org/oclc/155131850.jsonld). This parallel publishing allows for both human- and machine-readable metadata at the same address.⁴ All of these efforts are the latest in the long history of libraries working to improve access by normalizing, enhancing, and connecting library resource metadata. Although the medium of cataloging has changed from print catalogs to cards, to electronic records to linked open data, the aim has been the same—namely, to make information accessible to users. Linked open data takes this to a new level by publishing individual components of a bibliographic record in a machine-readable format, making new forms of user discovery and collection analysis possible.

EXTRA-SPECIAL COLLECTIONS

In the information ecosystem, bibliographic metadata is just the tip of the iceberg. Having copies of the same book in multiple libraries means that metadata about that book could be shared to improve access. But what happens when resources are truly unique? How do we make cultural heritage materials more discoverable? Archivists are familiar with this barrier to access, but experiments with linked open data in archives and special collections are showing the potential for new methods of discovery—ones that shine light on the relationships and contexts implicit within archival materials.

At the University of Nevada, Las Vegas (UNLV), Cory Lampert and Silvia Southwick led a team to add linked data to the UNLV University Libraries' Southern Nevada Jewish Heritage Project. This linked data initiative led to the creation of the

Chapter One: Linked Open Data in Libraries

Jewish Heritage Project Navigator, a pilot search and browse interface (http://lod.library.unlv.edu/nav/jhp/). By using external relationship vocabularies to connect people, organizations, subjects, and materials, the UNLV team was able to create an interface that allows users to browse the collections in a nonlinear way. For example, connections between family and community members are described using predicates like "parentOf," "childOf," "neighborOf," and so on. This is in turn connected to materials, creating a rich context for users to explore the project's digital collection. This type of exploratory interface will become much more common in the next five years as libraries and archives seek to enhance their collections. To date, relevance-ranked keyword searches were the best researchers could hope for. But with the advent of linked open data in libraries and archives, researchers will have immediate access to additional contexts that can save both time and energy when exploring digital collections.

The Linked Jazz project (http://linkedjazz.org) takes this same work a step further by using linked open data to connect the relationships in the jazz community described in oral histories. These relationships come alive in the Linked Jazz Network Visualization Tool, where users can explore how various jazz artists, producers, and educators connect (http://linkedjazz.org/network/). This visualization is possible because Cristina Pattuelli and her team of researchers took transcripts from fifty-four oral histories and identified more than nine thousand entity names through automated and human analysis. This list of names was then connected to other linked open data vocabularies like DBpedia, VIAF, and MusicBrainz (http://musicbrainz.org). However, because some of the people mentioned in the oral histories were not in any of the other vocabularies, the Linked Jazz team had to publish (a.k.a. "mint") their own linked open data URIs to represent those people.[5] As more archival institutions mint their own URIs and connect them, it will become possible to see relationships within collections, across collections, and even across archival institutions.

This last kind of connection is particularly needed, as researchers often have difficulty locating materials about the same person or organization held at separate archives. The Social Networks and Archival Context (SNAC) Cooperative aims to help solve this problem through its website (http://n2t.net/ark:/99166/w6gk06z2). For example, 318 different library collections have materials about the influential and prolific activist W. E. B. Du Bois (http://snaccooperative.org/view/67874817). By harvesting metadata records at archival institutions, the SNAC website makes it possible to identify records connected to Du Bois. Like libraries, linked open data in archives and special collections is made possible because of metadata standards and schemata. Archives have been using XML to create Encoded Archival

PART I: Data

Description (EAD) finding aids since 1998, and more recent creations like SNAC make use of the Encoded Archival Context-Corporate Bodies, Persons and Families (EAC-CPF) standard.[6] By publishing standardized authority records for entities, new linked open data connections—and therefore new methods of discovery—become possible.

THE FUTURE: MOVING FROM CODE TO TOOLS

Publishing and integrating linked open data is the future trend for cultural heritage organizations, but until recently, taking advantage of these standards required planning a discrete project and hiring programmers to do the coding. But library vendors have also been paying attention to emerging standards and schemata, so tools are now being designed with linked data standards in mind. It will take the availability of both open source and proprietary linked open data library tools before broad adoption can happen.

Archives and special collections have seen the popular digital exhibit tool Omeka launch a new, completely rewritten version of the tool in late 2017 dubbed Omeka S (http://omeka.org/s). This version includes the ability to integrate with external vocabularies, create custom vocabularies, publish linked data URIs, and use templates designed to work with DPLA's MAP data model. There is a plug-in for an International Image Interoperability Framework (IIIF) server to assist in processing and sharing images (see chapter 13 for more on this framework). Additionally, Omeka S administrators can install plug-ins to connect to other popular tools like Fedora 4 and DSpace.

Institutional repositories had a linked data overhaul in 2015, when DSpace version 5 came out with linked data capabilities, and that trend has continued with version 6 (http://dspace.org). It is important for scholars, researchers, and academic librarians to make research and its associated metadata as widely available as possible. By including RDF metadata and a SPARQL endpoint, DSpace provides researchers with the ability to increase the findability and impact of their research while also opening up repositories for large-scale data analysis.

Digital repository vendors are also adding linked data capabilities to their tools. Since Fedora is the backbone of several digital repository programs, its inclusion of linked data capabilities with the Fedora 4 release had a large impact on future development of tools like Islandora (http://islandora.ca/CLAW) and Samvera

Chapter One: Linked Open Data in Libraries

(http://samvera.org). Fedora 4 also supports the Portland Common Data Model (PCDM), a model for sharing content in digital repositories and institutional repositories (http://pcdm.org).[7]

The standards and technologies at the core of linked open data are being integrated into an increasing number of library schemata and software; as these tools become more available, the entire landscape of information seeking and retrieval will change.

SCI-FI SEARCH

Through the early research into linked open data by the projects mentioned earlier, we're already beginning to see how linked open data will impact libraries. The discovery and contextualization of information are being reshaped, and new possibilities for research are becoming broadly available.

In the near future, resource discovery will take on new dimensions for users and researchers alike. Context clues will be scattered throughout bibliographic records as libraries pull in biographical information from public databases to tell students about the backgrounds of authors. Underrepresented populations will get new levels of exposure, as users will be able to narrow down authors and subjects by new facets enabled by richer metadata provided through linked open data, like with Stacy Allison-Cassin and Dan Scott's pilot project to improve visibility for Canadian musicians.[8] We can imagine other examples where students will be able to limit search results by an author's gender, allowing women's studies and queer studies students to quickly locate research by women or nonbinary authors. With large sets of archival metadata online, historians will be able to study changes in the patterns of human communication and behavior as publications, correspondence, and photography open for analysis in aggregate.

For public domain materials, there is no need to limit linked open data to bibliographic records. Text mining and machine learning can be put to work to unlock tabular data from old books and archival manuscripts and publish them online as linked open data. Further in the future, we could see historical weather patterns published from the daily diaries of manuscript collections, helping us study the direction of climate change. Social justice advocates could query historical demographic information en masse, revealing patterns of disenfranchisement that have previously been hidden from view in scattered tables and maps. Special collections and archives will be publishing their own locally controlled vocabularies

PART I: Data

and ontologies and connecting them across institutions. This work will require metadata experts to wrangle messy data sets, connect them, and maintain those connections over time. But because of this effort, the lives of historical figures who have previously been passed over will find new light as authority records are connected across the world.

The next five years will be both exciting and a tad chaotic for libraries. Linked open data has slowly matured over the seventeen years since the concept was first introduced. But now that linked data is entering mainstream use in libraries, we will need to contend with larger problems that have been easy to overlook in the past. Disambiguation will require renewed urgency and care as information professionals connect resources together. The importance of metadata standardization will only increase as we link our data together, and gray areas of interpretation and bias in description will need refreshed scrutiny. As libraries start minting new URIs to represent resources, we must make a long-term commitment to preventing link rot (see chapter 3 for more). The library community will need to balance data models that describe library resources in depth while also connecting to outside search engines; we must accept that some tools will work and others will go the way of dodo birds and Betamax tapes. Within all these challenges, however, are opportunities to further express our core value of helping people connect with the information they need.

Experiments with linked open data in libraries are giving us glimpses of a tantalizing future where users have increased access and context for interacting with information. But even more, building the infrastructure of library linked open data will make information available for remixing and reusing in ways that we can't yet imagine. Those new uses will be discovered not only by librarians and archivists but by the users we serve, making linked open data a top technology that every librarian needs to know.

NOTES

1. Sally H. McCallum, "BIBFRAME Development," *JLIS.it* 8 (September 2017): 71–85, https://doi.org/10.4403/jlis.it-12415.
2. Karen Coyle, "Mistakes Have Been Made," filmed November 24, 2015, at Semantic Web in Libraries, Hamburg, Germany, www.youtube.com/watch?v=d0CMuxZsAIY, 37:30.
3. Richard Wallis, Antoine Isaac, Valentine Charles, and Hugo Manguinhas, "Recommendations for the Application of Schema.Org to Aggregated Cultural Heritage Metadata to Increase Relevance and Visibility to Search Engines: The

Case of Europeana," *Code4Lib Journal* 36 (April 2017), http://journal.code4lib.org/articles/12330.

4. Carol Jean Godby, Shenghui Wang, and Jeffrey K. Mixter, *Library Linked Data in the Cloud: OCLC's Experiments with New Models of Resource Description*, Synthesis Lectures on the Semantic Web: Theory and Technology, vol. 4, no. 5 (Williston, VT: Morgan & Claypool, 2015), https://doi.org/10.2200/S00620ED1V01Y201412WBE012.

5. M. Cristina Pattuelli, Karen Hwang, and Matthew Miller, "Accidental Discovery, Intentional Inquiry: Leveraging Linked Data to Uncover the Women of Jazz," *Digital Scholarship in the Humanities* 32, no. 4 (2017): 918–24, https://doi.org/10.1093/llc/fqw047.

6. Hilary K. Thorsen and M. Cristina Pattuelli, "Linked Open Data and the Cultural Heritage Landscape," in *Linked Data for Cultural Heritage*, ed. Ed Jones and Michele Seikel (Chicago: ALA Editions, 2016), 5.

7. Erik T. Mitchell, "Library Linked Data: Early Activity and Development," *Library Technology Reports* 52, no. 1 (January 2016): 24.

8. Stacy Allison-Cassin and Dan Scott, "Wikidata: A Platform for Your Library's Linked Open Data," *Code4Lib Journal* 40 (May 2018), http://journal.code4lib.org/articles/13424.

Chapter Two

Everything Is Online
Libraries and the Internet of Things

Matthew Connolly

Internet of Things (IoT) is a blanket term for the concept of uniquely identifying real-world items and networking them together so that software systems can act on them in different ways. Put another way, it involves the connection of physical objects to the Internet. On the face of it, that might not sound very exciting—until you realize that with today's technology, pretty much anything can be Internet enabled. And if it can be networked, it probably already has been. Toasters, egg trays, toothbrushes, farm equipment, security cameras, temperature sensors, location beacons, clothing, conference name tags, programmable buttons, activity trackers, GPS tracking tags, "intelligent assistants" like the Amazon Echo, and many, many more devices can be obtained today with built-in Internet connectivity. And it doesn't end there; "connection to the Internet" includes passive objects, such as individual books, that are tracked by an Internet-connected system.

Many of the more frivolous IoT devices are the result of a perceived gold rush by manufacturers. However, what remains after eliminating those from consideration

PART I: Data

is a large array of useful, potentially life-changing technologies that are already finding their way into people's everyday lives—in homes, workplaces, businesses, vehicles, and yes, libraries as well. Like it or not, the Internet is becoming embedded throughout our environment. Technically inclined homeowners who aren't tempted by networked toothbrushes are investing instead in home-automation products, where disparate, "smart" light bulbs, outlets, thermostats, and sensors can be linked together and orchestrated by a "home" app from Apple, Google, or Amazon. Stores are using iBeacons to lure passersby inside with special sales broadcasted to individual smartphones, and some, such as Seattle's Amazon Go grocery store, are experimenting with self-checkout systems enabled by IoT devices.[1] Networked GPS trackers on a car, train, or bus can be used in conjunction with an app to predict when the next vehicle will arrive to pick up passengers. And libraries are doing all sorts of things: using the Amazon Echo to respond to verbal catalog searches, using Internet-connected sensors to monitor the availability of public spaces or study rooms, gathering metrics on usage of services, providing navigation within library stacks and guiding patrons to the exact shelf location of a book, and enabling self-checkout for items tagged with radio-frequency identification (RFID) chips.

The challenge today is not to find Internet-enabled technologies to use but rather to discern how to use and connect them into systems that bring real value to the work of librarianship and the services that libraries offer to patrons. This is a great opportunity for imaginative, creative thinking. All the tools are in place. Even if a library isn't inclined to invest in devices that have built-in connectivity, a technically inclined librarian or library worker can use a microcontroller like the Arduino or a microcomputer like the Raspberry Pi to network all sorts of things. And a variety of online services, like If This Then That (IFTTT), let users create automated workflows based on the input from IoT devices. By adopting these tools wisely, libraries can offer a variety of exciting new and enhanced services to their users.

IOT TECHNOLOGY

The term *Internet of Things* was coined in 1999 by Kevin Ashton, who was then working on RFID technology at MIT's Auto-ID Center.[2] RFID was a key technology in the original concept of the IoT. The development of tiny, passive RFID "tags" that could be embedded into almost any physical object for a few cents apiece made it feasible to uniquely identify any number of such objects in a given system. A passive RFID tag uses no power, requires no batteries or connections, and can withstand a fair amount of abuse. Each tag stores a small amount of data (e.g., a serial or catalog number, a status code, etc.) that can be read or changed by a scanning device. In commercial and industrial applications, RFID has already been implemented on a massive scale and used to track inventories, shipment routes, and expiration dates. RFID tags have also found their way into passports, credit cards, and "smart" personal ID cards. The data stored on an RFID tag varies from application to application, but a standard for identifiers exists in Auto-ID's Electronic Product Code (EPC).[3] In addition to physical tags and scanners, RFID systems need software that can make use of the data the tags provide and act on it in useful ways. There is nothing exotic about such software, though; once an RFID tag is scanned, its contents can be utilized by a software program like any other piece of data.

While the tagging and unique identification of physical objects is crucial to the IoT concept, that aspect of the IoT has been overtaken in recent years by the explosive growth of Internet-connected electronic devices, which could be said to form the second wave of the IoT. This growth is a natural result of the relentless pace of computer miniaturization. Just as computers themselves have shrunk from room-sized calculation machines to devices that can be worn on a wrist, so also the specific electronic components that enable communication with the Internet can now be squeezed into the tiniest corner of a tiny circuit board. As consumers have grown to expect all their devices and gadgets to provide online connectivity and respond to one another, device manufacturers have answered by including such functionality in just about anything they produce—in some cases, "just because."

Traditional computers have an inherent advantage for the IoT's principle of unique identification: any networked computer already has such an identifier in the form of an IP address. And network-enabled devices that don't come in the form of traditional computers—a "smart" thermostat, for example—by necessity already include the software required to translate whatever data or input it may provide into a usable form and to transmit that information out across the network. Thus they're a natural fit for the Internet of Things—even if their utility is rather dubious in some cases.

As an example, home automation is a growing consumer market for IoT devices. Home-automation technology has been around for decades, but the ability to easily network and control a set of connected devices has greatly enhanced its appeal. These days, "smart" home devices—light bulbs, thermostats, door locks, security sensors, cameras, smoke alarms, temperature and humidity sensors, power-usage monitors, and so on—have started to appear in the homes of casual users. Coupled with the power of smartphones and tablets, these devices can provide a wealth of information about the state of a house and the power to control its functions. (They also entail serious privacy and security considerations, which will be detailed later.)

Although basic patterns for using RFID and IoT technologies for inventory control and process management in a commercial-industrial setting are well established, those of the second-wave IoT are not. The personal Internet of Things today is, in a sense, an untamed frontier. For any given application, there are usually numerous competing products and formats that can attain similar ends. Many of these employ proprietary hardware and software, hearkening back to such classic format battles as VHS versus Betamax or Blu-Ray versus HD DVD. To take just one example, Philips gained an early lead in the "smart" light bulb market with its line of Hue LED bulbs that can be programmed and automated to glow in different colors or at set times of day. As the technology matured and the cost of hardware dropped, other classic lighting suppliers as well as home-automation vendors rushed to compete. A customer now has to consider not just Philips or GE or Sylvania or other offerings but which larger home network system—Apple or Google or Amazon or other—their bulbs are compatible with.

A user of IoT devices, though, is typically less concerned with which proprietary system she is buying into than with being assured that all of her devices will work with one another. This is a necessary consideration in the library world as well. Many major library software systems are proprietary, not easily modified or connected to other systems, and predate the IoT revolution. Until the dust settles and the IoT becomes a more integrated part of our technological surroundings, individuals and libraries alike must often depend on third-party services to provide some sort of glue to connect disparate pieces of an IoT system.

One library-specific example of such a tool is the SELIDA project (http://selida-project.isi.gr). SELIDA is a Greek acronym that translates to "Printed Material Management Using Radio Frequency Identification Technology"; *selida* (also the Greek word for "page") has been used successfully at the University of Patras Library in Greece to integrate RFID item management and cataloging with the Koha ILS.[4] The project also has larger ambitions for facilitating more general physical-electronic document management.

For the larger world of IoT integration, users can avail themselves of popular workflow automation tools like IFTTT (https://ifttt.com) and Zapier (https://zapier.com). IFTTT in particular offers connections to a wide assortment of physical IoT devices, such as more than twenty different types of lighting systems. These tools make it simple to create triggers or workflows to control your IoT devices without having to understand the technical details of each individual device ecosystem.

USES OF THE IOT IN LIBRARIES

The technologies and specific devices and applications of the Internet of Things are changing rapidly, but the future prospects of the IoT are indisputably bright. The present-day IoT provides a vast assortment of different tools—an assortment that will only grow over the next few years. Conservative estimates put the number of Internet-connected devices over the coming years in the tens of billions. The challenge for any library interested in taking advantage of these tools is to decide what to do with them—to figure out which ones are useful and to dream up innovative uses or improvements to services that they enable. This challenge actually predates the concept of the IoT as we understand it today. It's really a question about what to do with ubiquitous computing. When our view of what a computer is evolves to the point that anything we can see in our physical environment is, in a sense, a computing device, then what new possibilities does that afford?

The original idea of the Internet of Things focused on unique identification and tracking of physical objects by means of RFID. When applied to a library, this idea immediately focuses on books. Cataloging. Inventory of a library's physical collections. And to be sure, the thought of tagging each individual item in the library catalog with an RFID chip and using it for tracking purposes is not, at this point, a new one. Enough libraries have adopted RFID tech for inventory control, or at least expressed interest in doing so, that major businesses now offer RFID solutions tailored to library needs.[5] Even though the prospect of adopting RFID can be daunting for larger library collections, the potential benefits it enables can make it a reasonable long-term solution. Besides simply replicating existing library workflows using bar codes, RFID tagging can provide the following:

> **Better self-checkout systems.** A book's status (charged or not) can be stored directly on its RFID tag, coordinated with the LMS's check in/out functionality, and checked by an RFID reader at the entrances to provide basic security. This also opens up the possibility of users checking out their own books using an app on their smartphones, a natural progression of the basic concept. In some cases, this technology has even been

PART I: Data

> used to set up remote, unstaffed kiosks that patrons can make use of to borrow popular items (e.g., the Hillsboro, Oregon, public library's Book-O-Mat, www.wccls.org/libraries/hillsboro).
>
> **Better shelf organization.** An RFID scanner that's run across a shelf of books can reveal not only which items are present or absent on the shelf but also the exact order of those items. Misfiled books can be easily identified and reordered.
>
> **Real-time inventory monitoring.** Permanently mounted RFID scanners on shelves (or even at a large-scale, room-size deployment) can track the removal of a particular item from its shelf or room, providing better availability information to others trying to find the same item.

The same basic principles can be applied to other "inventories" as well, such as for use in room reservations, availability status display, and access. Think of modern hotel room key cards—though again, an innovation already appearing in high-end hotels is to do away with cards altogether and provide access using a smartphone.

Another IoT technology not yet touched on here can be used to improve library navigation and "advertising." So-called iBeacons are small powered devices that constantly broadcast an identifying Wi-Fi signal that can be picked up and interpreted by a beacon-aware system, like a smartphone with a corresponding app. Beacons are used to identify a place; apps that make use of them can determine when a person is within a few tens of meters of a particular beacon. In commercial use, they are often deployed in stores to provide ads to customers. For example, an iBeacon app might see that you were walking past the front door of Target and suggest that you might want to stop in and check out their sale on gloves. In the library world, the same setup could be used to remind a library patron about an overdue fee as he passes by the entrance. Inside the library, beacons could be positioned in the stacks at intervals to provide information about resources located in a particular place, or they could be integrated with a shelf-finding app that could guide a user to a specific item she's trying to locate.

iBeacons can also have their broadcasting power reduced to the point where a beacon-sensitive device has to be pressed up right next to it in order to read its information. In this mode, beacons could be placed next to individual items in an exhibition or collection and used to provide enhanced information in the form of a web page or audiovisual resource about the subject on display. (This same functionality can also be provided by RFID tags or QR codes; it's simply a matter of choosing your preferred technology.) Beacons become less useful for this purpose

Chapter Two: Everything Is Online

when the distance between discrete items narrows (e.g., among items stacked on a shelf). In those cases, though, RFID still works perfectly well. Imagine being able to scan a book's RFID tag with a smartphone and pull up all kinds of related content for it: reviews, suggested materials, related items, individual research notes, and more. With uniquely identifiable items, a framework that enables that kind of metadata linking offers virtually unlimited possibilities.

Always-on "assistants" are at present a nascent technology in the Internet of Things. Spurred on by voice-activated systems like Apple's Siri and Google's OK Google, these new devices are taking the shape of speaker-studded cylinders or screens intended to be placed in a home. Always on, always listening for their trigger keyword, implementations like the Amazon Echo, Google Home, and Apple's HomePod are intended to invoke the sense of an omnipresent, helpful AI in your environment (although the first-generation HomePod's Siri assistant is highly constrained compared to the functionality of the Echo and Google Home). Although the presence of a speaker actively listening to conversations and connected to a cloud service somewhere outside your control has raised privacy concerns, the ability to control devices and get answers to queries using only your voice is undeniably useful in many contexts. Some libraries have begun experimenting with these devices as a means of providing simple information to visitors. At the Murray Hill Middle School Library in Maryland, for instance, librarian Gwyneth Jones has introduced an Amazon Echo to her students both as an interesting technology experiment and as a potential means of compensating for reduced staffing. Through its default connections to the Internet and Amazon, the Echo is capable of answering simple queries about books and authors (albeit less obscure ones).[6] More intriguingly, the Echo's capabilities can be expanded through programming for specific domains; it's easy to foresee a future in which Echos or other assistants are connected to library catalogs and are able to aid users with more complex queries and research.

The Internet of Things also affords libraries new ways of managing their environments. By utilizing off-the-shelf IoT components, many intended for home automation applications, it's possible to create more efficient and effective library spaces, monitor environmental conditions and energy usage, and painlessly connect users to services like printing and public computing.

Study and conference rooms, small theaters, and exhibits can all benefit from the use of IoT lighting and networked audiovisual equipment. With the proper setup, lighting can be adjusted by the tap of a button (or voice command) to dim in parts of the room for a presentation or highlight certain areas. You could also use colored bulbs like the Philips Hue collection to set the mood for a public exhibit, subtly adjusting the lighting color to match the displays. Group meetings and presentations can also benefit from wireless access to projectors and monitors. A TV plug-in like the Roku, Apple TV, or Google Chromecast makes it trivial to mirror a laptop monitor or stream media on a big screen that everyone can share.

Thermostats, temperature and humidity sensors, moisture alarms, and energy-monitoring "smart plugs" offer new ways for libraries to save money, energy, and even library collections. A vault or rare manuscript collection could be monitored with environmental sensors that trigger an alarm when conditions deteriorate. IoT-connected plugs, thermostats, and lighting can be used to shut down energy consumption in places where or times when rooms and devices are not in use.

Finally, don't forget about the IoT devices you may very well have already in your library. Networked printers are a good example of a practical, well-established model for providing users with services that can easily be reconfigured or replaced. These days, users often don't even have to worry about printer drivers or network configuration; their phones and tablets are able to scan the network, discover an available printer, and use it as an output source.

Many libraries today are embracing the makerspace movement, providing education and tools to the public to enable users to play, experiment, and create new electronic systems of their own. Cheap, easy-to-use microcontrollers like the Arduino and single-board computers like the Raspberry Pi often feature in such projects; they also happen to be functional components of the Internet of Things, able to serve as bridges between "less-smart" devices and the greater Internet. It's natural to consider ways to add IoT-specific workshops and devices to library outreach sessions and makerspace projects. One organization already implementing them is North Carolina State University Libraries, which now provides IoT-specific content in its D. H. Hill Library makerspace.[7]

SECURITY CONCERNS AND IMPLICATIONS FOR PRIVACY

While the future of the IoT promises great things for how libraries will change and evolve to provide better, more personalized services to their users, the present technology comes with significant caveats relating to online security and privacy. The threat that the IoT poses to the library's traditional values of user privacy should not be underestimated.

Chapter Two: Everything Is Online

The first problem is that in the rush to bring new IoT-ready devices to market, some manufacturers have overlooked basic principles of computer and networking security. You wouldn't leave your personal laptop—filled with private photos, messages, and financial data—sitting out in public with your username and password written on a sticky note affixed to the monitor. That is, however, almost exactly what some vendors have done with their IoT devices. Any sensor, camera, scanner, or light bulb that connects to a network on its own is a networked computer, subject to the same vulnerabilities that a full-scale laptop or desktop machine has. If the "smart" device ships with a standard default log-in that is not later changed by its owner, it's a sitting duck. Malicious hackers can scan the Internet for any such connected devices that are using the manufacturer's known defaults and easily take control of them. This has become a growing concern over the past few years as consumer IoT devices have proliferated without proper safeguards or instructions for securing them. Hackers have taken advantage of the abundance of vulnerable IoT devices to create botnets, collections of thousands or even hundreds of thousands of devices infected with malware that can be controlled as a system and used for various illicit purposes.

The botnet problem peaked most recently in 2016 with the so-called Mirai botnet, which discovered and infected unprotected IoT devices with unprecedented speed. Mirai was so successful that its creators (three college-age men trying to gain an unfair advantage in the lucrative world of services built around the game Minecraft) found themselves with an army of six hundred thousand networked devices—an online weapon so powerful that it overwhelmed websites and systems used to dealing with smaller, more conventional botnets. Released as open source malware, other authors used Mirai's base code to launch an attack against Dyn, a major provider of the Domain Name System functionality that makes the Internet work. Their attack brought down large swathes of the Internet in the United States.[8]

For the time being, there is no clear regulation or certifying authority that can ensure that IoT devices are safe in this way. The burden is on the consumer to somehow know that a device has been secured. It's also important to consider the manufacturer's commitment to supporting its products and updating them to protect against future threats. The usual way of doing this for an IoT device is by means of a firmware update that rewrites all or part of the software embedded in its processor. Unfortunately, the steps involved in executing a firmware update vary greatly from system to system and are commonly arcane or opaque to the user. For these reasons, libraries should proceed with IoT deployment with great caution, engaging the help of IT staff to determine the vulnerability of, and ability to update, a particular device or device family.

A second concern for libraries relates to the growing success of the Internet of Things. As the technologies of the IoT mature, the amount and disparate types of data collected by IoT sensors and gadgets will increase exponentially. IoT software will become more efficient and effective at making sense of this data, combining and differentiating it in unexpected ways to gain new insights into whatever real-world objects are at the far end of the system inputs. The threats that big data aggregation and analysis pose to the privacy of individuals are not new, but the growing influence of the IoT will amplify them. Librarians and library workers will have to carefully discern the happy medium between the use of IoT devices to improve their work and the risks those same devices pose to the privacy of their users.

THE IOT-CONNECTED LIBRARY OF THE FUTURE

The Internet of Things isn't going anywhere. In fact, it's coming to you whether you like it or not. Despite threats to privacy and security, we already live in a world of interconnected devices, tools, and sensors that have changed the way we live and work. Although some uses of the IoT are frivolous, the technology can be immensely beneficial when used sensibly and thoughtfully. The challenge of libraries over the next few years is not to decide whether to use the IoT but rather to determine how to deploy IoT in a strategic way that maximizes the positive changes to library operations and services while mitigating the risks to users.

Overall trends in IoT over the next few years will most likely focus on voice control, better integration of disparate devices, and unobtrusiveness. In the near term, for example, advances in voice-recognition technology and improved, low-cost, Echo-like products could lead to a library installing one in each of their individual research rooms, providing a hands-free way for users to query library systems, reserve items, and explore links between different pieces of library content. However, the real future is not for libraries to provide kiosk-like systems that users have to approach to interact with; rather, IoT devices will interact directly with the IoT-capable devices users already have on their persons. That includes not only smartphones and tablets but also wearables like smart watches and some types of augmented-reality glasses (like Google Glass, only much better). Location-aware devices that are able to communicate with library IoT systems open up a wealth of new possibilities and conveniences for reserving rooms, navigating to locate physical items in the library stacks, viewing or previewing digital copies of nearby materials, sharing content, and using library facilities. Beacons can also be deployed outside the library, in university dorms or on city streets, to provide unique contextual information or announcements about library services and events to people who might otherwise not think to visit the library.

Future library collections will become increasingly IoT aware and managed. Embedding RFID tags into every item in a catalog will streamline checkout and check-in procedures, enable self-checkout, provide researchers with quick access to aggregated metadata, and allow real-time availability and location data. Library spaces will also be managed for convenience and efficiency. Merging with improved voice-assistant features, conference rooms can provide complete control over their environments and AV equipment. Those rooms, as well as larger public spaces, will report data about their use—times, number of occupants, equipment or services employed—that will be aggregated to supply precise and detailed statistics for library reporting.

The availability of so much data of so many different kinds will lead to novel ways of collecting and analyzing it all (see chapter 7). Such an analysis could affect the scheduling of public-outreach sessions (or even library service hours), collection building, and more. As always, library administration will have to take care not to let the numbers occlude the human needs of their users that can't be understood by automated systems—nor to let them triangulate and identify specific individuals within the agglomerated data.

This is a boom time for the Internet of Things. IoT concepts are being realized today through the convergence of many advanced technologies: ubiquitous, high-speed Internet service; machine learning and AI; sophisticated software; improved sensors; and augmented and virtual reality. The future of IoT is for it to disappear into our environment and become a part of our everyday world. Just as children growing up today will press their fingers against a computer monitor or TV screen with the expectation that it will respond to their touch, the children of tomorrow will expect the world around them to interact with them in ways that are only now starting to emerge. And when they start using libraries, they'll expect those to behave in the same way.

NOTES

1. Exactly which IoT technologies the Amazon Go store is using is unclear. Amazon's own information speaks of "computer vision, sensor fusion, and deep learning" (https://go.amazon.com) that helps the store track individual items as they are taken off the shelves and associate them with a particular shopper. RFID might be in use as well.

PART I: Data

2. J. E. Ibarra-Esquer, F. F. González-Navarro, B. L. Flores-Rios, L. Burtseva, and M. A. Astorga-Vargas, "Tracking the Evolution of the Internet of Things Concept across Different Application Domains," *Sensors* 17, no. 6 (2017): 1379, https://doi.org/10.3390/s17061379.
3. See the EPC standards page at www.gs1.org/epc-rfid.
4. Kyriakos Stefanidis and Giannis Tsakonas, "Integration of Library Services with Internet of Things Technologies," *Code4Lib Journal* 30 (2015), http://journal.code4lib.org/articles/10897.
5. Such as 3M's system: http://solutions.3m.com/wps/portal/3M/en_WW/Track_Trace/home/Products/one/one.
6. Gwyneth Jones, "There's an Echo in My Library!" *Daring Librarian* (blog), June 24, 2015, www.thedaringlibrarian.com/2015/06/echo-in-my-library.html.
7. "NCSU Libraries Offers 'Internet of Things' Support with Help from OIT," OIT News, NC State University, 2015, https://oit.ncsu.edu/2015/11/24/ncsu-libraries-offers-internet-of-things-support-with-help-from-oit.
8. Garrett Graff, "The Mirai Botnet Was Part of a College Student Minecraft Scheme," *Wired*, 2017, www.wired.com/story/mirai-botnet-minecraft-scam-brought-down-the-internet/.

Chapter Three

Link Rot, Reference Rot, and Link Resolvers

Justin M. White

From the earliest days of the web, users have been aware of the fickleness of linking to content. In some ways, 1998 was a simpler time for the Internet. In other ways, like basic website design principles, everything old is new again. Jakob Nielson, writing "Fighting Linkrot" in 1998, reported on a then recent survey that suggested 6 percent of links on the web were broken. The advice given then hasn't changed: run a link validator on your site regularly and update or remove broken links. Also set up redirects for links that do change. The mantra for Nielson was "You are not allowed to break any old links."[1] Several years later, partly in response to Nielson, John S. Rhodes wrote a very interesting piece called "Web Sites That Heal." Rhodes was interested in the causes of link rot and listed several technological and habitual causes. These included the growing use of content management systems (CMSs), which relied on back-end databases and server-side scripting that generated unreliable URLs, and the growing complexity of websites, which was

PART I: Data

leading to sloppy information architecture. On the behavioral side, website owners were satisfied to tell their users to "update their bookmarks," websites were not tested for usability, content was seen as temporary, and many website owners were simply apathetic about link rot. Rhodes also noted the issue of government censorship and filtering, though he did not foresee the major way in which government would obfuscate old web pages, which will be discussed below. Rhodes made a pitch for a web server tool that would rely on the Semantic Web and allow websites to talk to each other automatically to resolve broken links on their own.[2] Although that approach hasn't taken off, there are other solutions to the problem of link rot that are gaining traction.

What is link rot? Link rot is the process by which hyperlinks no longer point to the most current or available web page. However, this isn't the only problem facing users: content on web pages isn't static. As authors and editors update and edit web pages over time, the original URL may stay the same, but the page at that URL may be about something very different. This evolution of a page's function has been termed *content drift*. When combined with link rot, this creates *reference rot*. In general, when linking to a resource as a reference, the author is faced with a twofold problem: the link may no longer work, and even if it does, the material being referenced may no longer exist in the same context.[3]

Luckily, the technological solution for reference rot is already at hand. Rather than relying on link checkers, website owners can use link resolvers and decentralized web preservation through software like the Amber project (http://amberlink.org). The Amber project, out of the Berkman Klein Center for Internet and Society, works from a simple enough premise. When a web page is published, the software goes through it, takes a snapshot of each linked page, and saves it locally or to a centralized web-archiving platform, such as the Internet Archive or Perma.cc. When it detects that a link is broken or misbehaving, Amber suggests the archived version to the user. Amber emphasizes decentralized web archiving as a philosophical commitment to the need to avoid centralized responsibility of a few organizations for preserving the web. There are also link checkers that have begun to integrate web archiving into their workflows, but they still tend to function in the same "scan for issues, change broken links" paradigm that Nielson described back in 1998.

The scope of the problem is extremely wide. The average life span of a URL is forty-four days, according to the Internet Archive's Brewster Kahle.[4] This number is hard to estimate and will vary widely depending on who is asked and what context the links exist in. As it stands, there is too much dependence on platforms that have no mandate to do the work of preservation. Consider the third-party vendors that libraries and their institutions rely on for data management. Where will they be in five years? And if they find data to be objectionable in some way, what is to stop them from deleting it? This is part of the problem that the Amber project responded to by creating independent snapshots of web pages rather than relying on the Internet Archive and Perma.cc. Clifford Lynch gave a speech in 2016 about the shift from print news media to broadcast and web news, in which the preservation systems previously put in place began to break down. Now that news organizations rely on links to underlying evidence rather than utilizing extensive summaries, their context relies on information that is not controlled by them.[5] It's easy to imagine a situation in which a website owner realizes his work has been linked to in a way he disapproves of and changes the context as a "response" to the linked work.

Link and reference rot have a particular history in scholarly communication. In 2014, a group of researchers found that one in five articles suffers from reference rot.[6] A 2016 study found that three out of four Uniform Resource Identifier (URI) references led to content that had been changed since the study cited it, leading to the possibility of malicious changes to undermine a citation (particularly in legal decisions). Most preservation is concerned with the long-term preservation of journal articles themselves, not the content referenced in them.[7] Much like in the news world, there is a reliance on the publishers of data to preserve information, not libraries or other "faithful guardians of immortal works."[8] The larger trend of citing web sources means that scholarly communication will have to focus its priorities on larger web preservation.[9] In 2017, the Coalition for Networked Information's Clifford Lynch gave an opening plenary on "Resilience and Engagement in an Era of Uncertainty." Lynch emphasized that the crisis was in the preservation not of scholarly literature itself but of information that scholars will use in the future. Lynch also covered difficulties in our current preservation assumptions and questioned whether the government was a reliable steward of research data.[10]

Legal scholars have been particularly prominent in the discussion over reference rot, particularly as it affects the citations in legal decisions. The most prominent paper is that by Jonathan Zittrain, Kendra Albert, and Lawrence Lessig in 2014, but a year before their landmark paper, Raizel Liebler and June Liebert had surveyed the life span of web links in US Supreme Court decisions from 1996 to 2010. They found that 29 percent of websites cited in these decisions were no longer working, with no discernible pattern of which links were most likely to rot.[11] Zittrain, Albert, and Lessig looked at the legal implications for link rot and found reasons for alarm. The authors determined that approximately 50 percent of the URLs in Supreme Court opinions no longer linked to the original information and that a selection of articles in legal journals, including the *Harvard Law Review*, published between 1999 and 2011 had a link rot rate of 70 percent. The authors of the 2014 study suggest that libraries be involved in the publishing process and take on the "*distributed*, long-term preservation of link contents" (emphasis added).[12]

HOW LINK ROT AND WEB ARCHIVING APPLY TO LIBRARIES

What does link rot mean for libraries? Many libraries are not involved in academic or legal publishing but rely extensively on web resources for their users. Approaching the issue from a basic educational approach, a 2003 study found that link rot seriously limited the usefulness of web-based educational materials in biochemistry and molecular biology.[13] It is not much of a stretch to imagine this issue is broader than the biological sciences.

The Chesapeake Project is a collaborative digital preservation initiative undertaken to preserve legal references. In exploring the materials preserved by the project, Sarah Rhodes measured rates of link rot over a three-year period. Rhodes found that links most libraries would consider stable—government and state websites—degraded at an increasing rate over time.[14] With the Whitehouse.gov reset at the beginning of the Trump administration, approximately 1,935 links on Wikipedia broke at the flip of a switch.[15] Librarians who maintain LibGuides and Pathfinders to government information know the value of link checkers to their guides, as any government shake-up can mean that many of their resources now live somewhere else, even in another government agency, with no overriding link routing system. While it is best practice to link to the most up-to-date information, a regime change can mean that valuable studies and data can be deliberately or unintentionally obscured. For example, IRS tax statistics recently moved from www.irs.gov/taxstats/index.html to www.irs.gov/statistics with no redirect, even though this change was within the same domain. As the author is responsible for government information at his library, he would also note the fickleness of presidential libraries' websites despite the preservation role of the libraries they represent online.

The Environmental Data & Governance Initiative (EDGI) sprang up in the face of new hostility from the incoming Trump administration to climate science and other scientific fields that rely on open government data. From its earliest days, EDGI attempted to "preserve publicly accessible and potentially vulnerable scientific data and archive web pages from EPA, DOE, NOAA, OSHA, NASA, USDA, DOI, and USGS" utilizing the Internet Archive and DataRefuge. Visitors to the page can find a task in the preservation workflow that suits their skill sets (e.g., general librarians might be tasked with checking metadata).[16]

Libraries should also keep in mind the growth of open access (OA) journals and their reliance on these journals to supplement their traditional paid subscriptions. While very large OA journals like the *Public Library of Science* (*PLoS*) have the scale and thus the notice of archival organizations, small OA journals are often run with shoestring budgets and few faculty supporters. Clifford Lynch pointed out that libraries are unlikely to advocate or financially support OA journal preservation when they are already relying on the fact that OA journals are free to access.[17]

Audrey Watters warned in a recent article that copyright enforcement also stands in the way of preservation efforts.[18] This is particularly a problem in preservation efforts in new mediums and platforms, which may have digital rights management (DRM)–protected content that prevents copying and access. Librarians will also have to deal with the various data and information generated by their library systems—such as internal communication, statistics, and customer management—that rely exclusively (at the moment) on the stability of the vendor.

SOLUTIONS ON HAND

The technology for avoiding and repairing link rot is already on hand, just waiting for individuals and institutions to adopt it. The previously mentioned Internet Archive and Perma.cc are available for widespread use. These two particular services even have browser add-ons that can make archiving for scholarly reference as simple as a single click. Even more effective is software that can be built to utilize these systems for automatic web preservation and link routing. CMSs like WordPress have many plug-ins that allow for automatic preservation of links that are in a post. These add-ons can scan new posts for links, submit them to the IA for preservation (creating a new snapshot that represents that page at the moment it was preserved), and automatically route broken links to archived copies. The Amber project's WordPress plug-in can utilize the IA, Perma.cc, or local copies to automatically preserve and reroute broken links.[19] It seems reasonable to assume that link checkers in more CMSs will begin to follow this pattern of preservation and link routing, and librarians should engage with their vendors to ensure that their web content remains accessible.

PART I: Data

However, it is a dangerous assumption that these technologies, particularly the Internet Archive, are truly archiving the web. The IA can only archive the "surface" of the web, referring to the largely static web pages that the IA can capture, as opposed to the PDFs, videos, Adobe Flash objects, and so on that make up the web's content. The IA and Perma.cc have to be considered within the limits that they exist, and other approaches to preservation are required for a true solution to link and reference rot.[20]

Studying legal citations, particularly those of the US Supreme Court, has been a growing field since the first comparative analysis of citations of secondary sources by Sirico and Margulies in 1986. With the added stakes of being the highest court in the land, the accessibility of citations by the Supreme Court has garnered more attention than academic reference rot generally. As mentioned above, it is nearly impossible to predict with any certainty what links will break, whether gauging them by source or by format. Independent and decentralized digital archiving is extremely important to ensuring the long-term viability of access to digital materials. For example, Liebler and Liebert's 2013 study of Supreme Court citations generated a list of invalid URLs: they found that only 68 percent of those broken citations could be found on the Internet Archive. A partnership between the court and the IA or another digital archiving group would improve this number tremendously. Creating digital backups on already existing systems such as Public Access to Court Electronic Resources (PACER) does improve digital archiving but hinders access in a way that more open-access preservation doesn't.[21]

One common approach to preventing link rot is to create permanent URLs. In its most basic form, a permanent URL is an address that remains consistent while it can point to new homes where the content it represents lives. This requires a lot of upkeep but also lacks the advantage of preservation approaches. A permanent URL can be updated when the content moves, but merely updating the URL does not track when the content itself has been changed in some way. Permanent links help address link rot but not reference rot.

Memento links, in their most basic definition, are snapshots of a website with time/date information. Mementos have the advantage of including human- and machine-readable information on what version of a preserved site is being viewed within the link URI itself.

This temporal context information has, so far, been included in a way that is helpful for human consumption. Despite the many variations in expressing the information that is relevant for a web citation, a user can interpret it and connect the dots. Also, temporal context information has so far only been included in formal web citations. However, because all links are subject to reference rot, the addition of such information should not be limited to formal citations of web resources but should rather be applicable to all links to web resources.[22]

Thus rather than saying "(link) was accessed on 10-11-2015," the link itself contains temporal information within the HTML element <a>, using the `versionurl` and `versiondate` attributes.[23] A Memento with machine-readable information as an in-line link would look something like this HTML code:

```
<p>It allows writers and editors to capture
and fix transient information on the web with
a <a href = "http://blogs.law.harvard.edu/
futureoftheinternet/2013/09/22/perma/" versionurl =
"http://perma.cc/0Hg62eLdZ3T" versiondate = "2013-10-
02">new, permanent link</a>.</p>
```

The words *new, permanent link* would thus become a clickable link to a new resource, but the information in that link is more than a typical URL provides.

With all of the tools mentioned, from centralized platforms for preservation like the Internet Archive and Perma.cc to decentralized projects like the Amber project and Memento protocols, it is possible right now to build platforms that incorporate best practices to prevent reference rot. Perma.cc, for instance, has recently received an Institute of Museum and Library Studies (IMLS) grant to help scale up its operations and could become a major player in concert with the Internet Archive as a first option for web archiving.[24] Specific examples of how these approaches will look will be discussed in the next section. In general, we can expect that all digital platforms will begin to incorporate solutions that scan and preserve web links; create backups on the Internet Archive, Perma.cc, or locally; and automatically reroute users to the archived copies when the platform's link checker detects that the link is no longer functioning. We can also expect that institutional repositories will be scanned for web links, and those will be automatically preserved in a similar manner, though reading through references in scholarly papers is a bit trickier. Utilizing the Memento protocols for linking, with machine-readable dates, might be the solution to ensuring that the same version of the web page is presented for various versions of a paper, such as a preprint compared to a postprint. All of these efforts will inevitably come up against issues in copyright, which is why it is imperative that librarians are on hand to advocate for fair use defenses and technological adaptations that allow for preservation and access to be maintained when copyright law creates a barrier.

PART I: Data

WHAT WILL REFERENCE ROT PREVENTION LOOK LIKE?

Ultimately, changes in habits are required in the many ways we think about linking and citing web resources. In citations, it is tempting to follow current style guides and have only one URL, which a reference rot–conscious writer would prefer to use. However, it's important to maintain the original context of the page cited. For the moment, we can focus on the Internet Archive and Perma.cc, which create new URLs for archived web pages, and set aside the machine-readable versioning approaches that the Hiberlink project utilizes. Original URLs serve as references that archived versions of web pages use as their ultimate context. If these are removed in citations and the archived link no longer works, there is no opportunity to find another archived version. While waiting for citation manuals to catch up or come up with new standards for Mementos and computer-readable Memento links, the best option for now is including both the original URL and the archived version's URL (see notes for examples).[25] In the realm of citation, authors are largely self-reliant in creating archival versions of their web sources, though institutions can support this role by hosting and promoting Perma.cc and its browser extension or building a web archive with the Internet Archive.

On the topic of institutions supporting their authors, the rise of institutional repositories and small-scale journals has moved many libraries into the unfamiliar territory of acting as publishers. As in the publishing world, library-hosted and supported journals will rely on the library's efforts at preventing link rot. For example, Perma.cc has specifically marketed itself as compliant with the requirements for the Bluebook uniform system of citation for library-hosted journals. With the wide and growing variety of content management systems for hosting scholarly work, libraries will also want to consider what kind of automated web-archiving processes are built into their platforms to make the task of preservation manageable.

Because a lot of cited materials are news related, news preservation is another area of focus for memory organizations. For those news organizations, particularly those that do not self-archive, there is a need for digital as well as physical preservation. However, many news organizations are not geographically localized, and so the issue of who should preserve them remains an open question.[26] Social media presents a similar challenge, magnified by the ephemerality of most social media posts and the variety of formats presented.

Although it's possible that learning management systems (LMS) will adopt some form of link preservation in the near future, it will probably be after libraries start tackling this problem. Librarians who are involved in course design and support will be useful resources for teaching faculty about reference rot and helping with the preservation of web materials used in courses. For those courses that eschew LMSs, other content management systems like WordPress already have link resolvers built in that utilize the Internet Archive and Perma.cc, along with server storage space for local copies (see the Amber project mentioned above).

CONCLUSIONS

So far, we've covered a wide range of applications for web archiving, some more specialized than others. This is because web archiving, and link rot prevention in general, is going to become a fundamental aspect in dealing with online resources of almost every kind. The areas in which most librarians will come into contact with web archiving can be broken down into a few categories. Library websites, with their Pathfinders/LibGuides, often link out to web resources that change with regular frequency (particularly things like government web resources, which change with every administration or agency restructuring). The CMSs that libraries use should begin or be pressured to adopt web-archiving technologies that automatically preserve links that are added to the library website and, like current link checkers, note when a website is being nonresponsive and give the user the option to view a (preferably locally) archived version. With the falling costs of virtual server space thanks to competition between Amazon Web Services and its rivals, librarians should expect their CMSs to make space available for locally archived copies of web resources.

Another area in which librarians at larger institutions can expect to interact with web archiving is through their institutional repository or other CMSs that handle publications. This is particularly true of those libraries that are acting as the homes of academic journals. When papers with web references are submitted to the journal's repository software, librarians should anticipate that their vendor can provide a link-checking and archiving tool that will make copies of all linked materials, either locally or in Perma.cc or even the university's web-archiving tool (e.g., the Internet Archive's paid service, Archive-It). The legal profession has led the way in looking at how to provide snapshots (Mementos) of web resources that are properly timestamped in a machine-readable way, and although that might be too much for most journals to take on at once, there are plenty of institutions that libraries can partner with to learn about these new approaches while instituting their own procedures for preventing reference rot.

PART I: Data

There are other possibilities for preventing link rot that will be even more challenging to approach but still should be considered. This includes vendor links to e-resources that the library subscribes to. Although this creates copyright issues, there is a strong argument to be made that libraries should have redundant copies available for when links break or are not redirected properly, as those libraries have made significant payments to have access to these materials and lack the first-sale rights they enjoy with printed materials. Making e-resources more reliable could depend on coming to agreements about creating archives of subscription materials.

The difficulties facing libraries in web archiving are often not technological but legal in nature. Copyright and anticircumvention laws prevent the creation of perfectly reasonable archives. This is particularly problematic in the archiving of media resources that are not simply text but include embedded video, audio, or interactive media.

The current trends in web archiving have yet to reach the level imagined by John Rhodes's "Websites That Heal" in 2002, but the rapid expansion of web materials will require a concurrent expansion in institutions that take part in archiving those materials to preserve users' access to them. As mentioned, this will require a change in habits from citations to web design, but with current tools, there are many ways that librarians can educate themselves about and prevent reference rot in every web-related realm they currently operate in.

NOTES

1. Jakob Nielson, "Fighting Linkrot," Nielson Norman Group, June 14, 1998, www.nngroup.com/articles/fighting-linkrot/. Archived at http://web.archive.org/web/20171213072929/https://www.nngroup.com/articles/fighting-linkrot/.

2. John S. Rhodes, "Web Sites That Heal," WebWord, March 10, 2002. Archived at http://web.archive.org/web/20160315090512/http://www.webword.com/moving/healing.html.

3. Martin Klein et al., "Scholarly Context Not Found: One in Five Articles Suffers from Reference Rot," *PLoS ONE* 9, no. 12 (2014): e115253, accessed December 31, 2017, https://doi.org/10.1371/journal.pone.0115253. Archived at http://web.archive.org/web/20171021142905/http://journals.plos.org/plosone/article?id=10.1371%2Fjournal.pone.0115253.

4. Audrey Watters, "Memory Machines and Collective Memory: How We Remember the History of the Future of Technological Change," *EDUCAUSE Review*, October 23, 2017, accessed December 31, 2017, https://er.educause.edu/articles/2017/10/memory-machines-and-collective-memory. Archived at https://web.archive.org/web/20171231180450/https://er.educause.edu/articles/2017/10/memory-machines-and-collective-memory.

5. Clifford Lynch, "Born-Digital News Preservation in Perspective," *Digital Technology & Culture* 46, no. 3 (2017): 94–98, doi:https://doi.org/10.1515/pdtc-2017-0012.
6. Klein et al., "Scholarly Context Not Found."
7. Shawn M. Jones et al., "Scholarly Context Adrift: Three out of Four URI References Lead to Changed Content," *PLoS ONE* 11, no. 12 (2016): e0167475, accessed February 24, 2018, https://doi.org/10.1371/journal.pone.0167475. Archived at http://web.archive.org/web/20170719082055/http://journals.plos.org:80/plosone/article?id=10.1371/journal.pone.0167475.
8. Paraphrase of John Milton.
9. Klein et al., "Scholarly Context Not Found."
10. Clifford Lynch, "Resilience and Engagement in an Era of Uncertainty," YouTube, December 22, 2017, https://youtu.be/TBApuajS6ZU.
11. Raizel Liebler and June Liebert, "Something Rotten in the State of Legal Citation: The Life Span of a United States Supreme Court Citation Containing an Internet Link (1996–2010)," *Yale Journal of Law and Technology* 15, no. 2 (2013), accessed January 1, 2018, http://digitalcommons.law.yale.edu/yjolt/v0115/iss2/2. Archived at https://web.archive.org/web/20180101213208/http://digitalcommons.law.yale.edu/cgi/viewcontent.cgi?article=1085&context=yjolt.
12. Jonathan Zittrain, Kendra Albert, and Lawrence Lessig, "Perma: Scoping and Addressing the Problem of Link and Reference Rot in Legal Citations," *Harvard Law Review Forum* 127, no. 176 (2014), accessed June 7, 2017, https://dx.doi.org/10.2139/ssrn.2329161.
13. John Markwell and David W. Brooks, "'Link Rot' Limits the Usefulness of Web-Based Educational Materials in Biochemistry and Molecular Biology," *Biochemistry and Molecular Biology Education* 31, no. 1 (2003), accessed February 25, 2018, https://doi.org/10.1002/bmb.2003.494031010165. Archived at http://web.archive.org/web/20171227011827/http://onlinelibrary.wiley.com/doi/10.1002/bmb.2003.494031010165/full.
14. Sarah Rhodes, "Breaking Down Link Rot: The Chesapeake Project Legal Information Archive's Examination of URL Stability," *Law Library Journal* 102 (2010): 581, accessed January 1, 2018, http://scholarship.law.georgetown.edu/digitalpreservation_publications/6/. Archived at https://web.archive.org/web/20180101230246/http://scholarship.law.georgetown.edu/cgi/viewcontent.cgi?article=1005&context=digitalpreservation_publications.
15. Adrianne Jeffries, "The Whitehouse.gov Reset Broke Wikipedia Links En Masse: Here's What Editors Are Doing about It," *Outline*, January 26, 2017, https://theoutline.com/post/959/whitehouse-gov-switch-broke-wikipedia. Archived at http://web.archive.org/web/20171223224726/https://theoutline.com/post/959/whitehouse-gov-switch-broke-wikipedia.

16. "Archiving Data," EDGI, accessed February 24, 2018, https://envirodatagov.org/archiving/. Archived at http://web.archive.org/web/20170905141512/https://envirodatagov.org/archiving/.
17. Lynch, "Born-Digital News," 95.
18. Watters, "Memory Machines."
19. See https://wordpress.org/plugins/amberlink/.
20. Lynch, "Born-Digital News," 96.
21. Liebler and Liebert, "Something Rotten."
22. Herbert Van de Sompel, Martin Klein, Robert Sanderson, and Michael Nelson, "Thoughts on Referencing, Linking, Reference Rot," Memento Project, December 28, 2013, http://mementoweb.org/missing-link/#linkrot. Archived at http://web.archive.org/web/20171215212526/http://mementoweb.org/missing-link/.
23. Ibid.
24. Kim Dulin and Adam Ziegler, "Scaling Up Perma.cc: Ensuring the Integrity of the Digital Scholarly Record," D-Lib Magazine 23, nos. 5–6 (2017), https://doi.org/10.1045/may2017-dulin. Archived at http://web.archive.org/web/20170726113714/http://www.dlib.org:80/dlib/may17/dulin/05dulin.html.
25. Klein et al., "Scholarly Context Not Found."
26. Lynch, "Born-Digital News," 96.

BIBLIOGRAPHY

Dulin, Kim, and Adam Ziegler. "Scaling Up Perma.cc: Ensuring the Integrity of the Digital Scholarly Record." D-Lib Magazine 23, nos. 5–6 (2017). https://doi.org/10.1045/may2017-dulin.

Jeffries, Adrianne. "The Whitehouse.gov Reset Broke Wikipedia Links En Masse: Here's What Editors Are Doing about It." Outline, January 26, 2017. https://theoutline.com/post/959/whitehouse-gov-switch-broke-wikipedia. Archived at http://web.archive.org/web/20171223224726/https://theoutline.com/post/959/whitehouse-gov-switch-broke-wikipedia.

Jones, Shawn M., Herbert Van de Sompel, Harihar Shankar, Martin Klein, Richard Tobin, and Claire Grover. "Scholarly Context Adrift: Three out of Four URI References Lead to Changed Content." PLoS ONE 11, no. 12 (2016): e0167475. https://doi.org/10.1371/journal.pone.0167475. Archived at http://web.archive.org/web/20170719082055/http://journals.plos.org:80/plosone/article?id=10.1371/journal.pone.0167475.

Klein, Martin, Herbert Van de Sompel, Robert Sanderson, Harihar Shankar, Lyudmila Balakireva, Ke Zhou, and Richard Tobin. "Scholarly Context Not Found: One in Five Articles Suffers from Reference Rot." PLoS ONE 9, no. 12 (2014): e115253. https://doi.org/10.1371/journal.pone.0115253. Archived at http://web.archive.org/web/20171021142905/http://journals.plos.org/plosone/article?id=10.1371%2Fjournal.pone.0115253.

Liebler, Raizel, and June Liebert. "Something Rotten in the State of Legal Citation: The Life Span of a United States Supreme Court Citation Containing an Internet Link (1996–2010)." *Yale Journal of Law and Technology* 15, no. 2 (2013). http://digitalcommons.law.yale.edu/yjolt/v0115/iss2/2. Archived at https://web.archive.org/web/20180101213208/http://digitalcommons.law.yale.edu/cgi/viewcontent.cgi?article=1085&context=yjolt.

Lynch, Clifford. "Born-Digital News Preservation in Perspective." *Digital Technology & Culture* 46, no. 3 (2017): 94–98. https://doi.org/10.1515/pdtc-2017-0012.

———. "Resilience and Engagement in an Era of Uncertainty." YouTube, December 22, 2017. https://youtu.be/TBApuajS6ZU.

Markwell, John, and David W. Brooks. "'Link Rot' Limits the Usefulness of Web-Based Educational Materials in Biochemistry and Molecular Biology." *Biochemistry and Molecular Biology Education* 31, no. 1 (2003). https://doi.org/10.1002/bmb.2003.494031010165. Archived at http://web.archive.org/web/20171227011827/http://onlinelibrary.wiley.com/doi/10.1002/bmb.2003.494031010165/full.

Nielson, Jakob. "Fighting Linkrot." *Nielson Norman Group*, June 14, 1998. www.nngroup.com/articles/fighting-linkrot/. Archived at http://web.archive.org/web/20171213072929/https://www.nngroup.com/articles/fighting-linkrot/.

Rhodes, John S. "Web Sites That Heal." *WebWord*, March 10, 2002. Archived at http://web.archive.org/web/20160315090512/http://www.webword.com/moving/healing.html.

Rhodes, Sarah. "Breaking Down Link Rot: The Chesapeake Project Legal Information Archive's Examination of URL Stability." *Law Library Journal* 102 (2010): 581. http://scholarship.law.georgetown.edu/digitalpreservation_publications/6/. Archived at https://web.archive.org/web/20180101230246/http://scholarship.law.georgetown.edu/cgi/viewcontent.cgi?article=1005&context=digitalpreservation_publications.

Van de Sompel, Herbert, Martin Klein, Robert Sanderson, and Michael Nelson. "Thoughts on Referencing, Linking, Reference Rot." Memento Project, December 28, 2013. http://mementoweb.org/missing-link/#linkrot. Archived at http://web.archive.org/web/20171215212526/http://mementoweb.org/missing-link/.

Watters, Audrey. "Memory Machines and Collective Memory: How We Remember the History of the Future of Technological Change." *EDUCAUSE Review*, October 23, 2017. https://er.educause.edu/articles/2017/10/memory-machines-and-collective-memory. Archived at https://web.archive.org/web/20171231180450/https://er.educause.edu/articles/2017/10/memory-machines-and-collective-memory.

Zittrain, Jonathan, Kendra Albert, and Lawrence Lessig. "Perma: Scoping and Addressing the Problem of Link and Reference Rot in Legal Citations." *Harvard Law Review Forum* 127, no. 176 (2014). https://dx.doi.org/10.2139/ssrn.2329161.

Chapter Four

Engaging Libraries with Web Archives

Todd Suomela

There are two major ways to view the World Wide Web, now twenty-five years old, from the perspective of a librarian. The first view is the web as a distribution channel. The delivery mechanism for a research journal has shifted from paper publishing to online publishing in PDF, but the formatting and layout of the text are mostly unchanged. A scholar in 1990 would recognize a research article published in 2015 just by looking at it, whether on-screen or in print. Other media such as books, video, and audio are similar to the journal article. The file formats have become digital, but the surrounding contexts of creation, production, and distribution are still the same. For example, the production process for many e-books is almost identical to that of a printed book. Most libraries purchase books from a distributor, which has a relationship with a publishing house, where it was edited by an editor, formatted by a designer, and then distributed via the web. We read it on a tablet or an e-reader, but the content could be published as a printed book

PART I: Data

with minimal transformation. The web has changed how we access information, but the types of content would still be familiar to a librarian from thirty years ago.

A second view of the web is as a venue for new forms of expression that have no analog to previous materials that used to be put into a library. These new forms are becoming increasingly important to the history of the modern world, and we, as librarians, need to pay more attention to them. The new forms include objects such as social media, discussion boards, e-mail chains, and comment threads. There may have been analogs to some of these media objects fifty years ago in the form of bulletin boards or letters to the editor, but past librarians from the twentieth century treated them as forms of ephemera. Now they are the bedrock of many people's experience of the world.

Popular magazines and newspapers are a particularly interesting example of media transformation that libraries are struggling to manage in the new web era. Twenty-five years ago, libraries could sign up for a subscription to a newspaper or magazine and expect to have a physical copy printed and delivered for processing into the collection. Nowadays, the newspaper is constantly updated on the web. Few libraries make any attempt to capture the web versions of contemporary newspapers. Many libraries still subscribe to printed copies if they are available, which are useful for capturing a static snapshot of journalism but fail to capture the dynamic way that most people consume media. A robust strategy for preserving born-digital journalism will include web-archiving tools and partnerships with news organizations.[1]

The current chapter begins by defining what a web archive is and then describes the process of creating a web-archiving program in a library. The challenges, both technical and institutional, are described in the next two sections. The continual innovation that takes place on the web presents serious challenges and demands rethinking the traditional roles of librarians and archivists. A final section of the chapter discusses the challenges for web archiving when we look beyond the archive or library out to the wider world.

DEFINING WEB ARCHIVES

At the most general level, web archiving is the process of collecting material from the World Wide Web, regardless of its digital format, for future preservation and research. According to the International Internet Preservation Consortium (IIPC), "Web archiving is the process of collecting portions of the World Wide Web, preserving the collections in an archival format, and then serving the archives for access and use."[2]

The benefit of using a broad definition of web archiving is that it helps us understand the complex set of challenges that we still need to resolve in order to attempt such a project. It also focuses on the overlapping goals of the library and the archive. The IIPC describes the archiving process as an overlapping set of activities: selection, harvest, preservation, and access. Selection describes the choices made by libraries and archives about what material will be collected as part of a web archive. Harvesting is the activity of downloading the material from the web and placing it into a platform that can reproduce the website as it was captured. Preservation is the long-term process of protecting the harvested content and ensuring that it is not modified. Access is providing the means for people to use the archives, whether it be viewing the websites in a page-by-page interface or through programmatic processing of the data collected during the harvesting process.

The World Wide Web has changed significantly over the past twenty-five years as it has grown in size and popularity. The technologies and standards on which the web is based have also changed, creating a series of challenges for web archivists. The technical and institutional challenges will be addressed later in this chapter, but first I will describe some common practices for starting a web-archiving program in a library or archive organization. Good planning for such a program will include a needs assessment as well as collection, metadata, and quality-control policies. Each of these steps will be discussed in the next section.

STARTING AND OPERATING A WEB ARCHIVE

The first step when starting a web-archiving program is to conduct a needs assessment. What is the purpose of the program for the institution? Who will it be serving? What types of content will it collect? How will access be provided? These and other questions should be asked in order to determine if web archiving is a service that an institution will, or is able to, provide.

Part of assessing the need for a web-archiving program must include evaluating the kind of technical infrastructure the institution will have available. If there is a significant technical staff with deep expertise in administrating operating systems, storage, and software configuration, then it may make sense for the library to install its own web-crawler software. Otherwise, outsourcing the archiving software gives the library the opportunity to curate the materials and scope of the web archive without having to worry about the maintenance of computer hardware and software updates. One of the most popular outsourcing solutions is the Archive-It service developed by the Internet Archive. Outsourcing allows institutions without significant technology resources to develop a web-archive program and apply their expertise where it will count the most—as information curators.

The curation process begins with defining a collection policy and deciding on the scope of the archiving project. Example collection policies can be obtained from the IIPC and modified to reflect the particular legal and organizational needs of the web-archiving program.[3] Once the collection policy is in place, the scope of the program can be set.

The traditional approach to collection management in libraries is based on a subject area, such as nonfiction, young adult, engineering, or some other topic. Web-archiving programs don't have this option; there is no technical way for a web archive to simply follow the results of a search about a particular topic because most search engines limit the activity of web crawlers or redirect links through other URLs, thus blocking the web crawler from capturing anything beyond the search results. So the librarian who is trying to set up a subject-based collection must actively choose the seed URLs where the web crawler will begin and then determine the optimum depth of the web crawl in order to capture a representative amount of information.

Some technical terms need to be defined at this time to help explain the process. The Heritrix web crawler, which forms the base for the majority of web-crawling platforms, including Archive-It, begins with a seed. The seed is a URL that usually takes the form of a top-level website (www.example.com). The next parameter to set is the scope. The web crawler works by going to the seed URL, downloading the page, following links to other web pages based on the scope rules set for the crawl, and then downloading those new URLs it has followed. The collection manager can set the scope to include everything from the initial domain (e.g., all the URLs that can be followed from the seed and are still in the domain of example.com), or the depth can be limited—for example, if the collection manager only wished to capture the home page of a particular website. In some cases, the scope can be set to follow all links on a page, including ones that are not in the original seed domain, but this configuration is risky because it may quickly exceed the storage capacity of the web crawler. The collection manager must establish a balance between breadth and depth in order to fulfill the particular goals of the collection policy.

As the web crawler proceeds, it will download individual pages and treat them as files. These files are stored by the web-archive software in the Web ARChive

(WARC) file format. WARC files are similar in purpose and style to BagIt and ZIP files because they encapsulate the different digital assets that make up a web page. A typical web page could contain multiple digital assets, including HTML, JavaScript, image files, audio, video, and so on. The WARC file format concatenates these digital assets along with a WARC record that contains metadata about the web request, content type, content length, and other named fields. WARC was recognized as an ISO standard in 2009 and was updated in 2017.[4] The Internet Archive's Wayback Machine works as an index and interface to these WARC files, which are rendered in the browser whenever a user attempts to access an archived web page. These archived snapshots usually have their own URL or Memento to indicate the date of capture.[5]

Metadata is an important consideration for many librarians and should be taken into account when dealing with web archives. Within the Archive-It system, there are three levels of metadata that can be entered. The most general level is the collection. This level contains a description of the collection along with the collection owner / organization name. It may also contain some basic Dublin Core information, which is optional. The next level is the seed metadata. This follows a basic Dublin Core set of attributes such as author/publisher, title, geographic area, date, and so forth. The final and most granular level is the document level, which again uses a subset of Dublin Core fields. The typical librarian's expectation may be to try to describe everything at the document level, but for even a small crawl of fewer than ten seeds, the crawler could download thousands of documents. Most web archivists confine themselves to seed-level metadata and only enter document metadata in specific circumstances because of the limited resources and time available for the task.

Another common issue facing a web archivist is quality control. Librarians and archivists want to ensure that the information they are collecting is accurate, especially if they are going to be providing users with access to that information in the future. But performing quality control on a web archive with thousands (or millions) of documents presents a unique challenge. It is impossible for an individual human being to review every document or page collected in a web archive and compare them to the current version of the web page. Moreover, the current version of the web page may have changed since the web crawler captured it. The best option is to make sure that as little information is missing from the web crawl as possible. Archive-It offers tools to perform patch crawls, which can fill in missing pieces of data on some pages. Large-scale quality control requires automatic evaluation; unfortunately, the tools currently available are crude and only report on links that could not be followed or pages that may need a patch crawl.

PART I: Data

TECHNICAL CHALLENGES FOR LIBRARIANS

The major technical challenges for web archiving include infrastructure, changing technical standards, format diversity, dynamic content presentation, and platform lock-in.

Infrastructure

Web archiving requires significant infrastructure and resource allocation, ranging from data storage to software development. The sheer size of the World Wide Web presents the biggest challenge for any web-archiving program. The Internet Archive and some national libraries are the only groups that have attempted any large-scale archive efforts. But even they are struggling with the demands for building an infrastructure capable of managing such a massive collection. The Library of Congress and Twitter agreed to transfer an archive of tweets to the library in 2010, but so far the actual progress toward providing access to the archive has been minimal.[6] One reason for this is the scale of the data challenge—one that even relatively well-funded public organizations may not be able to manage. And there is no sign that any of the private companies involved in the web, such as Google or Facebook, are taking up the slack.

The software needed to crawl and copy the web seeds that one intends to archive is another infrastructure challenge for would-be web archivers. The number of reliable web crawlers that could be deployed on a production system is limited, and there is no concerted commercial effort to develop such programs. Heritrix, the software used by the Internet Archive, depends on the open source community for updates. Although it has the longest track record by far, it still struggles with the constantly changing nature of content delivery on the web.

Standards

Tim Berners-Lee first proposed the HTML and HTTP standards in the early 1990s. Since then, the number of standards that have been added to the web is remarkably large. Some standards—including Cascading Style Sheets (CSS), Really Simple Syndication (RSS), Extensible Markup Language (XML), and JavaScript—have achieved widespread deployment. However, many other specialized standards—such as Web Ontology Language (OWL), Resource Description Framework (RDF), and Simple Object Access Protocol (SOAP)—have been proposed but adopted only in limited applications.

Web-crawler software needs to be updated in order to respond to constant changes in the web, and each change needs extensive testing. Different browsers may implement the standards in diverse ways, making it much more difficult to capture the experience of individual users on the web.

Format Diversity

Not only do the standards for the display and delivery of content change over time; the standards behind the file formats that are delivered also change over time. RealAudio streams were the typical way to deliver audio over the web twenty years ago, but today that technology is obsolete. Playing a RealAudio stream from an archived web page is almost impossible. The only way to address this challenge is to emulate the browser and web-server software that were in use twenty years ago. Strides are being made to make this technologically achievable, but even then much of the content may already be lost.

One of the keystone activities for digital preservation is format migration. Best practices suggest that old digital file formats should be transferred to newer formats as they become available. In many libraries, there is no time and no budget for digital format migrations because web archiving is struggling just to keep up with ingesting new material.

Dynamic Content

Dynamic online content is another challenge for web archivists. Social media platforms present a difficulty because of their technological structure, constantly changing content, and commercial ownership. The speed of updates on social media requires specialized tools to download content, especially in large quantities. An archivist needs a deep technological knowledge of these tools and the application programming interface (API) provided by the website in order to build a reliable and useful corpus. On the legal side, the commercial terms of service affect the types of information that can be gathered by archives and how those data can be analyzed or shared.

Other commercial sites, such as news media websites, often host comment threads where Internet users can post their opinions on the topics covered in the main story. Downloading the main content of a news story posted on the web is relatively trivial, but collecting the comment stream presents a problem because the comments can be hosted by another website service or displayed dynamically as a user scrolls further through a web page. In such cases, the default web-archiving tools will not be sufficient.

Finally, another major form of dynamic content on the web is advertising. This content most often is served from domains that may be outside the scope of the seed list provided to the web-crawling software. Furthermore, there is no way to know which ads are being shown to which users because that information is proprietary and controlled by the major corporations that run advertising on the web.

Platform Lock-In

The dominance of major commercial companies in the information sector is also a challenge for web archiving. Facebook, Google, Amazon, Apple, and Microsoft are all near monopolies, and their behavior can have significant impacts on the technology needed for web archiving. Technology changes implemented by single companies can break existing web-archiving software. As companies become dominant, they can develop and implement their own "web standards" that benefit themselves and make it harder (inadvertently) for librarians and archivists to do their job. Even the bounds of fair use law might not help. Digital rights management (DRM) is one example of a software technology that may make it much harder for web archivists to capture content from the web.

FROM SPECIAL COLLECTIONS TO MAINSTREAM

The technological challenges of archiving material from the web are sometimes obvious, but the most difficult problems may be institutional and organizational. In this section, I discuss three institutional challenges for web archiving: assigning responsibility, disciplinary changes in library and archive science, and collaboration with nonlibrary professionals.

Responsibility

To be effective, both librarians and archivists must take responsibility for web archiving. Without cooperation, professional expectations may limit the perspectives of either role. An archivist may be focused on creating or managing a fixed record of a particular situation. She might look at a web page and concentrate on preserving a copy for the future. But the archival aspiration of creating a fixed record for the web is impossible because resources are limited, and the technical architecture of the web constantly changes. Furthermore, there is no single web that everyone sees and thus no archival record that we can declare as authoritative or official.

A librarian may be focused on the collection, deciding what types of material should be included and how they should be accessed. He might want to emphasize patron access and fulfilling information needs. But the librarian who views the web as a collection of resources runs the risk of becoming an index builder who merely directs users to resources they immediately need. Commercial search engines, such as Google and Bing, have usurped this role.

By working together, librarians and archivists can respond to the broader context of web archiving. We know that political influence shapes the type of information published to the web by official governments. Conservative Stephen Harper's web-content streamlining project led to the disappearance of Canadian government information. The same thing happened during the political transition from the Obama to the Trump administration in the United States.[8] Pointing patrons to a collection of web resources is not sufficient if librarians wish to play a role in preserving the public record.

Disciplinarity and Professions

In addition to deciding who is responsible for web archiving, there is the question of how web archiving is treated by the library and archive professions. Is web archiving considered a core part of the education of new librarians or is it treated as an elective? Discussions of web archiving in libraries often begin as part of a larger discussion about digital materials in general, without a specific focus on the diversity of the web itself. The novelty and challenge of managing digital materials may lead to a premature focus on the technical aspects of digital formats instead of a focus on what content we should be trying to collect.

The problem may be too large for librarians and archivists to handle alone. Clifford Lynch argues that the personalization of the web based on big data algorithms can never be captured through the static storing of documents or even the emulation of current browsers because the background resources devoted to creating the web as it is shown to users is too large. Furthermore, there is no commercial incentive to do any of this work. He proposes that the problem requires us to look beyond the standard response of preserving digital artifacts, perhaps leading to a "new discipline and profession of Internet documentation."[9]

Collaboration

The skills needed for web archiving are too broad and too distributed for any one person to manage or even understand, so collaboration is needed in order to build any kind of significant web-archiving program. Collaboration between librarians and technologists is especially important. Librarians are dependent on software engineers to update the harvesting programs that drive web-archiving projects because of the constant technical changes to web architecture. Academia and non-profits such as the Internet Archive are the sources for most of the web-archiving software currently available. Librarians should pay close attention to these areas and offer their input and support where appropriate.

Researchers and academics who are interested in working with web-archive collections or even developing their own collections are another audience with which librarians can collaborate. Librarians are in a perfect position to explain to researchers how web archives work and how they are different from search engines. The hardest difference to explain is that a web archive is not a traditional subject-based collection. Content on the web changes quickly, and past content may only be accessible if someone was actively collecting it while it was available.

Publishers are another constituency that librarians may need to cooperate with. For rapidly updating, ephemeral media such as newspapers, the only way to preserve a record of the changing presentation of news—as it is being edited and revised by journalists—will be to preserve the content management database used by the publication. This cannot be accomplished by librarians alone. In addition, robot.txt files present another issue related to publisher cooperation. These can be used by website owners to instruct web-crawler software to ignore parts of, or the complete whole, of a website. Librarians may argue for fair use or the documentary significance of born-digital content and harvest these sites without the consent of the owner. However, such an approach rapidly runs into ethical challenges and raises issues about what it means to publish or put content into the public discourse. There are no easy answers for this problem or any of the other institutional challenges presented by web archiving.

IMPROVING ACCESSIBILITY

For Researchers

The Twitter archive at the Library of Congress demonstrates some of the technical difficulties that libraries face when trying to provide access to web archives. Even the Library of Congress may not have enough clout to command the resources needed to manage the big data generated by a site such as Twitter. But a larger problem may be communicating to researchers what types of access can actually be achieved.

Researchers will often frame their questions about web phenomena by describing a topic that they wish to study. But the architecture of the web is built on the key idea of a website, a particular set of files that may include many different types of media—including text, images, and video—and is hosted by a particular business, institution, or individual. The tools used to archive the web are built on this technical background for dealing with URLs, APIs, REST, RSS, and other interfaces that human beings do not usually explicitly interact with. In the language of web-archive software, the unit of research is the seed, or base URL, from which data can be harvested. For the researcher, the unit of work is the topic. Negotiating between these two conceptions of how online research should work is a major communication challenge for any type of Internet research.

For Communities

Small communities face resource shortages that may prevent web archiving. The technical ability needed may be far beyond the capability of anyone in the organization. Many of these communities must turn to other cultural heritage organizations, such as libraries or archives, and ask for their assistance in preserving their digital traces.

Another alternative is to build DIY solutions for community archivists. Some projects, such as the Preserving Digital Objects with Restricted Resources (POWRR) project, are attempting to do this,[10] but these efforts are vulnerable to the vagaries of funding, training, and infrastructure.

CONCLUSION

Web archives are important because they represent the major record of how contemporary life is lived. Saving them means providing the future with a better sense of how the contemporary world works, what it thinks about, and how it moves through history.

PART I: Data

We can also use web archives to better understand ourselves by looking at the cultural traces of people around us. Understanding a social movement in the contemporary world means understanding how technology platforms like Facebook, YouTube, and Twitter affect the collective discourse of many different people and groups.

Libraries, in their role as memory institutions, are in a position to provide more than just access to information. Librarians can shape the understanding of that information by helping people comprehend the context in which information comes to them and how to evaluate that information for accuracy and truthfulness.

The library profession needs to think in more depth about the ethical implications of web-archive collection policies. Librarians can hold the government and other organizations accountable by providing a robust record of these entities' actions over time. They can also be engaged in questions about the representation of groups in the archive. Who should determine the material that is saved for future generations? How should librarians respond to these ethical challenges? The traditional response may be to emphasize freedom of access, but it's not at all clear that this is a sustainable position.

Libraries are important stewards of cultural heritage. The profession must recognize that more and more of our culture is created and distributed on the web and provide ways to collect, preserve, and access that material today and in the future. Web archives are a crucial tool for achieving that mission.

NOTES

1. Abbey Potter, "Dodge That Memory Hole: Saving Digital News," *The Signal* (blog), Library of Congress, June 2, 2015, https://blogs.loc.gov/thesignal/2015/06/dodge-that-memory-hole-saving-digital-news/.
2. "Web Archiving | IIPC," International Internet Preservation Consortium (IIPC), n.d., http://netpreserve.org/web-archiving/.
3. "Collection Development Policies | IIPC," IIPC, n.d., http://netpreserve.org/web-archiving/collection-development-policies/.
4. "WARC File Format," International Organization for Standardization (ISO), 2017, www.iso.org/standard/68004.html.
5. The Memento framework provides a protocol for exchanging date times between different archives and for fulfilling client requests. It is not designed to provide a fixed identifier like a DOI. H. Van de Sompel, M. L. Nelson, and R. D. Sanderson, "HTTP Framework for Time-Based Access to Resource States—Memento," Memento Project, 2013, http://mementoweb.org/guide/rfc/.
6. The Library of Congress announced at the end of 2017 that they would no longer be collecting all of the tweets published by Twitter but would continue to selectively

archive tweets going forward. Niraj Chokshi, "The Library of Congress No Longer Wants All the Tweets," *New York Times*, December 27, 2017, www.nytimes.com/2017/12/27/technology/library-congress-tweets.html.

7. Eli Pariser, *The Filter Bubble: What the Internet Is Hiding from You* (New York: Penguin, 2011); Cass R. Sunstein, *Republic.Com* (Princeton, NJ: Princeton University Press, 2001).

8. Anne Kingston, "How Ottawa's War on Data Threatens All That We Know about Canada," *Maclean's*, September 18, 2015, www.macleans.ca/news/canada/vanishing-canada-why-were-all-losers-in-ottawas-war-on-data/; Terrence O'Brien, "Trump's Quiet War on Data Begins," Engadget, March 20, 2017, www.engadget.com/2017/03/20/trumps-quiet-war-on-data-begins/.

9. Clifford Lynch, "Stewardship in the 'Age of Algorithms,'" *First Monday* 22, no. 12 (December 2, 2017), https://doi.org/10.5210/fm.v22i12.8097.

10. "About POWRR," Digital POWRR, last modified August 22, 2017, http://digitalpowrr.niu.edu.

BIBLIOGRAPHY

Chokshi, Niraj. "The Library of Congress No Longer Wants All the Tweets." *New York Times*, December 27, 2017. www.nytimes.com/2017/12/27/technology/library-congress-tweets.html.

Kingston, Anne. "How Ottawa's War on Data Threatens All That We Know about Canada." *Maclean's*, September 18, 2015. www.macleans.ca/news/canada/vanishing-canada-why-were-all-losers-in-ottawas-war-on-data/.

Lynch, Clifford. "Stewardship in the 'Age of Algorithms.'" *First Monday* 22, no. 12 (December 2, 2017). https://doi.org/10.5210/fm.v22i12.8097.

O'Brien, Terrence. "Trump's Quiet War on Data Begins." Engadget, March 20, 2017. www.engadget.com/2017/03/20/trumps-quiet-war-on-data-begins/.

Pariser, Eli. *The Filter Bubble: What the Internet Is Hiding from You*. New York: Penguin, 2011.

Potter, Abbey. "Dodge That Memory Hole: Saving Digital News." *The Signal* (blog), Library of Congress, June 2, 2015. https://blogs.loc.gov/thesignal/2015/06/dodge-that-memory-hole-saving-digital-news/.

Sunstein, Cass R. *Republic.Com*. Princeton, NJ: Princeton University Press, 2001.

Van de Sompel, H., M. L. Nelson, and R. D. Sanderson. "HTTP Framework for Time-Based Access to Resource States—Memento." Memento Project, 2013. http://mementoweb.org/guide/rfc/.

PART II

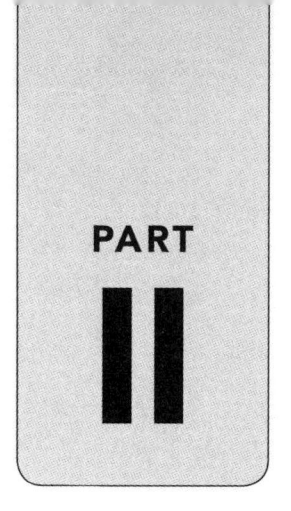

Services

Chapter Five

Privacy-Protection Technology Tools
Libraries and Librarians as Users, Contributors, and Advocates

Monica Maceli

The average Internet user is highly concerned with privacy and perceived loss of control over the collection and use of personal information.[1] However, research findings indicate that most users take little action to protect their privacy, either by making behavioral changes or by using privacy-enhancing tools.[2] In this complex and often paradoxical landscape, librarians and information professionals play a vital role in explaining technical topics and advising their users and patrons as to what privacy-protection tools to employ; the importance of this role will likely dramatically increase in the coming years.

Privacy-protection tools include specialized software such as web browser plug-ins to block ads and behavioral tracking, the Tor browser, virtual private network (VPN) clients, and password managers as well as techniques such as using encryption and avoiding social-engineered attacks. Through a variety of workshops, tool kits, guides, and handbooks, the library community has disseminated information on such tools—both within their peer group and to their patrons and other users. Though organizations such as the Electronic Frontier Foundation (EFF), the Library Freedom Project (LFP), the Institute of Museum and Library Services grant programs, and the American Library Association (ALA) have taken strong stances in favor of privacy-protection policies and supportive technology tools, more work remains in spreading this message throughout libraries and their patron communities. Such technical topics are generally not given extensive coverage within master of library science program curricula beyond ALA's long-standing policy of commitment to protecting patron privacy generally.[3] The increasing complexity of technological environments has led to many individuals feeling overwhelmed by the plethora of personal privacy-protection options.

LIBRARIES AND PRIVACY-PROTECTION TECHNOLOGY TOOLS

The rapidly changing technological landscape has posed myriad challenges to librarianship, such as providing appropriate technology education, keeping pace with job requirements, and posing new privacy-related threats and concerns. Privacy- and computer security–related topics dominate the news cycle on a consistent basis. At the time of writing this chapter, a major data breach was reported at a consumer credit reporting agency, Apple rolled out controversial facial-recognition software, and malware was distributed inside a popular Windows utility program. Given that there are no comprehensive data protection laws in the United States, its citizens are at particular risk of their data being unknowingly collected, commodified, hacked, or shared with third parties. Outside of the US, the General Data Protection Regulation (GDPR) passed within the European Union in 2016 and took effect in May 2018. The GDPR requires data collectors to protect their customers' data and privacy as well as give EU citizens greater control over how their data are used. As many Internet companies operate throughout the world, they have chosen to deploy these changes across all their customers worldwide, potentially giving US citizens more future control of their data and privacy. However, with the general prioritization of corporate interests over those of individual citizens, particularly within the United States, libraries and human rights organizations are the main influencers left to assist communities in protecting themselves when other societal structures may not.

With these trends in mind, the information landscape in the next three to five years is poised to become deeply engaged with the use of and education about privacy-protection technologies, driven by the increasing popularity of such tools as well as the larger societal concerns about protecting one's privacy. This chapter will provide an overview of key privacy-protection technologies, highlight novel efforts in this area within libraries, and suggest future possibilities for libraries to become leaders in this realm.

OVERVIEW OF PRIVACY-PROTECTION TECHNOLOGY TOOLS

The current reality is that no one privacy-protection technology tool provides complete protection against all potentials threats. Determining one's personal priorities, tolerance for risk, and willingness to expend time and money will dictate the tools chosen or the particular scenarios, such as a coffee shop with open Wi-Fi, in which such tools will be employed. A similar needs assessment must be conducted in suggesting tools for use by our patrons and communities more generally. And as in other realms of technology, the tools themselves are not a panacea; rather, they are best combined with human behavioral changes (e.g., only using websites offering HTTPS and valid SSL certificates), so knowing the *why* is as important as learning the *how*.

WEB BROWSING AND BROWSER SAFETY

For many users, implementing privacy-protection tools within their web browser is an immediately tangible, simple, and low-cost starting point. Such browser plug-ins typically provide real-time feedback as to the blocking or protection actions taken by the tool at any given moment. A common protection provided by such plug-ins is the ability to choose what categories of behavioral trackers to allow or block. Tracking may be used for a variety of purposes, from saving personalization preferences or shopping cart contents to collecting browsing habits or determining users' characteristics, such as geographic location, across entire browsing sessions. Fortier and Burkell provide useful background on online behavioral tracking, noting the importance of digital literacy education in this area to help patrons protect their privacy against such threats.[4]

Privacy-protecting plug-ins are available for a variety of browsers and facilitate blocking of advertising, site analytics, social media, and customer interaction

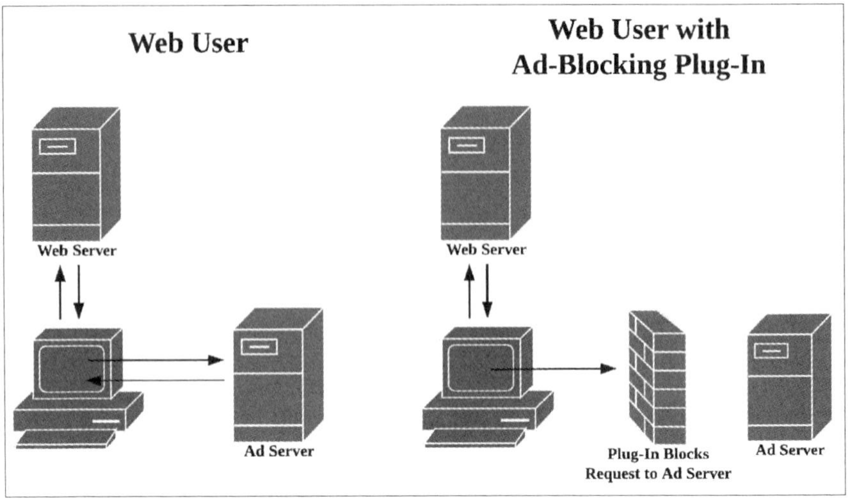

PART II: Services

FIGURE 5.1
Process of blocking ads.

trackers, among other things. This blocking is accomplished by severing the connection between the various trackers and the page the user has requested (figure 5.1), which typically (hidden to the end user) contains extensive code connecting out to other servers to deliver ads, analytics, and other features. Due to a loophole in the security behavior of web cookies, these third-party sites are thus allowed to place a cookie on the user's computer, which can be used to assist in tracking their subsequent site visits.

The Electronic Frontier Foundation (EFF), an influential nonprofit defending digital privacy, free speech, and innovation, offers several browser-based privacy-protection tools created by their organization or in partnership with others.[5] Notable offerings include the HTTPS Everywhere (www.eff.org/https-everywhere) browser plug-in, which rewrites web page requests to ensure usage of the HTTPS-secured version of the site, in which web page data are encrypted in transit between the originating server and the user's browser. Another EFF offering, Privacy Badger (www.eff.org/privacybadger), analyzes and blocks trackers and ads, particularly those that track without user consent. A popular, more general-purpose blocker is UBlock Origin (www.github.com/gorhill/uBlock), which is an open source software released under the GNU General Public License. UBlock Origin can be customized to provide a variety of levels of protection, including preventing the web page from connecting to third-party servers or even blocking the web page's JavaScript from running at all. Though many plug-ins exist in this broad domain, understanding the philosophy and business model behind their creation and use can assist librarians in assessing its true protective abilities and data collection policies.

Incognito mode, available in all modern browsers, can be leveraged to protect against later users of the same computer viewing your stored browsing data, though it is limited in the protection it affords users. In the web browsing realm more generally, users may seek out sites that provide needed services within the framework of a more consumer-focused privacy policy. One such growing service is DuckDuckGo (www.duckduckgo.com), a privacy-protection search engine that does not track searches or store users' personal information.

SECURITY WHILE TRAVERSING NETWORKS

As briefly mentioned in the previous section, behavioral choices, such as using sites that offer HTTPS to secure web data as it travels back and forth from the user's computer, assist in protecting privacy of data in transit. Many web users are unaware of the inherent insecurity of the Internet and the relatively trivial task of intercepting unencrypted web page data using tools such as packet sniffers. In response to these issues, several important privacy-protection tools have gained popularity in providing robust protection of data as it travels unsecured networks. A virtual private network (VPN) serves to encrypt users' traffic between their computers and the VPN server within a secure "tunnel," providing protection while traversing an open wireless network or from Internet service providers (ISPs) snooping into their traffic. Additionally, VPNs are commonly used to allow off-site access to companies' internal private networks. As detailed in figure 5.2, the user's traffic is lastly sent over the insecure network from the VPN server to their ultimate destination server. To the destination server, the traffic appears to originate from the VPN server itself as opposed to the user's actual machine (and associated IP address).

Due to growing concerns about surveillance and data collection from a variety of entities (governments, ISPs, malicious users on open Wi-Fi networks, etc.), VPNs have seen a steep increase in use in the consumer realm. However, using a VPN necessarily entails trusting the VPN provider with one's traffic and browsing history, so selecting a reliable option with clear policies regarding log retention and data collection activities is of the utmost importance. Troublingly, a recent study found that many VPN apps entirely failed to encrypt traffic or even injected malware.[6] Understanding both the role of the VPN and what assurances to seek out in the provider's policy are important skills for the future information professional. The

PART II: Services

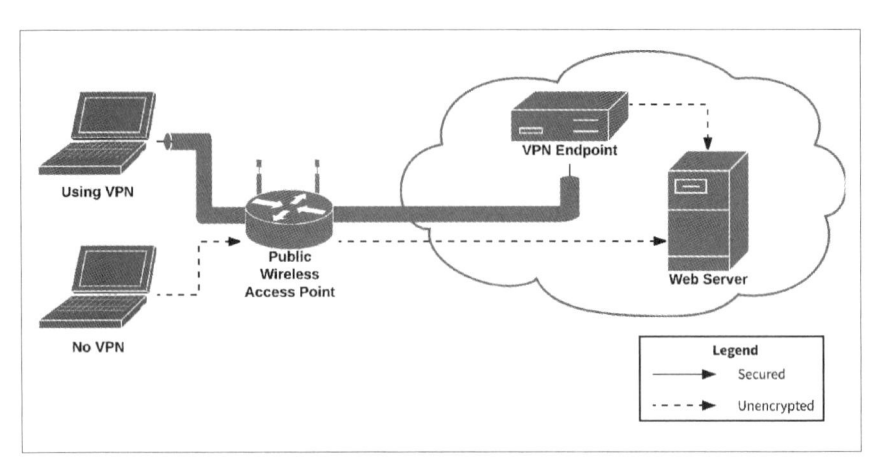

FIGURE 5.2
Function of a virtual private network (VPN).

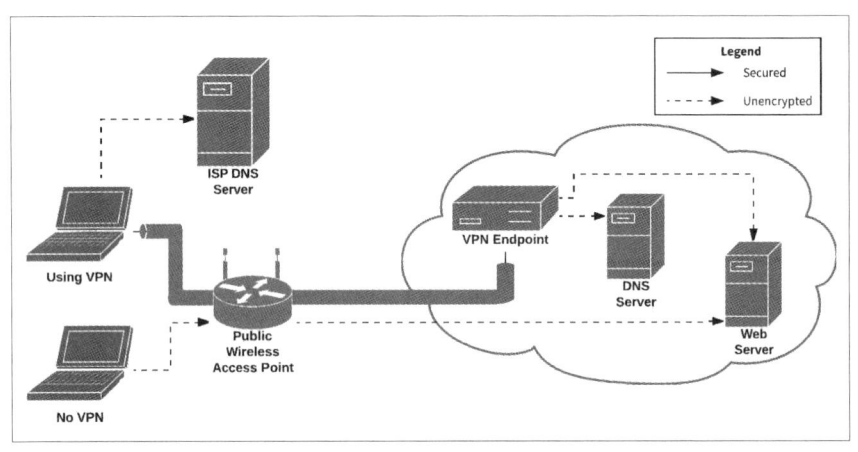

FIGURE 5.3
DNS leaking while using a virtual private network (VPN).

EFF maintains information (www.ssd.eff.org/en/module/choosing-vpn-thats-right-you) to assist users in the difficult process of choosing a VPN, and a variety of sites rank and assess VPNs based on a number of characteristics, including jurisdiction, logging, security, and pricing.

In using a VPN, additional privacy threats may emerge, such as Domain Name System (DNS) leaking (figure 5.3). In order to retrieve the destination server's IP address, the user's web browser must first contact a DNS server to translate the symbolic domain name (e.g., www.google.com) into its corresponding IP address

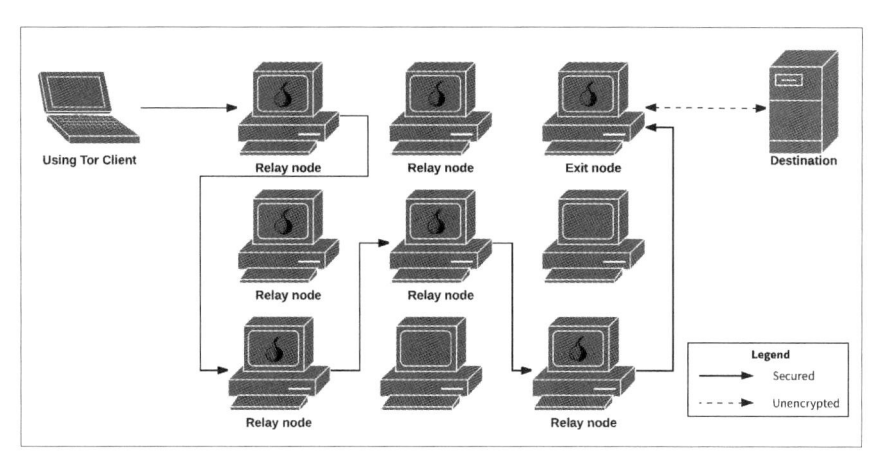

FIGURE 5.4
The Tor anonymity network.

(e.g., 74.125.28.147). Typically, the DNS servers are set by the user's Internet service provider, and thus the information of sites visited can be collected by the ISP (and in the United States as of March 2017, may legally be resold by the ISP).

Changing one's DNS servers to a public option or seeking out a trusted VPN that automatically changes network settings to use the VPN's DNS servers can combat this threat.

The Tor Project is a volunteer-run network that provides anonymity for users browsing the web. While VPNs can be a useful tool for securing your browsing behavior from others on an unsecured network or your Internet service provider, depending on the protection and policy of your VPN provider, your actions can be easily traced back to you. In contrast, the Tor software was developed to hide users' identities by routing their traffic through a series of other computers, known as Tor relays, thus allowing for the high level of anonymity needed by those avoiding censorship and surveillance (activists, journalists, whistle-blowers, military intelligence gathering operatives, etc.). Instead of the usual routing mechanism of traversing the Internet in which a direct path is taken, the Tor network seeks to obfuscate the destination and origin of traffic by taking a random pathway through several Tor relays, each "hop" of which is encrypted and unaware of the previous path taken by the data (figure 5.4). Most of the relays are volunteer-run personal computers and can be run on any operating system, with approximately 6,388 Tor relays as of May 2018 (metrics.torproject.org).

The Tor network does contain weaknesses and potential pitfalls. Some arise from technical exploits, whereas others result from Tor users' inadvertently identifying actions (e.g., peer-to-peer downloading or logging in to personally identifying social media sites). Novice Tor users may be most vulnerable to such privacy threats, highlighting the need for education alongside use.

The Tor Project also provided financial support in developing a security-focused Linux distribution—the Amnesic Incognito Live System, known as Tails (http://tails.boum.org)—designed to run live on external media (a USB stick or DVD) for those seeking an even higher level of anonymity and security. The Tails operating system leaves no trace on the host computer and forces all traffic to be channeled through Tor. Tails also provides the user with a collection of cryptographic tools configured by default to provide highly secure use of common applications such as e-mail, web browsing, and instant messaging.

PRIVACY PROTECTION FOR ACCOUNT CREDENTIALS AND DATA

The privacy-protection technology tools explored above primarily focus on the security of data in transit across networks. Equal attention must be paid to the protection of data "at rest," when they are stored on personal or organizational computing devices, as well as to maintaining the privacy of ones' credentials used to access these systems. As with previous examples, such as HTTPs and VPNs, encryption plays a large role in maintaining privacy of data, with many operating systems increasingly providing built-in tools to encrypt files or the entire storage device (e.g., BitLocker for Microsoft Windows, FileVault for Mac OSX). Numerous third-party tools exist to encrypt data on a variety of devices. Full-device encryption is of particular importance for portable devices that can be easily lost or stolen. A popular open source option is the VeraCrypt (www.veracrypt.fr) utility for computers and devices running Windows, Mac OS X, or Linux, which improved on long-standing encryption features provided by its predecessor—TrueCrypt.

In addition to protecting data, many tools assist users in securely storing and keeping track of their numerous account credentials and aid in creating strong, unique passwords for each service used. Password managers (such as KeePassX, 1Password, or LastPass), combined with multifactor authentication, greatly improve the security and privacy of accounts. Two-factor authentication is an increasingly common offering of many websites and includes an additional log-in step, which may consist of entering a code sent via SMS to one's phone or using a software or hardware authentication device (e.g., the Google Authenticator, or Authy app; YubiKey security key; etc.).

Lastly, following general security best practices helps keep data and devices secure and private at both a personal and an organizational level. These practices include regularly running software updates, being careful about sharing settings on public networks, using built-in or third-party virus and malware protection tools, and avoiding social-engineered exploits (e.g., by deleting unknown attachments, checking digital signatures on downloaded files, and identifying phishing attempts). Robust digital literacy in computer security and privacy is often required to detect and avoid such threats, emphasizing the role libraries can play in educating patrons in this area. However, as to be expected in the fast-paced technology landscape, new vulnerabilities will be detected and compensated for, new privacy-protection technology tools will emerge, and best practices will shift as a result.

EARLY LIBRARY ADOPTERS OF PRIVACY-PROTECTION TECHNOLOGIES

Numerous exciting and thought-provoking projects have introduced privacy-protection technologies into the library landscape. As with earlier work in this area, the Library Freedom Project continues to play a prominent role in sponsoring, partnering, and otherwise facilitating and motivating such efforts. A few notable projects, either in progress or at their inception, that stand to have an impact in the coming three to five years are featured in the following section, including the use of Tor in libraries and several recent grants encouraging widespread privacy-related education in library communities.

TOR IN LIBRARIES

Providing patrons with the tools and knowledge necessary to protect their privacy in the online environment is an increasingly important function of libraries, which have provided public Internet services to their communities for decades. In the summer of 2015, the nonprofit privacy-focused Library Freedom Project announced a pilot program exploring the use of Tor in libraries, beginning with implementing and running a Tor relay in the Kilton Library of Lebanon, New

Hampshire.[7] Chuck McAndrew, IT librarian at the Kilton Library, collaborated with the LFP to implement the Tor relay. A process of experimentation was necessary to determine the appropriate level of the library's bandwidth to allocate to the Tor network so as to not negatively affect other library services. However, McAndrew reports that the relay was ultimately found to be generally low impact and require little technical maintenance once the project launched.[8]

The relay was then configured to serve as a Tor exit node. As detailed earlier (see figure 5.4), the Tor exit nodes provide access from within Tor to the larger Internet. These exit nodes represent a smaller subset of the total set of relays and often draw attention for illegal online activity, as traffic appears to be originating from the exit node used. Soon after its launch, the Kilton Library's Tor pilot received significant press coverage when both the Department of Homeland Security and the local police in New Hampshire demanded that the relay be shut down. The immediate public outcry against the relay's shutdown led the library board to unanimously vote to reinstate it. The exit node remains running to this day and over time has proven to be less controversial in practice. The library has received only a handful of security-related notifications from their Internet service provider, which were generated by the exit node's traffic. And, per McAndrew, the issues that have been flagged were commonplace, such as spam e-mail generation or Digital Millennium Copyright Act (DMCA)–related violations.

In addition to providing an exit node as a service to the wider Tor community, the Tor browser is currently installed on several public-use computers within the Kilton Library, and Tor workshops are offered for patrons wishing to learn more. Though the library does not track usage of the Tor client in-house, McAndrew has observed that the signage and mention of Tor serve as useful conversation points to spark discussion between library staff and patrons. Since the original Tor relay was launched, several other libraries have begun similar work, participating in running Tor relays and providing Tor client access on library machines. As libraries are already in the business of providing public Internet access, and have been for many years, McAndrew suggests that providing library-run VPN servers for use by library patrons could be another valuable service for libraries in the future.

To further affirm the right to run Tor within libraries, Alison Macrina, founder of the Library Freedom Project, worked with New Hampshire state representative Keith Ammon and other lawmakers to put forth a bill expressly allowing libraries to install and use cryptographic privacy platforms and software. In spring 2016, the bill passed the New Hampshire House of Representatives but ultimately stalled in the state senate.

INSTITUTE OF MUSEUM AND LIBRARY STUDIES SUPPORT FOR EARLY ADOPTERS

The Institute of Museum and Library Studies (IMLS) recently funded several grant proposals intended to further librarians' knowledge and use of privacy-protection concepts and technology tools. First, the aforementioned nonprofit Library Freedom Project has been a highly influential organization in the privacy domain, running privacy-related educational sessions for approximately 1,500 librarians per year since 2013.[9] In partnership with New York University (NYU), the Library Freedom Project was awarded a two-year grant that will "give librarians the practical, 21st century skills they need to safeguard patron privacy in the digital era" by training them to educate their peers and communities on privacy topics within their Library Freedom Institute (LFI). This work, which is just beginning, has the potential to broadly affect librarianship within the coming years and demonstrates the current recognition of privacy as a vitally important topic to the community.

A few years earlier, the IMLS funded the Digital Privacy Project, run by Brooklyn Public Library and several collaborators, with the goal of supporting librarians' professional development to assist in aiding patrons with their digital privacy and data-profiling questions and needs.[10] An earlier research project focusing on public perceptions of surveillance revealed that librarians and library staff themselves had many questions about digital privacy and data security.[11] To support digital-privacy training programs within libraries, the Data Privacy Project developed workshop curricula, online quizzes, and other educational materials to facilitate the reuse of their work, all available for free on their website.

Melissa Morrone of Brooklyn Public Library reports that their digital privacy materials were subsequently used for professional development workshops in Texas and California and formed the basis of the recently announced "NYC Digital Safety: Privacy & Security" initiative.[12] This partnership among New York City's three library systems and regional library resources council will run specialized trainings, both online and in person, on privacy and digital security for more than one thousand library staff by the summer of 2018, with strong support from local government officials.

PRIVACY-PROTECTION TECHNOLOGIES AND THE LIBRARY OF 2022

These early adopters and the larger societal trends toward privacy protection suggest an exciting and imminent opportunity for libraries to step to the forefront of this complex area as privacy-technology educators, practitioners, users, and advocates. The projects described above received more than half a million dollars of funding from the IMLS, signaling a strong commitment to the expansion of library services in the privacy area. Over the next five years, privacy-related concerns and anxieties are likely to continue to rise in the general public. The original vision of the open, democratic, and uncensored Internet is constantly under siege; users may be monitored, spied on, and tracked in nearly every aspect of their online lives, oftentimes with the law on the side of the data collectors. Though such tracking may be for relatively benign reasons, such as providing targeted advertisements or recommendations, users may still prefer that such companies do not collect their personal information. Libraries are perfectly positioned, alongside human rights and nonprofit organizations, to advocate for and to help protect the average citizen against such privacy threats and concerns.

Work in the area of privacy education is already under way in libraries, with great potential for the coming years. Just one of the funded projects mentioned earlier—the Library Freedom Institute—seeks to educate forty trainers who will then spread their privacy-related knowledge to their communities and peers. Were each of these trainers to reach even a fraction of the librarians who attended the original Library Freedom Project privacy-education sessions, many thousands of librarians will be trained in this area in the next five years.

Though the bulk of privacy-related efforts currently focus on continuing education for practicing librarians, there is an additional need to heighten the presence of these topics in the curriculum of library science degree–granting programs so that early career librarians enter the field with deeper knowledge in this area. Library science master's programs provide a broad range of technology education; however, privacy-protection technologies themselves have lacked prominence within curricula, with no programs demonstrating significant course offerings in this area.

Current technology trends in libraries, such as the makerspace, are a proof of concept for the library continuing to serve as a novel technology space. The makerspace has, in many libraries, become a permanent fixture and introduces patrons to everything from crafts to innovative do-it-yourself technologies, such as microcontrollers. In addition to formal privacy-education sessions, one can imagine similarly oriented, privacy-focused technology spaces becoming the norm, allowing users to experiment with Tor, VPNs, the TAILS operating systems, browser plug-ins, and the future privacy-protection tools that will invariably succeed (or complement) them.

Librarians on the front lines of reference may typically suggest technologies and techniques to protect users as well as demonstrate, configure, and assist in using such tools on the patron's own devices. Librarians will increasingly find themselves advocating for patron privacy and security in the context of using the numerous third-party tools such as e-book lending software or electronic journal vendors. It will likely fall to libraries, as customers of these companies, to pressure such organizations to respect our patrons' privacy and ensure adequate security practices.

Libraries will also contribute to privacy efforts for a worldwide collection of remote patrons through technological offerings such as running Tor relays, VPN servers, or even DNS servers. These systems may be used by any member of the public who desires such protections from a trusted source or wishes to support the libraries' organizational commitments to anonymity. Though such offerings incur costs over time—for example, through investments in staff, technology, and support—the willingness of influential granting bodies like the IMLS to fund privacy-related work is a promising sign that this may be possible on a wider scale in the future. And the eagerness of additional libraries to expand the Tor Project is a clear signal of both interest and perceived worth in serving remote patrons.

Lastly, librarians themselves must become personal users of such technologies on a consistent basis, as these issues affect us all. Robust knowledge in this area is built not only through participating in direct educational efforts but also through the deep familiarity arising from making privacy-protection tools part of daily life. Even if there are current barriers to expanding privacy-related offerings in one's particular library, librarians may still begin to use, experiment with, and build their hands-on understanding of the tools explained above. The excellent resources currently provided by the Library Freedom Project (http://libraryfreedomproject.org/resources/) offer an accessible starting point for librarians at all stages of their careers to prepare for the increase in privacy-protection technologies in the coming years.

NOTES

1. Mary Madden, "Public Perceptions of Privacy and Security in the Post-Snowden Era," Pew Research Center, last modified November 12, 2014, www.pewinternet.org/2014/11/12/public-privacy-perceptions/.
2. Delfina Malandrino, Vittorio Scarano, and Raffaele Spinelli, "How Increased Awareness Can Impact Attitudes and Behaviors toward Online Privacy Protection," *International Conference on Social Computing* (2013): 58, https://doi.org/10.1109/SocialCom.2013.15.
3. Monica Maceli, "Creating Tomorrow's Technologists: Contrasting Information Technology Curriculum in North American Library and Information Science Graduate Programs against Code4lib Job Listings," *Journal of Education for Library and Information Science Online* 56, no. 3 (2015): 202–9, http://dx.doi.org/10.12783/

issn.2328-2967/56/3/3; "Privacy," American Library Association (ALA), last modified September 25, 2017, www.ala.org/advocacy/intfreedom/librarybill/interpretations/privacy.

4. Alexandre Fortier and Jacquelyn Burkell, "Hidden Online Surveillance: What Librarians Should Know to Protect Their Own Privacy and That of Their Patrons," *Information Technology and Libraries* 34, no. 3 (2015): 59–68, https://doi.org/10.6017/ital.v34i3.5495.

5. "About EFF," Electronic Frontier Foundation, last modified February 6, 2018, www.eff.org/about.

6. Muhammad Ikram et al., "An Analysis of the Privacy and Security Risks of Android VPN Permission-Enabled Apps," *Internet Measurement Conference* (2016): 353–54, https://doi.org/10.1145/2987443.2987471.

7. Alison Macrina, "Tor Exit Relays in Libraries: A New LFP Project," Library Freedom Project, last modified July 28, 2015, https://libraryfreedomproject.org/torexitpilotphase1/.

8. Chuck McAndrew, personal communication, October 30, 2017.

9. "RE-95-17-0076-17," Institute of Museum and Library Services, last modified October 3, 2017, www.imls.gov/grants/awarded/re-95-17-0076-17.

10. "RE-06-15-0050-15," Institute of Museum and Library Services, last modified September 21, 2016, www.imls.gov/grants/awarded/re-06-15-0050-15; "Introduction," Data Privacy Project, last modified October 23, 2017, www.dataprivacyproject.org/about/.

11. Seeta Peña Gangadharan, "Library Privacy in Practice: System Change and Challenges," *I/S: A Journal of Law and Policy for the Information Society* 13, no. 1 (2017): 194–97.

12. Melissa Morrone, personal communication, November 22, 2017.

BIBLIOGRAPHY

Fortier, Alexandre, and Jacquelyn Burkell. "Hidden Online Surveillance: What Librarians Should Know to Protect Their Own Privacy and That of Their Patrons." *Information Technology and Libraries* 34, no. 3 (2015): 59–72. https://doi.org/10.6017/ital.v34i3.5495.

Gangadharan, Seeta Peña. "Library Privacy in Practice: System Change and Challenges." *I/S: A Journal of Law and Policy for the Information Society* 13, no. 1 (2017): 175–98.

Ikram, Muhammad, Narseo Vallina-Rodriguez, Suranga Seneviratne, Mohamed Ali Kaafar, and Vern Paxson. "An Analysis of the Privacy and Security Risks of Android VPN Permission-Enabled Apps." *Internet Measurement Conference* (2016): 349–64. https://doi.org/10.1145/2987443.2987471.

Maceli, Monica. "Creating Tomorrow's Technologists: Contrasting Information Technology Curriculum in North American Library and Information Science Graduate Programs against Code4lib Job Listings." *Journal of Education for Library and Information Science Online* 56, no. 3 (2015): 198–212. http://dx.doi.org/10.12783/issn.2328-2967/56/3/3.

Macrina, Alison. "Tor Exit Relays in Libraries: A New LFP Project." *Library Freedom Project*, last modified July 28, 2015. https://libraryfreedomproject.org/torexitpilotphase1/.

Madden, Mary. "Public Perceptions of Privacy and Security in the Post-Snowden Era." Pew Research Center, last modified November 12, 2014. www.pewinternet.org/2014/11/12/public-privacy-perceptions/.

Malandrino, Delfina, Vittorio Scarano, and Raffaele Spinelli. "How Increased Awareness Can Impact Attitudes and Behaviors toward Online Privacy Protection." *International Conference on Social Computing* (2013): 57–62. https://doi.org/10.1109/SocialCom.2013.15.

Chapter Six

Data for Discovery

Julia Bauder

Data visualizations—representations of numeric information in visual forms ranging from basic bar charts to dynamic, multidimensional graphics—have existed since at least 1786.[1] In that year, William Playfair published the first known bar chart, which displayed the volume of Scottish exports to and imports from seventeen countries.[2] A few years later, he also invented the pie chart, using it to show what proportions of the Turkish Empire's territory were in Asia, Africa, and Europe. For the next two hundred years, bar charts, pie charts, and a few other basic kinds of charts—relatively simple, static images conveying information on only one or two dimensions—were the dominant types of data visualizations. Even today, librarians might create a pie chart showing how much of a library's collection is fiction, nonfiction, juvenile, and so on or a bar chart showing the average number of patrons in the library at different hours of the day. Visualizations of this sort of operational data make it easy for library administrators to spot trends

PART II: Services

or problems and simple to demonstrate those issues to the library's staff, funders, or other stakeholders.

While simple visualizations of operational data remain common, librarians have only recently started to encounter another type of data visualization: interactive representations of library collections, search results, or individual titles. These interfaces, which are primarily intended for patrons and reference librarians rather than administrators, aim to help users navigate collections in some way. Some of them help patrons refine their queries by visualizing how the results of their searches cluster into various subtopics. Other interfaces allow users to see connections between documents in a collection, indicating which documents were most influential and whether later authors have engaged with or ignored specific earlier documents. Another type of visualization displays information about just one book, providing a richer sense of the book's contents and letting users home in on the particular chapter or passage that seems most relevant to their needs.[3]

If one origin of these visualized discovery interfaces is the data visualization tradition, another is the concept of so-called direct manipulation interfaces. The basic idea of direct manipulation interfaces is familiar to any mobile phone or tablet user today: use a finger on the screen to move the page up or down, drag and drop to move objects from one place to another, and otherwise directly operate on visual representations of the machine's virtual reality as similarly as possible to how one would do so in the physical world. However, in the early 1980s, before the 1984 release of the first Apple Macintosh computer, direct manipulation interfaces were a revolutionary idea of great interest to some researchers in the nascent field of human-computer interaction. One of these researchers, Ben Shneiderman, went on to spend more than thirty years expanding on these ideas in an attempt to make computer interfaces ever more user friendly. By the early 1990s, he and other researchers had applied direct manipulation principles to search interfaces, creating what he called *dynamic queries*: search interfaces where users manipulated sliders and other graphical controls to change search parameters and where the results of those changes were immediately displayed to them in some sort of visualization. A good early example of this is the FilmFinder.[4]

Although Shneiderman and others have been experimenting with search interfaces that incorporate visualizations such as these for decades, only now are they becoming common "in the wild." Today one major library database vendor, Gale, has a visualized search interface in production, and JSTOR has released its Topic**graph** interface for browsing books as a public beta. LexisNexis has purchased Ravel Law, a start-up company that designed a visual interface for exploring court decisions, and has promised to incorporate Ravel's visualizations into some of its products by 2018. Another start-up, Yewno, is actively promoting its visualized discovery layer, Yewno Discover, to both academic and high school libraries.[5]

This chapter will examine some of these interfaces in detail, including a discussion of the technologies that underlie them. The end of the chapter contains resources for libraries that are interested in incorporating these sorts of visualized search interfaces into their own services either by adding these visualizations to their own discovery layers or by helping their customers create visualizations such as these based on corpora selected by the patrons.

VISUALIZING SEARCH RESULTS: GALE TOPIC FINDER

The User Experience

Gale was the first of the vendors covered in this chapter to put a visualized discovery system into production. The company announced its intention to roll out term clusters in April 2013 as part of its new Artemis interface, and within a year, it made the tool available in many of Gale's databases.[6] The term-cluster interface was subsequently renamed Topic Finder to make it clearer to users, especially high school and undergraduate students, how and why they might want to use the tool.

After performing a search, users can click on the Topic Finder link on the search results page to see "a subset of [their] top results" clustered and visualized either as a sunburst chart (figure 6.1) or as a Voronoi treemap (figure 6.2).[7]

As can be seen in figures 6.1 and 6.2, which both show the results of a search for *pride* and *prejudice* in Gale's Academic OneFile database, clustering can help users isolate and ignore a large volume of irrelevant results at once. For example, a student who was assigned to write a paper about *Pride and Prejudice* for an English literature class is probably not going to find useful material in the texts in the "Zombies" cluster, which are about the 2009 novel *Pride and Prejudice and Zombies* and the 2016 film adaptation of the same name. The treemap visualization highlights two other sets of results that are irrelevant to our hypothetical student, which appear in the clusters "African Americans" and "Civil Rights." The documents in both of these clusters contain stories of people who faced prejudice and who either had pride or in whom their communities took pride—accurate keyword matches for *pride* and *prejudice*, but nothing to do with the novel.

Let's consider another example, one that better illustrates why the tool is named Topic Finder. A student who wants to write a paper about jaguars and searches

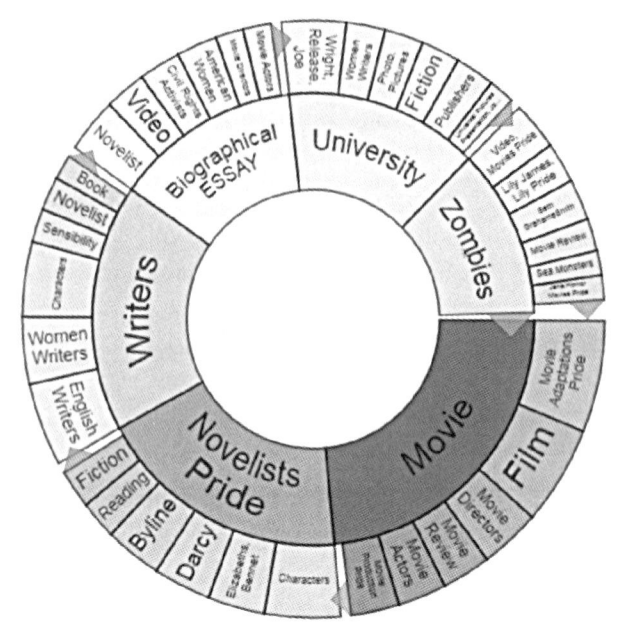

FIGURE 6.1
A screenshot of a wheel visualization
of a search for *pride and prejudice*.

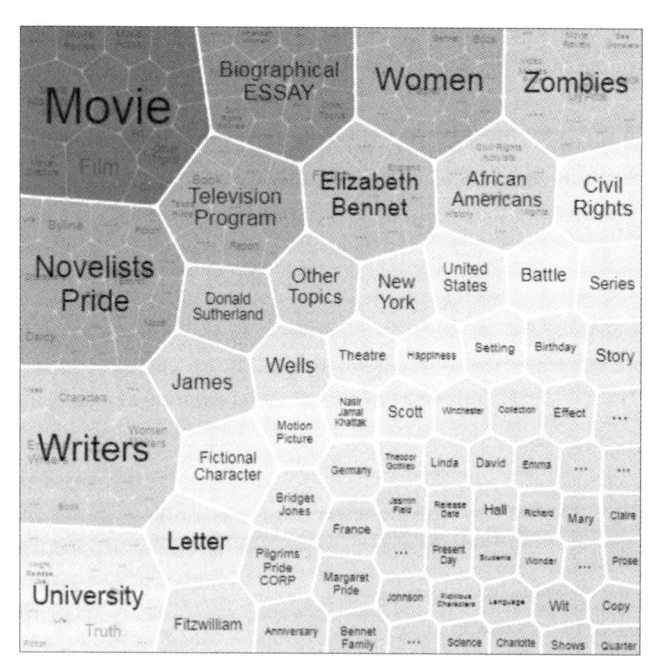

FIGURE 6.2
A screenshot of a treemap visualization
of a search for *Pride and Prejudice*.

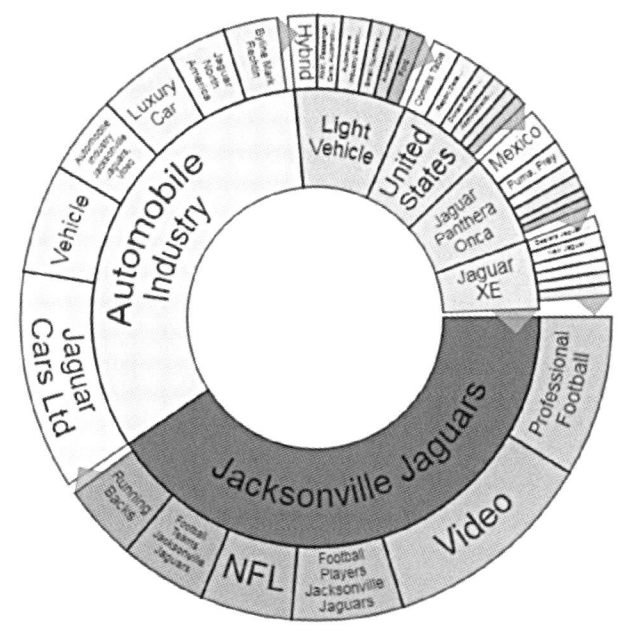

FIGURE 6.3
A wheel visualization of a search for *jaguar*.

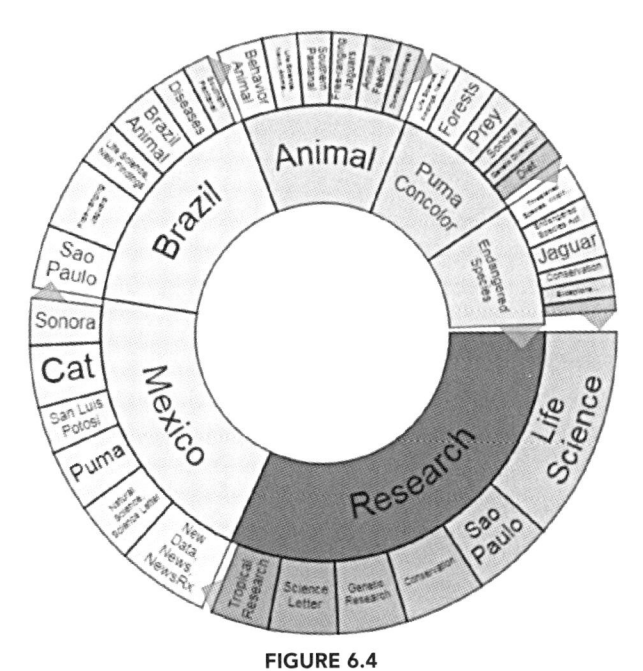

FIGURE 6.4
A wheel visualization of a search for *Panthera onca*.

with the simple term *jaguar* will see a wheel visualization like the one in figure 6.3.[8] Note that only the articles in the "Jaguar Panthera Onca" cluster are about the cat (whose scientific name is *Panthera onca*) rather than about the automotive company or the Jacksonville-based football team. If our hypothetical student sees this and searches again with the search term *Panthera onca*, the result will be the visualization in figure 6.4. Some of the topics in the outer wheel may represent viable, more focused paper topics for this student: genetic research (largely about genetic diversity in jaguar populations); the behavior of jaguars, feeding and otherwise; the role of wildlife corridors in jaguar conservation. Clicking on one of these clusters—or any other cluster in the inner or outer wheel—brings up the search results for articles in that cluster in a pane to the right of the visualization.

The Technology

Topic Finder is built using components from Carrot Search, a company that produces open source and proprietary code both for clustering documents and for visualizing the results of those clustering operations. The two visualization options, labeled "Wheel" and "Tiles" in Gale's interface, are Carrot Search's Circles (sunburst; see figures 6.1, 6.3, and 6.4) and FoamTree (Voronai treemap; see figure 6.2) visualizations, respectively.[9] Topic Finder uses Carrot Search's proprietary Lingo3G algorithm to perform the clustering. Since this algorithm is proprietary, very few details about how it works have been made publicly available. Speaking very generally, clustering algorithms create mathematical representations of documents based on whether words in the corpus appear in that document and, if they do appear, their relative frequency. These mathematical representations can then be compared for similarities, and representations that are most similar to each other and most different from the other representations can be gathered into a cluster.[10] In the case of algorithms like Lingo3G that create a hierarchy of clusters, an analogous process is used to group similar clusters together to form higher levels of the hierarchy or to break clusters apart into subclusters that are as dissimilar as possible.

Readers who are interested in further exploring clustering and visualization of search results but who do not have access to any Gale databases that support Topic Finder can experiment with Carrot Search's open source Carrot² "search results clustering engine." Carrot², which can be found at http://search.carrot2.org, allows users to search either the entire web or a few specific sites, including Wikipedia and PubMed, and view the results clustered using one of three different nonproprietary clustering algorithms. Results can be visualized either as Circles or as a FoamTree.

Chapter Six: Data for Discovery

VISUALIZING A SINGLE BOOK: JSTOR'S TOPICGRAPH

The User Experience

JSTOR's Topic**graph** interface, which was released in beta in December 2016, is more focused than Gale's Topic Finder. While the Topic Finder seeks to visualize large sets of search results, Topic**graph** visualizes the contents of a single book. As staff at JSTOR Labs have explained, the purpose of this visualization is not to replace the experience of reading a monograph; one of the goals that their advisory group gave them when designing the system was to "respect the integrity of the long-form argument as a complete narrative."[11] Instead, the goal is to help scholars who are searching for books on a topic decide more efficiently and effectively whether a given book is relevant enough to their work to merit reading in full. "Researchers told us that they usually look at anywhere from five to twenty pages of a monograph online before deciding to download the full book file or acquire a print copy," the JSTOR Labs staff reported. Thus they designed Topic**graph** to "allow users to target the pages they look at with greater specificity than the alternative, and then evaluate the usefulness of those pages to their research more quickly than they might otherwise."[12]

When a user opens a book in the Topic**graph** interface, they are presented with two panes. The pane on the left contains roughly twenty area charts, with each

FIGURE 6.5
Screenshot of *Burning Bright*, including the first six topics.

chart representing one topic covered in the book. As can be seen in figure 6.5, the x-axis is pages in the book, often with chapter breaks indicated; the y-axis represents how many of the words on a given page of the book are related to that topic. The pane on the right is a viewer that displays pages from the PDF of the book. Clicking on a page in one of the area graphs will bring up that page in the right pane, with words that are strongly related to the clicked-on topic highlighted. Users can also hover over an *i* icon next to the label for each graph to see which words the model has determined to be most indicative of writing about that topic. For example, hovering over the icon next to the label "Sculptors" reveals that the words most strongly associated with sculptors are "sculptor, sculpture, artist, marble, bronze, statue, art, plaster, sculptural, carved, studio, [M]ichelangelo, monument, carving, gallery, [and] portrait."[13]

The Technology

The topics used in the Topic**graph** are created by a method known as latent Dirichlet allocation (LDA), which treats each document that it analyzes as a "bag of words." The algorithms do not take into account any structure or syntax in the documents, nor do they attempt to infer the meaning of any given word in its context; their input is simply the number of times different words appear in different documents. (Note that a "document" in the context of LDA doesn't have to be a complete document as a human would understand that term. In the Topic**graph** example, each individual page in a book is treated as being one document.)

The topics created by LDA are also bags of words. Each topic created by the topic model is a set of words—like the ones associated with "Sculptors," mentioned above—and their relative frequencies (technically the probability that, if one chose a word at random from the words that are part of that topic, one would choose that word). Words can be part of more than one topic; to take one example, in the model used by Topic**graph**, *plaster* is a frequently occurring word in both the "Sculptors" and the "Surgical casts" topics.[14]

In addition to being bags of words, documents can also be thought of as bags of topics. Each document does not have to be (and typically is not) "about" a single topic in the topic model. For example, as can be seen in figure 6.5, many of the words on the first few pages of chapter 15 of *Burning Bright* belong to the topics "Engraving" and "Queens," but there are also a lesser number of words on those pages related to "Portraits." (Chapter 15, "Edward Harding and Queen Charlotte," is about a man named Edward Harding who worked as Queen Charlotte's librarian and who also helped operate a family publishing business that was known for selling engraved portraits.)

The math by which an LDA model gets from a set of documents to a set of topics and determines how much any given document is "about" any given topic involves Bayesian statistics. Speaking at a very high level, topic modeling with LDA starts by assuming that each document in the corpus was produced by randomly selecting words from a given number of topics, where each topic is a list of words and their probabilities. It then tries to work backward from the documents given to figure out what the topics are, from which topic or topics the words in each document were drawn, and what percentage of each document was drawn from each topic.[15]

VISUALIZING COURT CASES: RAVEL LAW

The User Experience

Ravel Law was founded by two students at Stanford University's law school who wanted to bring the sorts of high-tech analytical tools that are available in other industries to the legal field. Their Ravel platform uses a variety of algorithms to turn court rulings into different kinds of data. Only one set of data, which indicates how legal cases are related to each other, and its associated visualization are covered in this chapter. Other types of data created by Ravel, such as those used to analyze individual judges' rulings to help lawyers figure out which types of arguments each judge finds particularly persuasive, are beyond the scope of this chapter.

Ravel Law was purchased by LexisNexis in June 2017, and it is very possible that the experience of using Ravel may change as it is integrated into LexisNexis's platforms. The following describes the experience of using Ravel as it existed in 2017, before integration with LexisNexis.

When a Ravel user searches for court decisions, she is given the option to view the results in the traditional list view or switch to "visual search." In the visual search mode, the top seventy-five results, ranked by relevance, are displayed on a "Case Map," as can be seen in figure 6.6. The x-axis of the Case Map is always time, with more recent cases being displayed farther to the right. The user can choose whether to have the y-axis be based purely on the relevance ranking or to separate cases into multiple bands, with the top band representing cases from the Supreme Court and each lower band representing a lower court, such as district courts or state courts. Because the circles for the different levels of courts are different shades of blue, even when the cases are displayed purely by relevance on the y-axis, it's

PART II: Services

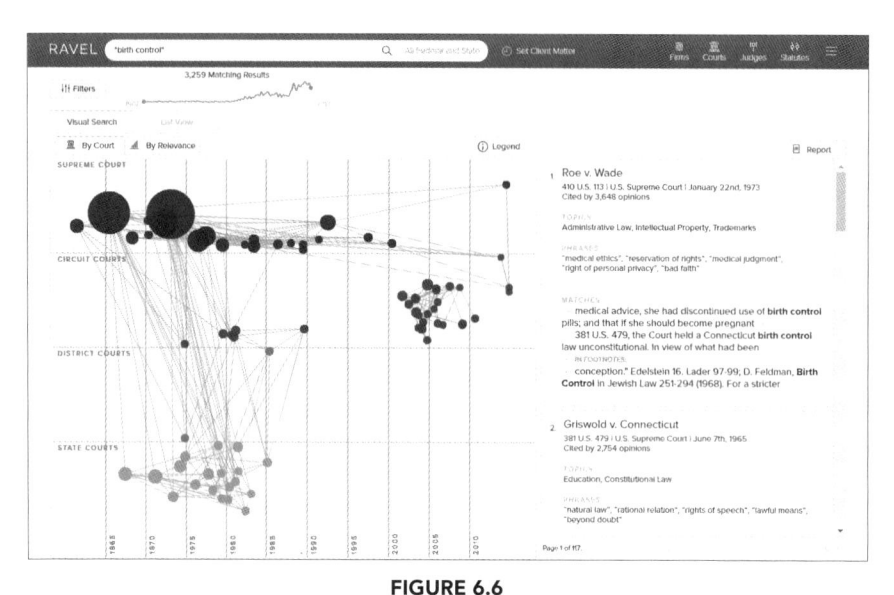

FIGURE 6.6
A screenshot of the Ravel Case Map for a search for *birth control*.

still clear to users which type of court heard each case. The more times a decision has been cited by other cases that also match the user's keyword search, the larger its circle on the Case Map. Faint gray lines indicate cases that cite each other. When the user hovers over a particular case's circle, the lines connecting that case to other cases that it cites or that cited it become darker, and the circles for cases that are not connected to the chosen case by citations fade into the background.

These visualizations allow users to quickly identify the most influential cases on a given topic. For example, in the search for *birth control* visualized in figure 6.6, the circles for the precedent-setting cases *Roe v. Wade* and *Griswold v. Connecticut* clearly stand out as much larger than the circles for the other cases. Users can also easily see that there are cocitation clusters in the birth control cases. For example, the large cluster of circuit court cases in the 2000s represents cases where Chinese citizens were seeking asylum in the United States because they feared that they would be persecuted for violating China's one-child policy. These asylum cases all cite each other and do not cite the cases outside of this cluster on the Case Map. Identifying these clusters through the Case Map is likely orders of magnitude faster than identifying them by reading through each of the individual cases and noting which other cases each one cites.

The Technology

Citations in legal cases are arranged differently from the citations in most academic research. Instead of all citations being gathered together in a bibliography, or at least having all citations in footnotes or endnotes, citations in legal rulings primarily appear in-line in the text. In order to create the citation data for Case Maps, Ravel must be able to automatically extract these citations. To do this, Ravel uses a technology called named entity recognition, which is designed to find *named entities*—most commonly people, places, and organizations—in natural-language texts. Fittingly for a company founded by Stanford graduates, their named entity recognition system is largely based on the Stanford Named Entity Recognizer (NER), one of several pieces of software produced by the Stanford Natural Language Processing (NLP) group that can be used to allow machines to parse normal human writing.[16] NLP software such as NERs can be "trained" on a small corpus of documents where named entities or other features have been marked by humans. They can also be programmed to look for specific patterns, such as "[Name] v. [Name]." Once the NER has learned how to identify the features of interest, it can find those features in previously unseen documents without human intervention.

HOW CAN LIBRARIES CREATE THEIR OWN VISUALIZED INTERFACES?

Tools to create the types of visualizations covered in this chapter—and, more importantly, to create the data underlying them—are freely available, although some require more technical skill to install and use than others.

Text clustering can be performed using various tools from the Carrot² Project. The easiest to use is the Carrot² Document Clustering Workbench, which is a desktop program with a GUI available for Windows, Mac, and Linux.[17] The Carrot² Document Clustering Workbench will perform both clustering and visualization of clusters. Libraries that are already using search tools based on ElasticSearch or recent versions of Solr can easily add document clustering to those systems via freely available Carrot²-based plug-ins and the Carrot² Circle and FoamTree visualizations.[18]

Topic models can be created online using the "Topics" function in Voyant Tools.[19] The topic model data can be visualized in Voyant Tools or exported and used with other data visualization software. For the more technologically adventurous, Machine Learning for Language Toolkit (MALLET) from the University of Massachusetts is another option for creating topic models.[20] MALLET is a command-line tool with no graphical interface, but the data it generates can be visualized using other programs.[21]

For named entity recognition, an online demonstration version of Stanford's NER is available. However, because it requires cutting and pasting text into a form on the site, it is only feasible to use for small amounts of text.[22] Users interested in making more robust use of named entity recognition can freely download the code for NER as well as for many other pieces of natural language–processing software developed at Stanford.[23] Associated visualization software can display some of the output created by this software, but users interested in creating a fully visualized interface will likely want to use other tools instead. Chapter 7 in this book provides many such options.

NOTES

1. As is covered in Elizabeth Joan Kelly's chapter in this volume (chapter 7), visualizations of spatial and temporal information predated Playfair by hundreds or thousands of years. Playfair, however, is believed to be the first person to visualize purely *quantitative* information.

2. This visualization can be seen at "Exports and Imports of Scotland to and from Different Parts for One Year from Christmas 1780 to Christmas 1781," Wikipedia, last modified September 20, 2018, https://en.wikipedia.org/wiki/William_Playfair#/media/File:1786_Playfair_-_Exports_and_Imports_of_Scotland_to_and_from_different_parts_for_one_Year_from_Christmas_1780_to_Christmas_1781.jpg.

3. Librarians are also rapidly becoming more familiar with digital humanities tools that allow researchers to perform "distant reading"—that is, using algorithms to discover and analyze themes, connections, or other aspects of textual corpora ranging from individual books to collections of millions of volumes. Although visualizations are not a requirement for distant-reading techniques, they are often incorporated into digital humanities tools that are used for distant reading, since visualizations of this data facilitate the exploration and interpretation process. Probably the most familiar examples of visualized distant-reading tools are ngram viewers, which show how frequently certain words or phrases appear in a corpus over time. These include the Google Books Ngram Viewer (https://books.google.com/ngrams), Bookworm (https://bookworm.htrc.illinois.edu/develop/), and the Term Frequency tool available in some Gale databases. Other, often less familiar, visualization tools in the digital humanities tradition include TextArc (www.textarc.org) and Voyant Tools (http://docs.voyant-tools.org/tools/). Although the visualizations produced by distant reading tools can be similar to the visualizations covered in this chapter, and in some cases they use the same underlying technologies and algorithms that are used by the tools covered in this chapter, the distinguishing factor is that the tools covered here are specifically intended to aid readers in the *discovery* process, whereas the

digital humanities tools are typically designed to help scholars in the *textual analysis* process.

4. Christopher Ahlberg and Ben Shneiderman, "Visual Information Seeking: Tight Coupling of Dynamic Query Filters with Starfield Displays" (technical research report, College Park, MD: Institute for Systems Research, September 1993), https://drum.lib.umd.edu/bitstream/handle/1903/5410/TR_93-71.pdf.

5. Yewno is not covered in detail in this chapter. Readers who are interested in learning more about Yewno may wish to consult the following webinars: Ruth Pickering, "Overview of Yewno Semantic-Analysis Engine for ASERL" (Atlanta: ASERL, August 10, 2016), https://vimeo.com/178369994; and Ruggero Gramatica and Michael Keller, "The Future of Discovery—Hyperknowledge" (Charleston, SC: Charleston Conference, November 3, 2016), www.youtube.com/watch?v=EX6hjJwY7i0.

6. "Gale to Unify the Humanities through *Artemis*," Cengage, April 2, 2013, https://news.cengage.com/higher-education/gale-to-unify-the-humanities-through-artemis/.

7. The quoted phrase can be found in text in the footer of the Topic Finder display. How this subset is chosen and how large the subset might be are not indicated. Treemaps, a visualization that uses nested polygons to represent the relative sizes of various items, are another of Shneiderman's inventions. They are designed to visualize items that are organized in what computer scientists call a tree: a set of items (leaves), hierarchically arranged, starting from a single root and branching out. One familiar example of a tree is a computer's filesystem, where the root is a disk, the branches are folders, and the leaves are files. In fact, treemaps were originally developed to help computer users manage their limited hard drive space by finding large files, but they are now used to visualize everything from the US federal government's budget to, as can be seen here, search results. For Shneiderman's work on treemaps, see Ben Shneiderman, "Tree Visualization with Tree-Maps: 2-D Space-Filling Approach," *ACM Transactions on Graphics* 11, no. 1 (1993): 92–99; and Ben Shneiderman and Catherine Plaisant, "Treemaps for Space-Constrained Visualization of Hierarchies: Including the History of Treemap Research at the University of Maryland," University of Maryland Department of Computer Science, last modified September 2014, www.cs.umd.edu/hcil/treemap-history/. The US federal budget visualized as an interactive treemap can be seen at Shan Carter and Amanda Cox, "Obama's 2012 Budget Proposal: How $3.7 Trillion Is Spent," *New York Times*, February 14, 2011, www.nytimes.com/packages/html/newsgraphics/2011/0119-budget/.

8. My use of *jaguar* as an example search term is not original. Because the word has so many distinct meanings, it is used as an illustration in many works on document clustering and term disambiguation, including more than one of the works cited in this chapter.

9. Free versions of the code for these visualizations can be downloaded from https://carrotsearch.com/circles/free-trial/ and https://carrotsearch.com/foamtree/free-trial/, respectively.

10. Those interested in the details of various algorithms that can be used for clustering should consult Christopher D. Manning, Prabhakar Raghavan, and Hinrich Schütze, *Introduction to Information Retrieval* (New York: Cambridge University Press, 2008), chaps. 16 and 17.
11. Alex Humphreys, Christina Spencer, Laura Brown, Matthew Loy, and Ronald Snyder, *Reimagining the Digital Monograph: Design Thinking to Build New Tools for Researchers* (New York: ITHAKA, 2017), 11.
12. Humphreys et al., 19.
13. Topic**graph** page for *Burning Bright: Essays in Honour of David Bindman*, https://labs.jstor.org/topicgraph/monograph/e992337a-246c-349c-a674-ca81e40f6167.
14. The labels used for the topics are not created by LDA; they are pulled from the JSTOR thesaurus. Humphreys et al., *Reimagining the Digital Monograph*, 18.
15. This explanation glosses over many, many mathematical details. Readers who are interested in fully understanding the algorithms behind LDA may wish to consult the following articles: David M. Blei, Andrew Y. Ng, and Michael I. Jordan, "Latent Dirichlet Allocation," *Journal of Machine Learning Research* 3 (2003): 933–1022; Thomas L. Griffiths and Mark Steyvers, "Finding Scientific Topics," *Proceedings of the National Academy of Sciences* 101 (April 6, 2004): 5228–35.
16. Jeremy Corbett, "Case Law and ML on Spark," San Francisco: Data by the Bay, May 18, 2016, www.youtube.com/watch?v=rQQrUjDOPdg. More information about the Stanford NER can be found on the website of the Stanford Natural Language Processing Group, https://nlp.stanford.edu.
17. The Carrot^2 Document Clustering Workbench, as well as other Carrot^2 applications, can be downloaded from http://project.carrot2.org/download.html.
18. Clustering in ElasticSearch requires a plug-in that can be downloaded from https://github.com/carrot2/elasticsearch-carrot2. A clustering plug-in comes bundled with recent versions of Solr; information about it can be found at https://lucene.apache.org/solr/guide/7_2/result-clustering.html.
19. Voyant Tools can be accessed at https://voyant-tools.org/; documentation on the Topic tool can be found at https://voyant-tools.org/docs/#!/guide/topics.
20. MALLET can be downloaded from http://mallet.cs.umass.edu/download.php. Shawn Graham, Scott Weingart, and Ian Milligan have written a user-friendly introduction to MALLET, "Getting Started with Topic Modeling and MALLET," that is available at https://programminghistorian.org/lessons/topic-modeling-and-mallet.
21. I am indebted to Liz Rodrigues for suggesting several of the resources mentioned in this paragraph and in the preceding note.
22. The Stanford NER online demonstration can be found at http://nlp.stanford.edu:8080/ner/.
23. The NER software can be downloaded from https://nlp.stanford.edu/software/CRF-NER.html. Links to other Stanford NLP software can be found at https://nlp.stanford.edu/software/.

Chapter Seven

Libraries and Information Visualization
Application and Value

Elizabeth Joan Kelly

Most librarians are accustomed to collecting data about their core functions, but they also need to be able to share those data with others in meaningful ways. A key method for making complex data and statistics more dynamic and digestible to a variety of stakeholders is information visualization, or the graphical representation of data. Librarians can improve understanding of what they do and how they do it using information visualization. Assessment of collections, public services, web traffic, or a myriad of other services offered by libraries can be made more quickly digestible, enabling users to recognize connections and patterns that could take hours to determine from raw data and text alone and exposing the most current data available (depending on the tools used). Thanks to the recent growth of available technologies, information visualization is an increasingly accessible method for librarians to share assessment data. From programming languages like R for statistical computing and graphics making, to commonly used programs like Google Sheets and Excel, to more complex data analysis tools like Tableau and

Voyant, there are many options both free and proprietary for librarians interested in information visualization, whether they are beginner or advanced users. Infographics can also be created from assessment data to promote and market library services in interesting and compelling ways. This chapter provides a brief history of information visualization, an overview of how libraries are using it, tools and tutorials for librarians, and a discussion of future implications for libraries.

THE BRIEFEST OF BRIEF HISTORIES

No discussion of information visualization is complete without a brief introduction to the history of visualization. This may not seem like a particularly difficult task, but data historians point to the beginning of visualization in widely varying time frames, from the precalendar era through the fifteenth century. Part of this disagreement stems from differing definitions of *visualization*, with some using data visualization and information visualization interchangeably, whereas others see the two as distinct. For the purposes of this chapter, I'll use a broad definition of *information visualization* to encapsulate both infographics and data visualizations, the primary difference between the two being that data visualizations are based purely on data (quantitative or qualitative), whereas infographics combine data visualization techniques with nondata descriptive elements.

With these parameters set, the birth of information visualization (IV) can be traced to the oldest known map, a nine-foot wall painting depicting a town plan created circa 6200 BC and found in modern-day Ankara, Turkey.[1] The most comprehensive history following the Catal Hyük map can be found in Michael J. Friendly's *A Brief History of Data Visualization* and corresponding website "Milestones in the History of Thematic Cartography, Statistical Graphics, and Data Visualization," which trace IV from tenth-century time-series graphs of planetary movements to eighteenth-century thematic mapping.[2] All other modern forms of data display—including bar graphs and pie charts, histograms, line graphs and time-series plots, contour plots, scatterplots, atlases, and natural and physical maps—emerged by the nineteenth century. Computer graphics were developed in the 1950s, and data analytics began to receive recognition in the 1960s as a legitimate branch of statistics thanks to information design pioneer John Tukey's critical article "The Future of Data Analysis" in the *Annals of Mathematical Statistics*.[3] Modern geographic information systems (GISs) and two- and three-dimensional statistical graphics provided new visualization methods and techniques for expressing statistics by 1975, followed by interactive computing systems, commercial and noncommercial software for visualizations, and innovations in computer hardware that have made IV an achievable goal even for those without computer science training. Finally, Edward Tufte's *The Visual Display of Quantitative Information*, published in 1983, is widely considered the preeminent text on modern visualization techniques and best practices.[4] As Friendly writes of his own work, "From this history one may also see that most of the innovations in data visualization arose from concrete, often practical goals: the need or desire to see phenomena and relationships in new or different ways. It is also clear that the development of graphic methods depended fundamentally on parallel advances in technology, data collection and statistical theory."[5]

SEEING IS REMEMBERING

It isn't an accident that visualization tools and techniques have become intertwined with conveying complex data. Out of all of the senses, vision is considered "very dominant" due to its high capacity for processing information.[6] Seeing something, as opposed to hearing about it, smelling it, touching it, or tasting it, has the ability to extend both memory and cognition. In reference to data, massive spreadsheets full of information may not enable individuals to understand and remember. Instead, visualizing data using graphs, charts, and infographics improves communication of the findings within. Stephen Few, a noted data visualization expert, advocates for clear and concise graphics because "seeing" is handled by the visual cortex faster and more efficiently than cognition.[7] In fact, vision can actually be *preattentive*; there are parts of visual processing that occur in the brain prior to any conscious awareness. In using visualizations for data analysis and communication, the creators of IV enable "intuitively, clearly, accurately, and efficiently conveyed information through visual perception."[8]

VISUALIZATION AND LIBRARIES

Hal Varian, Google's chief economist, posits that "the ability to take data—to be able to understand it, to process it, to extract value from it, to visualize it, to communicate it—that's going to be a hugely important skill in the next decades. . . . Because now we really do have essentially free and ubiquitous data." And while these abilities are essential to what Varian calls the "sexiest" job of the next ten years, statistics, they are also important skills for managers to be able to access and understand data.[9] Several industries have already firmly jumped into IV. Many of the tools discussed later in this chapter stem from business analytics in which past performance is used for data-driven decision-making. Data journalists also "must know how to find, analyze and visualize a story from data."[10] Geographers, geologists, environmental scientists, historians, and others use geographical information systems to visualize, analyze, and interpret location-based data. And projects in digital scholarship and the digital humanities use visualization techniques to create network analyses, digital exhibits, infographics, maps, and other visualizations from texts, metadata, digital surrogates, and more. Uses for IV in libraries include analyzing library services and collections, providing IV tools and instruction to patrons, and advocating to stakeholders for new and improved resources. The following are brief examples of potential IV projects for public, academic, school, and special libraries using select examples from library literature.

Usage and Public Service Data

Perhaps the most common use of IV by libraries up until this point is the creation of internally facing reporting of library services. Gate counts, reference requests, instruction sessions and workshops taught, circulation statistics, research guide views, electronic journal and database usage, digital collection downloads, and library website use statistics all easily lend themselves to IV. Once visualized, these seemingly basic, day-to-day activities are easily plugged into annual reports, library newsletters, meeting minutes, and even the library website in order to inform stakeholders about the library's work. Furthermore, IV can lead to quick decision-making in improving and revamping library services. Sharing IV that will be used to usher in change in a library benefits everyone involved. When the Brooklyn Public Library used Tableau to visualize common public services data like door counts, program attendance, and circulation, they were able to share this data with all library staff, creating transparency in decision-making as well as staff buy-in for making important decisions (see figure 7.1).[11]

One of the most referenced IV projects in professional literature is the Seattle Central Library's "Making Visible the Invisible" installation, which employed six LCD screens of live-updated circulation data from 2005 to 2014 and is possibly the longest-running dynamic data visualization project (see figure 7.2).[12] Seattle

FIGURE 7.1
"Brooklyn Public Library FY 18 Regional Branch Visits" visualization.

Courtesy Brooklyn Public Library.
https://public.tableau.com/profile/bpl.it#!/vizhome/BklynSTATVisits/MonthlyTotal.

FIGURE 7.2
Seattle Central Library installation, "Making Visible the Invisible."
"SPL Wall of Cool."

By Greg Careaga. Licensed under CC BY-SA 2.0.
www.flickr.com/photos/36053426@N08/3830905986/in/photolist-6QwoTd.

Central's installation was created by a professional digital media artist, George Legrady; however, the underlying data used by Legrady is commonly available data for libraries and could be used for many types of IV and to improve user experience and make resource recommendations.[13]

Metadata and Collections

Similarly, libraries can visualize their collections to inform collection-development decisions and budgets. Librarians at the College of Charleston used Microsoft Excel and Tableau to look at correlations between expenditures and course offerings in order to make decisions about budgetary allocations.[14] Similarly, librarians at the University of North Carolina at Chapel Hill created visualizations of electronic-resource usage data for electronic journal and electronic book titles to help make cancellation decisions.[15] The Kingsborough Community College Library web application SeeCollections collects data from the discovery system's application programming interface (API) to visualize the library's collections of books and e-books.[16]

Metadata visualizations can be used to identify common patterns along with usage data to better optimize search engines, internal indexes, and individual item metadata in order to improve the user experience and, in particular, item searching.[17] And an even more specified subset of IV can be created using data from archival collections. To combat user frustrations reading text-heavy and jargon-filled archives and manuscript-finding aids, Anne Bahde suggests creating visualizations for finding aids such as timelines, maps, and networks that are interactive to "enable users to participate in the process of analysis, to probe and explore further, and to remix and play with the data to achieve new understanding."[18]

Visual Search and Browse

Another method for libraries to utilize IV with their holdings is visual search and browse for users searching collections. A prototype of visual browsing for geographical areas and time periods in the Wilson Center's Cold War International History Project digital collection was praised by beta testers for its creativity and navigation, and after eight months, the visual browse page was the third most popular page on the digital collection website (see figure 7.3).[19]

Similarly, to combat student difficulties in constructing search terms, Jennifer Rosenfeld and Matt Conner at the University of California, Davis, tested undergraduates on four different search methodologies including a prototype called Visual Search. They found that Visual Search "inspired more use of subject terms"

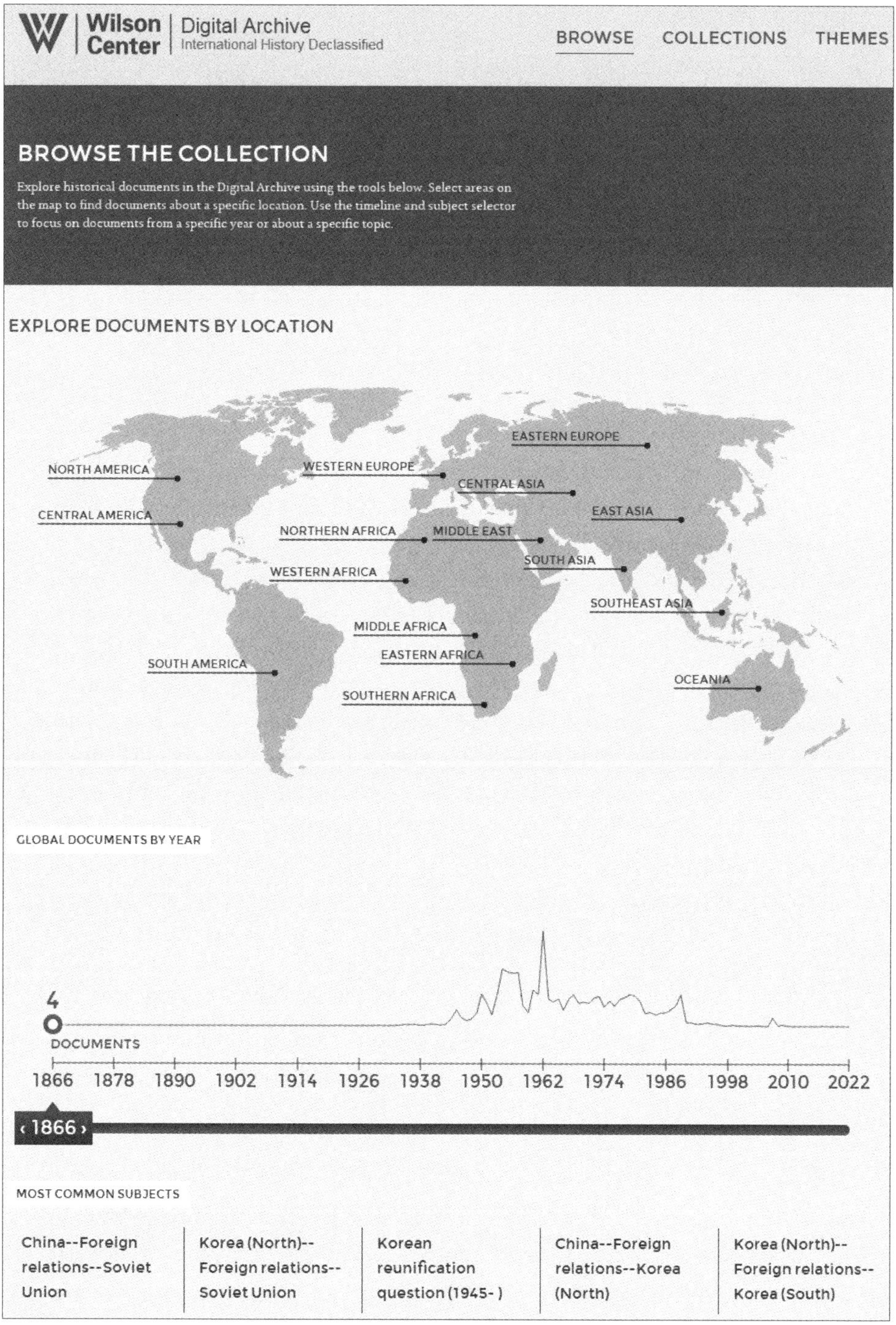

FIGURE 7.3
Screenshot of Wilson Center digital archive visual search.

Courtesy of Woodrow Wilson Digital Archive. http://digitalarchive.wilsoncenter.org/browse.

than text-based searches, generated more search attempts (meaning students were less likely to give up when using visual search), and was rated the most successful overall by the investigators.[20]

As a Library Service

Libraries also offer visualization tools and training as part of their service offerings. By providing users with the knowledge and infrastructure to create their own IVs, librarians are able to foster proficiency in data and visual literacy.

Instruction

Since libraries are already positioned as experts in information literacy, it is only natural for librarians and library staff to also take the reins in instruction for these literacies. Creating and understanding data visualizations, in particular, is one of a number of achievable data literacy skills. Charissa Jefferson posits that the higher-order thinking skills of Bloom's taxonomy, a framework for classifying learning objectives, can be achievable through spatial and data literacy instruction such as the creation of maps.[21] Jefferson explains that many library users are beginners in data visualization and map making and that spatial literacy aids students in better understanding their curricula. In this vein, and finding that accurately using data is increasingly important in medical decision-making, University of Houston librarians conducted GIS sessions for nursing and psychology students using real-life scenarios.[22]

While the integration of IV into college curricula has a natural partner in digital scholarship, it is also easily integrated into K–12 classes. Students can include graphs, charts, diagrams, mind maps, and more in written reports and class presentations, and the earlier they develop these skills, the better situated they will be to absorb IV quickly in their futures. MaryAnn Karre provides an example of teaching sixth and eighth graders how to create infographics for development reading and literature courses.[23]

3-D Printing

In order to support researchers' needs, libraries also provide the hardware, software, and training for users to engage in IV. The Health Sciences Library at the University of North Carolina at Chapel Hill partnered with Renaissance Computing Institute to enhance their Collaboration Center and offer IV as a service where researchers can work directly with experts to create custom applications for data analysis.[24] The Dalhousie University Libraries offer 3-D printing to students who have already had training in 3-D modeling in order to print building models, city models, and map topography. These skills are essential for engineers, architects, and urban planners, so providing access to 3-D modeling and printing infrastructure has particular significance for science, map, and geography libraries.[25]

Advocacy

While some of the previous examples have included librarians creating visualizations for internal use that incidentally became useful in advocating for the library's services, some libraries have created IV with the explicit purpose of drawing

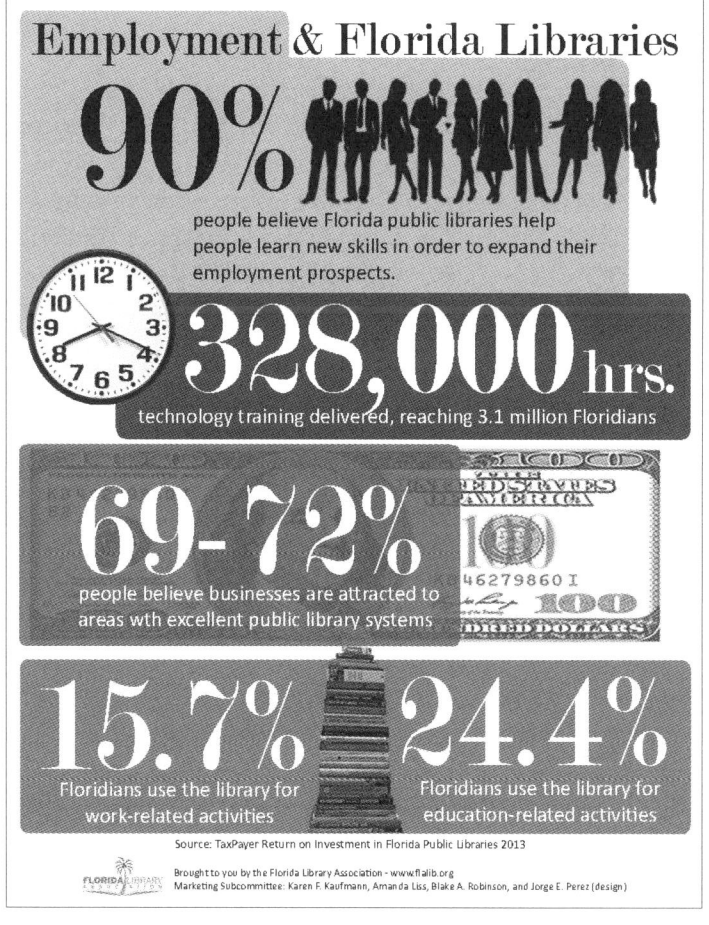

FIGURE 7.4
Florida Libraries 2016 education infographics.

attention to their value as a necessary partner in research and as a service provider. In 2016, the Florida Library Association Marketing Committee created infographics about education, employment, and entrepreneurship for Library Day at the Florida state capitol to provide data for legislators to use making decisions about funding (see figure 7.4).[26] In response to declining budgets in medical libraries, Daina Bouquin and Helen-Ann Brown Epstein advocate for the use of infographics to market library services.[27] Librarians may find that providing IV to stakeholders quickens and increases understanding of the library's significance to user communities and helps persuade administration and legislators to expand budgets for programs, collections, and staff.

GETTING STARTED

Are you convinced yet that developing IV skills can be a boon to librarians? If so, then your next step is to begin trying out different IV tools and methods. Those with proficiency in programming will be able to create data visualizations using programming languages like R and Python and JavaScript libraries like D3.[28] For those looking for more beginner-friendly and entry-level applications with a graphical user interface (GUI), however, there are still many options. Technology moves quickly enough that any summary of available tools will quickly become outdated, but what follows is a brief list of currently available applications for creating different kinds of IV.

Most of the tools listed have tutorials available for learning their basic functionality (see table 7.1). In addition to learning specific tools, however, librarians interested in IV should also understand what kinds of visualizations are best at conveying specific types of information. Some more general training opportunities follow to help librarians become acclimated with IV and scale their expertise based on personal interest and professional need.

TABLE 7.1

Information visualization tools.

Name	Functions	Description	URL	Free?	Alternatives
Google Sheets	Spreadsheet creation and charts and graphs	Web-based application for creating spreadsheets; includes chart and graph creation and integrates with Google Fusion Tables	www.google.com/sheets	Yes	Microsoft Excel, Apache Open Office Calc, Libre Office Calc
Mindmeister	Mind-maps	Web-based application for creating mind-maps	www.mindmeister.com	Includes both subscription and free products	
Piktochart	Infographics	Web-based application for infographics	https://piktochart.com	Includes both subscription and free products	Info.gram, Easel.ly, Canva, Adobe Creative Suite
Storymap JS	Maps	Web-based application for plotting events and media by location; integrates with Google Sheets	https://storymap.knightlab.com	Yes	Esri Storymaps
Tableau	Charts and graphs, maps, and dashboards	Available as desktop, server, or web-based application for creating charts, maps, network graphs, stories, and dashboards	www.tableau.com	Includes both subscription and free products (Tableau Public and Tableau Free)	Gephi
TimeMapper	Maps and timelines	Web-based application for plotting events and media by time and location; integrates with Google Sheets	http://timemapper.okfnlabs.org	Yes	Timeline JS
Voyant	Text analysis	Web-based application for "lightweight" text analytics like word clouds, frequency distribution plots, and more	https://voyant-tools.org	Yes	TAPoR

PART II: Services

Workshops and Materials

University of Wisconsin–Milwaukee, "Data Visualization Camp Instructional Materials (2017)" presentation materials, including activity handouts, from a one-hour workshop on choosing the right data and making better charts by librarian Kristin Briney (https://dc.uwm.edu/lib_staff_files/4/)

North Carolina State University, data visualization workshops: presentation files for various IV methods, from poster design, to infographics, to data visualization with R, to using Tableau (https://ncsu-libraries.github.io/data-viz-workshops/)

Data Science and Visualization Institute of Librarians: week-long course offered annually by North Carolina State University with the Coalition for Networked Information and Data Science Training for Librarians (www.lib.ncsu.edu/data-science-and-visualization-institute)

Tutorials

Data Visualizations and Infographics by Sarah K. C. Mauldin includes an entire chapter of visualization project tutorials for a variety of scenarios such as "Creating a Library Services Graphic," "Creating an Interactive Historical Timeline Two Ways," and "Creating Complex Data Visualizations," to name a few. Mauldin's instructions are very clear and walk readers through possible uses of each IV as well as step-by-step instructions using a recommended tool.[29]

WHAT'S NEXT?

What does the future hold for IV and libraries? We live in an increasingly visual world—we carry tiny computers with high-resolution screens in our pockets; television and computer monitors blast music videos and news broadcasts at us in stores, airports, and gas stations; and virtual reality is becoming less virtual and more real. This speaks to a society in which visual representations of information may be more easily received than textual ones, and research into visual perception and memory supports this. Mauldin hypothesizes that we may even see a future Pulitzer Prize for best infographics and data visualization in mass media in the near future.[30]

As the demand for IV increases, libraries may find themselves asked to create IV for their stakeholders and teach IV skills to their users. In order to keep up with this demand, librarians must pursue training in math and statistics, data analysis, and graphic design in order to understand basic principles of data manipulation and display. Hsuanwei identifies challenges to IV implementation, including a lack of expertise and skills, the need for "high levels of domain specialist knowledge," and attitudinal barriers.[31] She further posits that in order to become leaders in IV, librarians need a thorough understanding of math and statistics; knowledge of data storage, mining methods, front-end design, and development; and access to standardized data. This will require library and information science (LIS) programs to begin requiring coursework in these areas and even to offer specializations and certificate programs in visualization. Schools may also enlist the services of disciplinary faculty outside of LIS, including math and computer science, statistics, data science, and the visual arts, to train new librarians in these essential skills.

For librarians who have already completed their degrees, professional development opportunities in IV will need to increase in order to keep up with user expectations. Current course offerings in IV for librarians include DIY training materials and week-long intensive programs. On-demand and self-paced training for IV will be necessary for career librarians to increase their skills. Webinars from professional organizations, low-cost certificate programs aimed at continuing education through LIS programs, and massive open online courses (MOOCs) are all possible venues for such training, particularly if they can be crafted to meet the specific IV needs of librarians.

We also live in an age of lifelogging, or the quantified self, in which we use personal devices to gather data about our everyday lives, from wearable fitness trackers to continuous glucose monitoring systems to productivity apps. As we become data scientists of our own bodies, habits, and moods, our users may increasingly request visualization tools and training to understand, triangulate, and synthesize these complex results. Part of data literacy is also understanding where data come from, who has access to them, and who may benefit from them. Librarians will increasingly find the need to educate users on the nature of proprietary and open source software and hardware; the use of big data by corporations, governments, and other entities; privacy concerns inherent to contributing to big data; and more, particularly as these issues relate to lifelogging devices.

We as librarians may be able to use this same type of personalized data to visualize the needs and wants of our users. Visual search tools, such as those piloted at the Wilson Center and the University of California, Davis, will continue to improve and may someday interface with user data to offer personalized visualizations of material recommendations. Picture a system where a user can log in to his library account and instantly browse collections based on his previous searches, article downloads, or item checkouts using facets such as subjects, geography, and time. Network graphs will show the connections between resources tailored for individual users so that they can easily find even better resources. Then look further into the future to a visual collection browse so individualized that it utilizes colors, borders, and facets specific not only to the user's collection interests but also to the user's own abilities, transforming based on whether the user is color blind, has astigmatism, is sensitive to light, or otherwise.

Stephen Few even envisions a future in which IV is used not only for descriptive statistics but also for predictive analytics.[32] These predictions can refer to predicting user resources, but they can also be used by libraries to predict future usage and public service needs in order to better prepare staffing, professional development, library hours, instructions sessions needed, and more. However, the use of personalized data to improve library services opens up a can of worms that includes two areas of great significance for this discussion: accessibility and privacy.

Accessibility

As society moves toward a more visually interactive means of sharing and interpreting data, it is important to keep in mind those with visual impairments so that they are not left at a disadvantage. While the literature speaks to the many advantages of visualizing information, users with vision loss must necessarily be provided the same information as those absorbing the data through IV. Existing standards and best practices offer some guidance in this area, but there are significant hurdles to jump for librarians working with IV to make them truly technically accessible (not to mention as functionally and elegantly designed).

Current web and electronic design standards for accessibility require alternative descriptions for visual media such as "alt" tags and transcripts; these are not only best practices to make websites accessible; they are also required by law for many types of organizations. At the very least, librarians will need to add these sorts of alternative descriptions to IV so that they can be accessible to the visually impaired using screen readers. Increasingly sophisticated text- and touch-based alternatives that can be read with screen readers, accessed through tactile aids, and felt through force feedback devices, will improve accessibility for all users, not just those with special needs. IV that can be represented for a multitude of the five senses provides a host of opportunities for users with differing abilities to access the same data.

As enhancements to current library services begin to include more IV, libraries should factor in accessibility standards and provide alternative tools such as voice-dictated searching, descriptive analyses of data, and tactile representations of data like maps. Here, 3-D printing of tactile representations of visualization may provide solutions to make IV more broadly usable. By taking data and exhibiting it through visual, aural, and tactile depictions, librarians ensure they are offering the broadest and most equitable access to information that they can.

Privacy

No discussion of library data should occur without a stern caveat about user privacy. Librarians feel themselves to be proponents and protectors of user privacy and confidentiality.[33] This *should* include user's privacy concerning their material checkouts, search sessions, access to library websites, and item downloads, just to name a few. And with an increase in personal data collection due to lifelogging devices, we as a society are collecting more data than ever about personal health and habits that could potentially be used for nefarious purposes.

Any data collected by libraries about users should be anonymized, and patrons should be informed continually and thoroughly about what data are being collected about them. No IV should be created that could possibly point to an individual user's behavior and identity without their consent. Obtaining this consent may be inherently difficult. Doing so requires balancing not wanting users to feel that they are being spied on while also making them aware what data are being collected about them and how they are being used. Those who utilize user data for IV must receive training in protecting user identities and anonymizing data. While library systems collect a wealth of data about patrons that can be used to improve user services, libraries must always err on the side of protecting the patron over collecting potentially harmful statistics. Part of the future of IV in libraries, then, is digital confidentiality training. Resources such as those created and collected by the Library Freedom Project are already attempting to put these significant issues at the forefront of librarians' minds and will continue to expand and include guidance on protecting user data.[34]

CONCLUSION

Information visualization is a growing industry that holds many possibilities for libraries. From visualizing their own collections and services to providing data literacy instruction, librarians must be poised to support the visualization needs of a diverse user population. The examples provided in this chapter, as well as the training resources and tools detailed, should help librarians begin diving into the rich possibilities that visualization hold, whether at academic, public, school, or special libraries.

NOTES

1. J. Siebold, "100 Town Plan from Catal Hyük," Cartographic Images, n.d., http://cartographic-images.net/Cartographic_Images/100_Town_Plan_from_Catal_Hyuk.html.
2. Michael Friendly, "A Brief History of Data Visualization," in *Handbook of Computational Statistics: Data Visualization*, ed. Chun-houh Chen, Wolfgang Härdle, and Antony Unwin (Berlin: Springer, 2008), 16–48, http://citeseerx.ist.psu.edu/viewdoc/download?doi=10.1.1.446.458&rep=rep1&type=pdf; and Michael Friendly and D. J. Denis, "Milestones in the History of Thematic Cartography, Statistical Graphics, and Data Visualization," DataVis, 2001. www.datavis.ca/milestones/.
3. John W. Tukey, "The Future of Data Analysis," *Annals of Mathematical Statistics* 33, no. 1 (March 1962): 1–67, https://doi.org/10.1214/aoms/1177704711.
4. Mark Zachry and Charlotte Thralls, "An Interview with Edward R. Tufte," *Technical Communication Quarterly* 13, no. 4 (September 2004): 447–62.
5. Friendly and Denis, "Milestones," 30.
6. Michelle Chen Hsuanwei, "An Overview of Information Visualization," *Library Technology Reports: Information Visualization* 53, no. 3 (2017): 6.
7. Stephen Few, "Data Visualization for Human Perception," in *The Encyclopedia of Human-Computer Interaction*, 2nd ed., ed. Mads Soegaard and Rikke Friis Dam (Aarhus: Interaction Design Foundation, 2013), www.interaction-design.org/literature/book/the-encyclopedia-of-human-computer-interaction-2nd-ed/data-visualization-for-human-perception.
8. Few, "Data Visualization."
9. Hal Varian, "Hal Varian on How the Web Challenges Managers," *McKinsey & Company, High Tech* (blog), January 2009, www.mckinsey.com/industries/high-tech/our-insights/hal-varian-on-how-the-web-challenges-managers.
10. Jonathan Gray et al., *The Data Journalism Handbook* (Sebastopol, CA: O'Reilly Media, 2012), http://datajournalismhandbook.org/1.0/en/index.html.
11. Carrie O'Maley Voliva, "Data Visualization for Public Libraries," Public Libraries Online, April 20, 2015, http://publiclibrariesonline.org/2015/04/data-visualization-for-public-libraries/.
12. George Legrady, "Making Visible the Invisible DataVis at the Seattle Public Library" (Institute for Pure and Applied Mathematics Culture Analytics Workshop, University of California, Los Angeles, March 22, 2016), www.ipam.ucla.edu/abstract/?tid=13603&pcode=CAWS1.

13. Sumit Goswami et al., "Visualisation of Relationships among Library Users Based On Library Circulation Data," *DESIDOC Journal of Library & Information Technology* 30, no. 2 (March 2010): 26–39.
14. Jannette L. Finch and Angela R. Flenner, "Using Data Visualization to Examine an Academic Library Collection," *College & Research Libraries* 77, no. 6 (November 2016): 765–78, https://doi.org/10.5860/crl.77.6.765.
15. Megan Kilb and Matt Jansen, "Visualizing Collections Data: Why Pie Charts Aren't Always the Answer," *Serials Review* 42, no. 3 (July 2016): 192.
16. Mark Eaton, "Seeing Library Data: A Prototype Data Visualization Application for Librarians," Publications and Research, January 1, 2017, https://academicworks.cuny.edu/kb_pubs/115.
17. Corey A. Harper, "Metadata Analytics, Visualization, and Optimization: Experiments in Statistical Analysis of the Digital Public Library of America (DPLA)," *Code4Lib Journal* 33 (July 19, 2016), http://journal.code4lib.org/articles/11752.
18. Anne Bahde, "Conceptual Data Visualization in Archival Finding Aids: Preliminary User Responses," *Portal: Libraries and the Academy* 17, no. 3 (July 11, 2017): 487, https://doi.org/10.1353/pla.2017.0031.
19. Laura Deal, "Visualizing Digital Collections," *Technical Services Quarterly* 32, no. 1 (January 2015): 21, https://doi.org/10.1080/07317131.2015.972871.
20. Jennifer Rosenfeld and Matt Conner, "Navigating the Information-Scape: Information Visualization and Student Search," *Reference Services Review* 41, no. 1 (2013): 91, https://doi.org/10.1108/00907321311300901.
21. Charissa Jefferson, "Integrating Data and Spatial Literacy into Library Instruction," in *Data Visualization: A Guide to Visual Storytelling for Libraries*, ed. Lauren Magnuson (Lanham, MD: Rowan & Littlefield, 2016), 173–86.
22. Michelle Malizia Catalano, Porcia Vaughn, and Joshua Been, "Using Maps to Promote Data-Driven Decision-Making: One Library's Experience in Data Visualization Instruction," *Medical Reference Services Quarterly* 36, no. 4 (October 2017): 415–22, https://doi.org/10.1080/02763869.2017.1369292.
23. MaryAnn Karre, "Infographics Make an Impact," *School Librarian's Workshop* 35, no. 3 (January 12, 2014): 12–13.
24. Hsuanwei, "Overview of Information Visualization," 21–25.
25. Michael Groenendyk, "Emerging Data Visualization Technologies for Map and Geography Libraries: 3-D Printing, Holographic Imaging, 3-D City Models, and 3-D Model-Based Animations," *Journal of Map & Geography Libraries* 9, no. 3 (September 2013): 220–38, https://doi.org/10.1080/15420353.2013.821436.
26. Jorge E. Perez and Karen F. Kaufmann, "Data Visualizations: A Tool for Advocacy," *Florida Libraries* 59, no. 1 (Spring 2016): 25–28.
27. Daina Bouquin and Helen-Ann Brown Epstein, "Teaching Data Visualization Basics to Market the Value of a Hospital Library: An Infographic as One Example," *Journal*

of Hospital Librarianship 15, no. 4 (October 2015): 349–64, https://doi.org/10.1080/15323269.2015.1079686.

28. More information about R, Python, and D3 is available at www.r-project.org, www.python.org, and https://d3js.org.
29. Sarah K. C. Mauldin, *Data Visualizations and Infographics* (Lanham, MD: Rowman & Littlefield, 2015).
30. Mauldin, 4.
31. Hsuanwei, "Overview of Information Visualization," 26–27.
32. Few, "Data Visualization."
33. "Code of Ethics," American Library Association, last amended January 22, 2008, www.ala.org/tools/ethics.
34. See the Library Freedom Project website at https://libraryfreedomproject.org.

ADDITIONAL READING

Association of Research Libraries, Coalition for Networked Information, and the Scholarly Publishing and Academic Resources Coalition. *Research Library Issues: Data Visualization in Research Libraries*. No. 288. Washington, DC: Association of Research Libraries, 2016.

Few, Stephen. "Data Visualization for Human Perception." In *The Encyclopedia of Human-Computer Interaction*, 2nd ed., edited by Mads Soegaard and Rikke Friis Dam. Aarhus: Interaction Design Foundation, 2013. www.interaction-design.org/literature/book/the-encyclopedia-of-human-computer-interaction-2nd-ed/data-visualization-for-human-perception.

———. *Now You See It: Simple Visualization Techniques for Quantitative Analysis*. Oakland, CA: Analytics Press, 2009.

Magnuson, Lauren, ed. *Data Visualization: A Guide to Visual Storytelling for Libraries*. Lanham, MD: Rowan & Littlefield, 2016.

Mauldin, Sarah K. C., ed. *Data Visualizations and Infographics*. Lanham, MD: Rowman & Littlefield, 2015.

PBS Digital Studios. "The Art of Data Visualization: Off Book." YouTube, May 9, 2013. www.youtube.com/watch?v=AdSZJzb-aX8.

Thompson, Clive. "The Surprising History of the Infographic." *Smithsonian Magazine* (blog), July 2016. www.smithsonianmag.com/history/surprising-history-infographic-180959563/.

Tufte, Edward R. *The Visual Display of Quantitative Information*. Cheshire, CT: Graphics Press, 1983.

Chapter Eight

Virtual Reality
Out of This World

Austin Olney

As Gutenberg's printing press revolutionized the amount of information available to the public in the fifteenth century, so too has the information technology revolution of recent history supplied mass amounts of digital content to modern society. The way information is absorbed has remained wholly unchanged for centuries, but recent innovations have created new pathways to the mind. Virtual reality (VR) offers a high level of immersion by placing people in omnidirectional worlds, allowing them to receive information from all directions for educational, therapeutic, functional, and entertainment purposes. This innovative medium allows users to experience information in ways never before possible and boasts a vast, quickly growing network. There exists a rising demand for institutions to provide interactive VR experiences and content, and libraries now have the perfect opportunity to fill this need while upholding a core value of providing lifelong learning services for all. It could be beneficial for library professionals to

PART II: Services

understand both the logistical issues and exciting possibilities that accompany this rising form of technology, as we will explore in this chapter. We will also discuss how to incorporate VR into libraries and, most importantly, inspire staff to consider adopting this revolutionary technology.

LIBRARIES AND INNOVATION

Today, libraries across the world provide assistance to patrons in a wide variety of ways—everything from giving street directions and recommending books to teaching classes and providing résumé help. With the rise of the current "information age," many libraries have seized the opportunity to play a new role as the go-to information technology resource, supporting patrons with technical assistance and spreading knowledge.[1] It is not surprising that an innovative and promising medium such as VR has found its way into many of today's libraries. For example, nearly one hundred libraries in California are about to adopt the technology as part of a private initiative to spread awareness and distribute resources to the eager public.[2]

If you have not yet had the opportunity to try VR, you may be unsure of what it actually looks like and what components are involved. A VR user wears a physical headset, which resembles a futuristic pair of ski goggles, covering the eyes and ears to block out sights and sounds of the surrounding environment. The headset displays a digitally based world, created through the processing power of a computer, smartphone, or other digital device. The viewer has an omnidirectional, three-dimensional perspective of an artificial environment, and the visual content is relative to head movement. Audio is provided through headphones that are often built in to the headset. Interaction and gameplay are supported through various forms of input, oftentimes with a game controller or two, which makes it possible for the user to use his hands to physically influence happenings within the virtual environment. VR is "an artificial environment which is experienced through sensory stimuli (such as sights and sounds) provided by a computer and in which one's actions partially determine what happens in the environment."[3] It is essentially the practice of surrounding a user with reactive stimuli that foster the feeling of entering into an alternate world.

The birth of VR was brought about through a collaboration of technological breakthroughs, but it is rooted in the invention of the stereoscope by Sir Charles Wheatstone in 1838.[4] With this pioneering device, humans had their first taste of

Chapter Eight: Virtual Reality

simulated 3-D by viewing two hand-drawn illustrations, one for each eye, which "tricked" the brain into seeing a single three-dimensional image. The technology continued to advance with notable innovations (you may remember the classic "View-Master" stereoscope, which came on the market a century later) and brought about today's versions of interactive, three-dimensional, digitally artificial spaces.[5] With creative momentum, the technology continued to evolve and challenge traditional conventions.

Entering a virtual environment offers a substantially deeper experience than traditional visual displays or even an interactive console game. The technology consists of a hardware-synchronized digital world that tracks user head movement and neck angle and provides separate video feeds for each eye, enabling a three-dimensional perspective similar to Wheatstone's original stereoscope. The visual stimuli presented via the headset, in combination with auditory input through the earphones, create the impression that the user is entirely immersed in an artificial environment. The result is a remarkably realistic alternate reality—so realistic that the user may feel her stomach churn while riding a virtual roller coaster without ever leaving her chair. In this way, a VR user is invited to absorb content in a way never before possible, setting the stage for unprecedented practices in a multitude of different fields that expand beyond simple entertainment and gaming.

Critics of VR may claim it is just another amusement in today's mercurial technology scene; however, current business trends point to a future with VR at the forefront and with long-term potential. In 2014, the major social network corporation Facebook Inc. bought the company Oculus VR, which was starting to make waves in the VR field.[6] Facebook CEO Mark Zuckerberg believes it was a smart move in a world headed toward a future with virtual social networks.[7] While critics, such as *Forbes* contributor Erik Kain, say VR is nothing more than an "over-priced gimmick,"[8] it speaks volumes that an influential social media giant like Facebook would acquire what, at the time, was a relatively small VR company for billions of dollars. The future of VR is unknown, as the technology is still in its infancy, but even if it turns out to have been a gimmick, there are many benefits of incorporating the technology as it exists today into libraries.

VR is a whole new medium for content, and it might be wise for libraries to embrace it in the same way they have adopted other services beyond the realm of printed materials for decades. Sharing information was long achieved through print media (and before that, through stories told orally), but even traditions such as this derive from innovation. Five hundred years ago, the idea of capturing concepts and ideas in a physical book to be printed for the masses was essentially new technology, evolving from early papyrus scrolls.[9] The process of recording ideas on paper with marks is conceptually not far removed from modern methods of storing data on a computer with ones and zeroes. Today's libraries have expanded to lend everything from gardening tools and musical instruments to children's games and sports equipment; technology should not be an exception.

For decades, libraries have been expanding resources to include audiobooks, music formats, tablets, e-books, software, and more. Many patrons have now come to expect their local libraries to incorporate new mediums into their collections and services. It is partly this ability to adapt and cater to the evolving demands of the public that has led libraries to success in the first place. Physical books are the cornerstone of libraries and will likely remain that way in the foreseeable future, but other formats have proven that new mediums have the potential to thrive simultaneously.

Libraries that are able to keep up with modern technologies can provide patrons with knowledge and skills they may need in today's tech-driven world. Many patrons are interested in experiencing emerging technologies like VR because of the infinite possibilities and the deep level of immersion it offers, like diving into the atmosphere of a good book. The most basic and effective practice for library staff to employ with regard to VR is simply to expand awareness of the technology.

Educating the public about VR is the first step and could inspire today's patrons to harness one of the many applications of the technology or notify others who are simply interested. For example, libraries can inform the public how to access the technology at home with personal smartphones and inexpensive VR viewers—knowledge worth sharing.

EXCITING POSSIBILITIES

There are many potential uses of VR in libraries, and it is possible to offer the public a vast array of new and exciting services to benefit society.[10] From virtual conference meetings to educational media, digital exhibits to exposure therapy—the potential is limited only by imagination.

At this point, VR equipment is still relatively pricey, so it may be cost prohibitive for many library patrons to own it at home (although it is rapidly becoming more affordable). It would be convenient for patrons to be able to use library VR equipment for individual use, whether through a dedicated space in-house or by lending the equipment. Many public libraries have taken on the role of community centers in the areas they serve, and VR can also be a tool to bring people together. For example, a library could host a "Virtual Reality 101" night where patrons can come and use the equipment and learn how it works along with others who share an interest.

Although some of the more popular uses of VR are gaming and entertainment-based interactive experiences, libraries can support many other practices. With VR, there is a plethora of knowledge to impart and sufficient educational support ready to employ in libraries. For example, it is possible to give an educational virtual tour of the historic Giza Plateau where one can look at a virtual model of the Great Pyramid. Or better yet, one could provide virtual viewing of Giza using actual 360-degree footage for heightened realism. Imagine walking through top-class science museums and important cultural and historic landmarks around the globe—all from the comfort of your own local library. Patrons could research their family trees and visit their ancestral homelands virtually. Applications supply three-dimensional virtual viewpoints of the world, and resources are available to enrich educational perspectives in order to teach geography and much more. When equipped properly, libraries can provide substantial virtual resources to their communities.

Libraries can be magnificent places of creation by providing the required space and technology, and fostering the making of virtual spaces and simulations is an attractive aspect of VR. Utilizing VR equipment and free software, patrons of all ages can build worlds and explore creative possibilities. Children are able to make their own environments and virtually step inside after having learned basic development concepts.[11] Users can make worlds with minimal skills and delve as far into their creations as they wish. In addition, there are VR applications available today in which a user can use hand motions to physically sculpt three-dimensional models. Furthermore, without even stepping into a virtual environment, one can make an omnidirectional space using free modeling software that can then be exported and viewed with a headset.

With the recent rise of the maker movement, a new focus on cooperative growth and imagination is gaining popularity.[12] A makerspace provides the resources and tools necessary to design and build. Educational consultant Gary Stager writes how "the shift to 'making' represents the perfect storm of new technological materials, expanded opportunities, learning through firsthand experience, and the basic human impulse to create."[13] In the ideal makerspace, creation is unlimited, and new ideas can be pursued in a free and imaginative environment. Many libraries have seized the opportunity to support the creative inquiries of patrons and enrich concepts taught in schools (or, in many cases, not taught in schools due to budgetary limitations). In the case of VR, software development is the perfect arena to pursue such endeavors and could lead to additional innovations.

Patrons who have designed digital creations are able to present them in remarkable ways using VR technology. An architecture student could display a digital model of a proposed project in a virtual environment using a headset. An art student could design an artificial viewing room and display digital creations in a way never before possible. Patrons could stroll through a digital art gallery or science fair and observe the exhibits in a virtual atmosphere. A library could even share cooperative art and other projects by teaming up with local school districts or other institutions across the globe. Suffice it to say, library "displays" of the future have amazing potential.

VR has strong prospects for the future, and there may be a need to house equipment in a way not fit for individual homes. It is a need that private companies are beginning to fulfill, but libraries could be a resource as well. Modern arcades are already rising to the occasion, supplying the public with a place to use VR.[14] There are other interesting proposals, such as a Swiss motion-capture research institute planning to create large virtual spaces for multiple VR users in which they can join online worlds and digitally interact.[15]

Libraries with VR could become venues for live omnidirectional content. It is now possible to view real-time, 360-degree, omnidirectional footage with a VR headset. For example, singer-songwriter Paul McCartney has incorporated such footage for live concerts, allowing virtual attendees to watch him play on the stage.[16] Library patrons could virtually attend many different types of events—concerts, lectures, instructional demonstrations, the Olympics, or theatrical performances, to name a few—if libraries provide the proper equipment and spread awareness of the experiences.

VR is gaining popularity in the field of psychology and can be utilized at libraries for therapeutic purposes. Currently, a major use for VR is known as "exposure therapy," whereby a user is presented with specific environments in order to provoke potentially suppressed emotions for healing.[17] Participants may be victims of post-traumatic stress disorder or suffering from various phobias and fears. With a VR headset, it is possible for qualified therapists to use library spaces and equipment to bring a sense of atmosphere to a person that is simply not possible with other mediums and help him in innovative ways. A person with a fear of heights, for example, could benefit from a therapist using library resources to "expose" him to environments that appear to be high up.

Library patrons can also use VR to experience local history. As an example, it is possible to capture three-dimensional, omnidirectional footage of a person who experienced a historically significant event for later generations to benefit from and appreciate. It is even possible to create a virtual map of a town or city and artificially view it from ground level at different times in history. Imagine standing in your hometown as the landscape around you evolves over the course of decades or even centuries. Consider also how many local historic landmarks and institutions struggle to stay afloat due to lack of funding and resources. VR will be able to capture historically significant landmarks (such as Theodore Roosevelt's house) for all time even if the physical or financial realities change. VR offers a new way of not only experiencing but also re-creating history.

LOGISTICS OF INCORPORATING VR

Librarians and library staff must consider and plan for the logistics of incorporating VR, but if these plans are properly executed, patrons will have a great resource at their disposal. While there are resources available for libraries looking to implement VR, practical advice for library staff is still lacking.[18] Before purchasing any particular VR headset, it is prudent for staff to check safety information. For many headsets, the suggested minimum age of users is twelve or thirteen.[19] This and other important safety recommendations can usually be found on the particular manufacturer's website.

Patrons should also be made aware of the risks and health considerations involved with VR. For example, it is a good idea for patrons with epilepsy to be cautious about the technology and check with their doctor before use. Proteus VR Labs, maker of "FreeflyVR," advises that in general, the technology "is not suitable for those who are pregnant, have high blood pressure, suffer from motion sickness, inner ear infections or claustrophobia, had any form of recent surgery, pre-existing binocular vision abnormalities, heart conditions or epileptic symptoms."[20] In a phenomenon known as "cybersickness," patrons can get nausea after using VR due to "sensory and perceptual mismatches between the visual and vestibular systems," as described by analyst Judy Barrett.[21]

In order to recognize and adapt to the risks of VR, libraries should have a mandatory waiver available for anyone who wishes to use the equipment. It removes liability from the library and ensures that the patron knows the risks involved. It may be advisable to have the parent or legal guardian sign in person for patrons under the age of eighteen to avoid potential forgery.

Besides health considerations, it is crucial for library staff to have a solid understanding of the technology. Having knowledgeable staff can determine the success of VR implementation. Libraries should consider training existing staff members so they have the proper skills to assist patrons effectively, making it much more likely that the equipment will actually be used and not collect dust. Inviting VR developers to speak would also be beneficial so that staff and patrons alike can understand how exactly virtual content is created, which can help mitigate possible concerns about new technology and change.

Knowing what equipment to buy can be a major obstacle for librarians and make it feel rather intimidating to adopt VR. It is easy to become overwhelmed with the plethora of choices involved when shopping around for VR headsets and accessories. However, it ultimately comes down to a series of simple but important decisions relating to the vision of VR at any particular library.

In order to incorporate VR, there are several physical accessories and options to consider. Usually a six-by-six-foot area is sufficient for using a headset, especially if physical hand controllers are involved, and it is important to keep in mind the potential location of physical calibrated sensors, if required. Another factor for staff to consider is sanitation. After a VR headset has been used by a patron, it is a good practice to wipe down the equipment with an appropriate cleaning solution. It may be practical to include disposable face masks to be put on under the headset to protect both the equipment and the health of the patrons, although it is important to note that this is an ongoing expense.

At one end of the VR spectrum are relatively inexpensive headsets, essentially consisting of a smartphone strapped around a user's head. Unfortunately, the lower price tag often results in a lower-quality VR experience. It is also noteworthy that in order for a smartphone to work with this type of headset, it requires a common three-dimensional gyroscope built into the phone—not to be confused with an accelerometer, which can only detect one or two axes of movement. Users can refer to individual phone documentation to confirm.

There are multiple mobile VR viewers available on the consumer market, some of the most popular being Samsung Gear VR, Google Daydream, Merge VR, and Google Cardboard.[22] The *New York Times* actually bundled foldable Google Cardboards with copies of the newspaper in 2016 as a way to promote the technology.[23]

Chapter Eight: Virtual Reality

The proper software for these headsets is readily available on the device's associated digital stores (Apple's App Store, Google Play, etc.). If one was so inclined, there are even instructions on how to build one from scratch. With access to a 3-D printer, one could print out a headset frame, add two lenses of low-powered magnifying glasses, connect a head strap, insert a smartphone, and—voilà—have an inexpensive, "do-it-yourself" VR viewer.[24]

On the other end of the spectrum are high-end VR headsets that require substantial external processing power to function. For example, the Oculus Rift is a popular high-end headset that requires a high-powered PC to function (www.oculus.com/rift). It offers an exclusive content library and is owned by Facebook Inc. Another popular option is the HTC Vive, developed by HTC and Valve Corporation, which, like the Oculus Rift, also requires a high-powered PC (www.vive.com/us). In addition, a new Vive Pro version was recently released with superior performance at a higher cost. A third popular option is the PlayStation VR, made by Sony, but users must have a PlayStation 4 console to operate.

Users can refer to the manufacturer's recommended minimum system requirements to ensure they get an adequate PC, whether purchased preassembled or built from individual parts. There are several resources to aid in assembling a machine, such as PC Part Picker (www.pcpartpicker.com). One could potentially turn this process into a library class, in which patrons learn the skill of building a PC from scratch. It's wise to consider an external display connected to the PC running VR, in addition to the computer monitor, so onlookers can witness the user's virtual perspective too.

The days of needing substantial external processing power for VR may be numbered, however. There appears to be a new standalone style of VR headsets in which hardware to run VR is actually built into the headset itself. This can be seen with the recent release the Oculus Go headset (www.oculus.com/go), and Google has a similar one on the way.[25] These wireless headsets may set a new trend, making VR technology even more user friendly—but only time can tell.

The hardware and software of VR will continue to evolve over time, and this will open up even more possibilities. According to Moore's law, a prediction of how rapidly digital technology will advance, VR will soon become streamlined, wireless, and capable of photorealistic graphic environments.[26] With increased processing power and more efficient hardware, the possibilities for libraries will expand exponentially.

PART II: Services

FUTURE OF LIBRARIES

Libraries can continue to be relevant informative institutions in today's society, particularly as a venue for exploration and innovation, and VR can help toward this goal. An ideal library of the future, having successfully incorporated VR technology, would be one in which patrons could use relevant equipment at their convenience, borrow it for home use, learn about various subjects from within virtual environments, create worlds of their own, and more. It would be a library in which there are sufficient educational resources to support VR and classes that aim to enrich patron learning about the technology. With the right resources and support, the possibilities are endless.

Libraries can take advantage of innovative and technically advanced virtual outreach opportunities, such as streaming omnidirectional footage of a live event or a previous one for patrons to experience through VR headsets.[27] Future libraries may adopt a new concept of virtual conferencing rooms, supplying a new way of bringing people together. Video conferencing rooms are available in many libraries today, allowing users to communicate through video capture. Connecting users is at the core of the current information technology revolution, and online connections with VR exemplify this concept. With a virtual conference room, one could step into an artificial environment along with another user to communicate in an immersive way—potentially across great distances.

The social networking aspect of VR is gaining momentum, and people may be connecting virtually in the near future. The link between social networks and VR is tangible. As Nick Wingfield and Vindu Goel of the *New York Times* wrote, "Facebook sees the future—a 3D virtual world where you feel as if you are hanging out with your friends rather than staring at their pictures."[28] As the amount of VR users grow, there will likely be online virtual environments where users can connect.[29] Holding entirely virtual-based events for patrons at libraries may be common in the future, with participants joining via headset. Perhaps in the distant future, libraries will no longer be physical locations at all but vast virtual storehouses of information and a means of sharing resources and connecting people across the globe.

With an array of price points and capabilities, VR technology allows libraries to start small but dream big. VR has potential in a library setting, but it is up to the collective imaginations of library professionals to unleash it. It presents a great challenge for libraries to discover new ways to serve the public and provides an exciting opportunity to share knowledge and resources with patrons in ways never before seen. It may be in the best interest of libraries to keep pace with rapidly evolving modern technology by incorporating immersive digital experiences into their services. VR offers libraries the chance to not simply remain relevant in today's society but to play a critical role in its education and advancement. By embracing VR, libraries can encourage innovation and spark creativity that is out of this world.

NOTES

1. "Information Age: People, Information and Technology," National Museum of American History, 2006, www.si.edu/Exhibitions/Information-Age-People-Information-and-Technology-4069.
2. Adario Strange, "Oculus Installing Free VR Systems in Nearly 100 California Libraries," Mashable, June 7, 2017, http://mashable.com/2017/06/07/oculus-rift-library-project.
3. *Merriam-Webster*, s.v. "virtual reality," www.merriam-webster.com/dictionary/virtualreality.
4. Linda Lohr, "The Stereoscope: 3D for the 19th Century," University at Buffalo, University Libraries, 2015, http://libweb.lib.buffalo.edu/hslblog/history/?p=1512. Accessed November 1, 2017.
5. "History of Slide Projectors," Ithaca College, n.d., www.ithaca.edu/hs/vrc/history ofprojectors/?item=7305.
6. Nick Wingfield and Vindu Goel, "Facebook in $2 Billion Deal for Virtual Reality Company," *New York Times*, March 25, 2014, www.nytimes.com/2014/03/26/technology/facebook-to-buy-oculus-vr-maker-of-virtual-reality-headset.html.
7. Kathleen Chaykowski, "Mark Zuckerberg Has a Plan to Bring Facebook Users into Virtual Reality," *Forbes*, February 24, 2016, www.forbes.com/sites/kathleenchaykowski/2016/02/24/mark-zuckerberg-has-a-plan-to-make-virtual-reality-social.
8. Erik Kain, "Virtual Reality Is Just an Over-Priced Gimmick, Nothing More," *Forbes*, October 15, 2016, www.forbes.com/sites/erikkain/2016/10/15/virtual-reality-is-just-an-over-priced-gimmick.
9. "Early Writing," University of Texas at Austin, n.d., www.hrc.utexas.edu/educator/modules/gutenberg/books/early.
10. Madhumita Murgia, "How Virtual Reality Is Going to Change Our Lives," *Telegraph*, December 21, 2015, www.telegraph.co.uk/technology/news/12047279/How-virtual-reality-is-going-to-change-our-lives.html.
11. Leila Meyer, "Virtually There: Kids Are Using VR to Explore Worlds and Create New Ones," *School Library Journal*, September 29, 2017, www.slj.com/?detailStory=virtually-kids-using-vr-explore-worlds-create-new-ones.
12. Tim Bajarin, "Maker Faire: Why the Maker Movement Is Important to America's Future," *Time*, May 19, 2014, http://time.com/104210/maker-faire-maker-movement.

PART II: Services

13. Gary Stager, "What's the Maker Movement and Why Should I Care?," *Scholastic*, Winter 2014, www.scholastic.com/browse/article.jsp?id=3758336.
14. Alan Boyle, "Video Game Arcades Are Back—This Time, with Virtual Reality for the Masses," GeekWire, April 12, 2017, www.geekwire.com/2017/portal-virtual-reality-arcade.
15. Joseph Volpe, "The VR Arcade of the Future Will Look Something like This," Engadget, January 24, 2016, www.engadget.com/2016/01/24/the-vr-arcade-of-the-future-sundance.
16. Andrew Dalton, "Paul McCartney Adopts VR So Your Grandparents Don't Have To," Engadget, May 24, 2016, www.engadget.com/2016/05/24/paul-mccartney-adopts-vr.
17. Albert Rizzo, "Bravemind: Virtual Reality Exposure Therapy," USC Institute for Creative Technologies, 2005–, http://ict.usc.edu/prototypes/pts.
18. Troy Lambert, "Virtual Reality in the Library: Creating a New Experience," Public Libraries Online, February 24, 2016, http://publiclibrariesonline.org/2016/02/virtual-reality-in-the-library-creating-a-new-experience.
19. Sophie Charara, "A Super Quick Safety Guide to Letting Your Kids Use VR Headsets," Wearable, December 2, 2016, www.wareable.com/vr/guide-vr-headsets-children.
20. "Safety and Regulations for Using a Virtual Reality Headset," Proteus VR Labs, http://freeflyvr.com/safety. Accessed October 29, 2017.
21. Judy Barrett, *Side Effects of Virtual Environments: A Review of the Literature* (Edinburgh: DSTO Information Sciences Laboratory, 2004), http://pdfs.semanticscholar.org/ab1b/4153e44abb4c1a1fcac5f2aaee847d30ecf3.pdf.
22. "Gear VR with Controller," Oculus, n.d., www.oculus.com/gear-vr; "Homepage," Google Daydream, n.d., http://vr.google.com/daydream; "Homepage," Merge Labs, Inc., Merge Virtual Reality, n.d., www.mergevr.com; Google, "Homepage," Google Cardboard, n.d., http://vr.google.com/cardboard.
23. Kristen Hare, "The New York Times Will Send Google Cardboard to 300,000 Subscribers," *Poynter*, April 28, 2016, www.poynter.org/news/new-york-times-will-send-google-cardboard-300000-subscribers.
24. Alastair Jennings, "How to 3D Print Your Own Virtual Reality Headset," TechRadar, March 30, 2016, www.techradar.com/how-to/world-of-tech/how-to-3d-print-your-own-virtual-reality-headset-1317990.
25. Kyle Orland, "Google Announces Untethered, Fully Tracked, Standalone VR Headsets," arstechnia.com, May 17, 2017, http://arstechnica.com/gaming/2017/05/google-announces-untethered-fully-tracked-standalone-vr-headsets.
26. "Moore's Law and Computer Processing Power," datascience@berkeley, March 5, 2014, http://datascience.berkeley.edu/moores-law-processing-power.
27. Richard Nieva, "Facebook to Launch 360-Degree Live Videos," Cnet.com, December 12, 2016, www.cnet.com/news/facebook-is-launching-360-degree-live-videos/.

28. Wingfield and Goel, "Facebook in $2 Billion Deal."
29. Rachel Metz, "Virtual Reality's Missing Element: Other People," *MIT Technology Review*, June 14, 2017, www.technologyreview.com/s/607956/virtual-realitys-missing-element-other-people.

BIBLIOGRAPHY

Bajarin, Tim. "Maker Faire: Why the Maker Movement Is Important to America's Future." *Time*, May 19, 2014. www.time.com/104210/maker-faire-maker-movement.

Barrett, Judy. *Side Effects of Virtual Environments: A Review of the Literature*. Edinburgh: DSTO Information Sciences Laboratory, 2004. http://pdfs.semanticscholar.org/ab1b/4153e44abb4c1a1fcac5f2aaee847d30ecf3.pdf.

Boyle, Alan. "Video Game Arcades Are Back—This Time, with Virtual Reality for the Masses." GeekWire, April 12, 2017. www.geekwire.com/2017/portal-virtual-reality-arcade.

Charara, Sophie. "A Super Quick Safety Guide to Letting Your Kids Use VR Headsets." Wearable, December 2, 2016. www.wareable.com/vr/guide-vr-headsets-children.

Chaykowski, Kathleen. "Mark Zuckerberg Has a Plan to Bring Facebook Users into Virtual Reality." *Forbes*, February 24, 2016. www.forbes.com/sites/kathleenchaykowski/2016/02/24/mark-zuckerberg-has-a-plan-to-make-virtual-reality-social.

Dalton, Andrew. "Paul McCartney Adopts VR So Your Grandparents Don't Have To." Engadget, May 24, 2016. www.engadget.com/2016/05/24/paul-mccartney-adopts-vr.

Denning, Steve. "Do We Need Libraries?" *Forbes*, April 28, 2015. www.forbes.com/sites/stevedenning/2015/04/28/do-we-need-libraries.

Hare, Kristen. "The New York Times Will Send Google Cardboard to 300,000 Subscribers." *Poynter*, April 28, 2016. www.poynter.org/news/new-york-times-will-send-google-cardboard-300000-subscribers.

Jennings, Alastair. "How to 3D Print Your Own Virtual Reality Headset." TechRadar, March 30, 2016. www.techradar.com/how-to/world-of-tech/how-to-3d-print-your-own-virtual-reality-headset-1317990.

Kain, Erik. "Virtual Reality Is Just an Over-Priced Gimmick, Nothing More." *Forbes*, October 15, 2016. www.forbes.com/sites/erikkain/2016/10/15/virtual-reality-is-just-an-over-priced-gimmick.

Lambert, Troy. "Virtual Reality in the Library: Creating a New Experience." Public Libraries Online, February 24, 2016. http://publiclibrariesonline.org/2016/02/virtual-reality-in-the-library-creating-a-new-experience.

Lohr, Linda. "The Stereoscope: 3D for the 19th Century." University at Buffalo, University Libraries, 2015. libweb.lib.buffalo.edu/hslblog/history/?p=1512.

PART II: Services

Metz, Rachel. "Virtual Reality's Missing Element: Other People." *MIT Technology Review*, June 14, 2017. www.technologyreview.com/s/607956/virtual-realitys-missing-element-other-people.

Meyer, Leila. "Virtually There: Kids Are Using VR to Explore Worlds and Create New Ones." *School Library Journal*, September 29, 2017. www.slj.com/2017/09/technology/virtually-kids-using-vr-explore-worlds-create-new-ones.

Murgia, Madhumita. "How Virtual Reality Is Going to Change Our Lives." *Telegraph*, December 21, 2015. www.telegraph.co.uk/technology/news/12047279/How-virtual-reality-is-going-to-change-our-lives.html.

Nieva, Richard. "Facebook to Launch 360-Degree Live Videos." Cnet.com, December 12, 2016. www.cnet.com/news/facebook-is-launching-three-hundred and sixty degree-degree-live-videos.

Orland, Kyle. "Google Announces Untethered, Fully Tracked, Standalone VR Headsets." arstechnia.com, May 17, 2017. http://arstechnica.com/gaming/2017/05/google-announces-untethered-fully-tracked-standalone-vr-headsets.

Phillips, Heather. "The Great Library of Alexandria." Libraries at University of Nebraska–Lincoln, September 2010. http://digitalcommons.unl.edu/libphilprac/417/.

Rizzo, Albert. "Bravemind: Virtual Reality Exposure Therapy." USC Institute for Creative Technologies, 2005–. http://ict.usc.edu/prototypes/pts.

Stager, Gary. "What's the Maker Movement and Why Should I Care?" *Scholastic*, Winter 2014. www.scholastic.com/browse/article.jsp?id=3758336.

Strange, Adario. "Oculus Installing Free VR Systems in Nearly 100 California Libraries." Mashable, June 7, 2017. http://mashable.com/2017/06/07/oculus-rift-library-project.

Volpe, Joseph. "The VR Arcade of the Future Will Look Something like This." Engadget, January 24, 2016. www.engadget.com/2016/01/24/the-vr-arcade-of-the-future-sundance.

Wingfield, Nick, and Vindu Goel. "Facebook in $2 Billion Deal for Virtual Reality Company." *New York Times*, March 25, 2014. www.nytimes.com/2014/03/26/technology/facebook-to-buy-oculus-vr-maker-of-virtual-reality-headset.html.

PART III

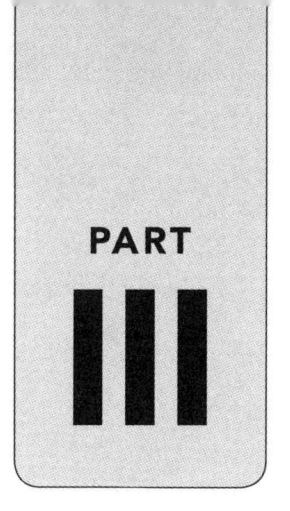

Repositories and Access

Chapter Nine

Digital Exhibits to Digital Humanities
Expanding the Digital Libraries Portfolio

Daniel Johnson and Mark Dehmlow

The digital libraries ecosystem consists of tools and services for digital asset management, digital resource curation and preservation, digital scholarship collection and preservation, digitization, content markup, optical character recognition, web-based discovery, and digital exhibits and collections. While the current instantiation of "digital libraries" was adopted as an area of focus for libraries within the last decade, ideas and projects that are representative of digital libraries have been around for well over half a century. Software that supports digital libraries includes the institutional repository, boutique websites for special collections or exhibits, data management systems, digital preservation systems, and current research information systems, to name a few. Current digital libraries projects frequently are distinct from traditional areas of library technology that focus on patron-facing discovery and delivery because they often focus inwardly on the intellectual output or special collections of an organization.

Digital humanities (DH) refers to a similar transformation of scholarly practice in humanistic and social science disciplines—not simply "applying" computational technology on top of traditional research but expanding the nature of evidence and argumentation itself. Digital humanities projects might include text encoding, text mining, geographic information system (GIS) mapping and layering, statistical modeling, bibliographic or full-text discovery, audio and visual analysis, and other advanced computational techniques.[1] The digital libraries field has evolved in parallel with the growing practices of digital humanities and, over time, has revealed many ways in which the two converge.[2] Increasingly, libraries are moving away from supporting research at the edges—helping researchers find materials and then acquiring new scholarship—to becoming collaborators at the center of scholarship: coordinating preservation of research materials, assisting in the creation of digital scholarship, and helping demonstrate the value of scholarship across the academy.

Given these trends in system convergence and service evolution, digital humanities represent a clear opportunity for libraries to offer significant value to the academy, not only in the areas of tools and consultations, but also in collaborative expertise that supports workflows for librarians and scholars alike.

TRACING THE DIGITAL LIBRARY TO DIGITAL HUMANITIES

The argument that libraries are a natural collaborator in the digital humanities endeavor has been a topic of discussion in the profession for nearly a decade. As Hitoshi Kamada writes in volume 71 of the *College & Research Libraries News*, digital humanities rely on the "skills and knowledge in collecting and organizing data, in which librarians have unique training and background."[3] In his article "What Is Digital Humanities and What's It Doing in the Library?," Micah Vandegrift further argues that libraries are uniquely suited to contribute to digital humanities "because the library already functions as a[n] interdisciplinary agent in the university . . . [and] DH projects involve archival collections, copyright/fair use questions, information organization, emerging technologies and progressive ideas about the role of text(s) in society."[4]

The trajectory for libraries to achieve that expertise can be tracked through the evolution of the "digital library." It has emerged through a long transformation wherein the various materials libraries collect were modified from their physical formats to digital versions. One origin for the digital library is the conversion of card catalog records to mainframe terminal connection–based systems in the 1960s and 1970s.[5] Then in the early 1990s, the transition toward digital content coincided with the proliferation of the Internet. Academic library literature saw the emergence of books and articles such as *Networking Information Products on Campus: Local Area Network and Campus Broadband* and "Electronic Editions of Serials: The Virtual Library Model," revealing the early transition of library content toward network-based CD-ROM indexes and the emanation of digitized serial literature.[6] At that time, *electronic library* and *virtual library* were being used to describe the migration of library collections to the digital environment as well as the effort to digitize texts.[7] For the next decade, library technology would generally focus on the discovery, delivery, and management of mainly traditional resources in digital formats, especially commercially acquired materials. While all of this gestures to the move of the library online, the term *digital libraries* would come to refer to the next big digital turn, which focused more on the creation of digital artifacts and collections through institutional repositories, the emergence of big data projects like the HathiTrust, and the emphasis on exposing institutional special collections. Increased attention in these areas has led to broad digitization, but in a world of billions of scholarly artifacts, projects themselves continue to need focus, curation, and purpose.

At the beginning of the twenty-first century, university libraries, seeing their dominant role as the center for scholarly research become eclipsed by the ubiquity of online content and freely available discovery indexes like Google Scholar, began exploring how they could enhance their overall value to the research endeavor and started evolving their roles from strictly collectors and gatekeepers of commercial content to curators of the scholarly output of their organizations.[8] This transition from intermediary of scholarly collections to a partner in aggregating and hosting scholarly output is one of the critical transitions for the digital library. It would position the profession as a more active participant in the research endeavor and is arguably the inflection point at which research libraries began deeper collaboration in the creation of scholarship. The developing relationships with faculty in the management of scholarly output can be linked easily to the creation of digital scholarship centers, spaces on campuses where scholars could consult with and collaborate on digital projects. The emergence of these centers would broaden the portfolio of deeply collaborative services offered in libraries, and it is at this time that libraries began to leverage their unique expertise, content, and position within the university ecosystem to contribute to new ways of supporting the research endeavor.

PART III: Repositories and Access

EVOLVING THE SCOPE OF OUR PORTFOLIO: DIGITAL HUMANITIES IN LIBRARIES

The emergence of what we now call digital humanities from concordancing, encoding, and rudimentary number crunching is fairly well known and rehearsed.[9] The sphere of potential activity, then as now, spans many dimensions, including scale (big data versus close textual analysis), kind (encoding versus publishing versus statistical modeling), and output (public humanities projects versus personal research datasets versus crowd-sourced archives). Rather than coalescing into a singular discipline or even a collection of techniques, the digital humanities have remained a plural entity, more a transdisciplinary community of practice such as "American studies" than a narrowly defined department such as "English."

Library work has always been central to this community, though it has often been performed by nonlibrarians. At whatever scale, kind, or output, digital humanities scholarship is especially librarian-like at the early stages: finding, accessing, and cleaning up data sources (whether commercial or open access). For those unused to the process, it can be time consuming and frustrating. Librarians who are prepared to help—and "traditional" collection development experience is good preparation—stand to gain trust as collaborators and, hence, as more involved partners across all stages of research and writing.

Take the Viral Texts Project (http://viraltexts.org). Team members reported in 2015 that the historic newspaper data they were using produced intriguing results, but the breadth of coverage was patchy. Drawing from the Library of Congress' open source "Chronicling America" newspaper archive, they were able to analyze 1.6 billion words from 132 newspapers printed before 1861, but even that impressive number demonstrated "significant gaps in [. . .] holdings."[10] One way the team hoped to expand analysis was by including commercial databases, such as ProQuest's American Periodical Series and Readex's America's Historical Newspapers, opening the door to direct collaboration with the library, which brokers relationships with these vendors.

Raw data from such databases, the team writes, "are typically not made available by default, even to subscribing libraries," but reticence is slowly melting.[11] Notre Dame's Hesburgh Libraries, for example, have successfully requested raw data on hard drives (along with written use agreements) from providers including Adam Matthew and Gale-Cengage. In fact, the latter is, at time of writing, beta testing a Digital Scholar Lab that promises to grant libraries data download access for subscribed "Primary Sources" databases.[12] Despite this increasing availability,

Chapter Nine: Digital Exhibits to Digital Humanities

challenges remain for departmental faculty: How exactly do I access the material? Who do I have to contact to use it and what agreements do I have to sign? What am I allowed to do with the data once I get it, and how long can I keep it? What are the publishing restrictions?

Again, these negotiations are clearly within the province of librarians, as are archiving, managing, and provisioning the data. But then someone must coerce the data into "information" that can be analyzed.[13] Advanced digital humanities scholars may wish to do this transformation for themselves, but even those who are capable can benefit from consultation with library specialists. "Many minds make light work" in data modeling, helping expose gaps and offering fresh perspectives . Librarians also bring knowledge of metadata standards that could open the work to unforeseen reuse and replication in other projects.

By all appearances, data gathering and data wrangling are in high demand. English professor Matthew J. Lavin (University of Pittsburgh) founded humanitiesdata.com to address the limited availability of humanities datasets in an environment chilled by "concerns about proprietary data, copyright, vendors' terms and conditions, and long-term data curation."[14] Such collection and cleaning efforts benefit the library too. For example, when vendors allow libraries to create and provision preservation copies of databases, anything added to those preservation copies will redound to future users. If an information professional collaborates with a departmental scholar by, say, writing a program that extracts author names and dates, that indexing could benefit many more patrons than just the original requester.

Challenges of data wrangling extend to the smaller, "close reading" end of the data scale as well, and libraries enjoy multiple advantages when they collaborate with faculty in using local special-collections strengths. Libraries, after all, have been digitizing their rare materials for years, offering unprecedented primary source collections for researchers. In 2011, Yale celebrated the digitization of its three hundred thousandth image, channeling Robert Frost to say that they have "many more to digitize before we sleep."[15] Unique material, beautiful metadata, all very accessible—but who is using it?

Librarians plugged in to their local digital humanities scene could float the idea of using special collections manuscript pages for a class on text encoding and scholarly editing. The teaching faculty would get a chance to jump to the top of the digitization queue and work with material that no one else holds. The library would see an uptick in special collections usage and gain student-generated metadata that might be incorporated back into finding aids. The students would learn archive navigation, practices of editorial close reading, and text-encoding standards. The completed project, showcased through digital exhibits and visualizations, would shine light on every collaborator; a win all around.

So collecting the data (whether a mass of digital newspaper articles or a few dusty physical manuscripts) requires a number of competencies that are particular librarian strengths, and it is a short step from collecting data to collaborating more deeply. Take that example of the text-encoding class based in special collections. Librarians might traditionally demonstrate how to read the physical page, how to decipher handwriting, or how to access a digital surrogate. Who will teach encoding, provide troubleshooting, or help visualize results? Perhaps the departmental professor is happy to expound on the Text Encoding Initiative (TEI) guidelines or the programming language R for students, but faculty members may feel that class time is better spent on discussing course content and criticism, so coding and encoding lessons could shift to the librarian.

This work need not be bare tools demonstration, or what librarians John E. Russell and Merinda Kaye Hensley call "buttonology."[16] As Laura Mandell writes in *Breaking the Book*, the "forms of attention that are required for hand encoding resemble and in fact reproduce those required by close reading."[17] Similar claims might be made for other digital humanities activities: each tool, methodology, and algorithm brings assumptions to bear on the object of study, from data collection to statistical modeling to data visualization, and hence provides the opportunity for critical reflection. Librarians equipped to engage at these levels have a stake in the project's intellectual design and scholarly payoff. DH therefore presents wonderful opportunities to develop deep partnerships in teaching and research, to move beyond "merely facilitating" DH collaborations, or "essentially moving jigsaw pieces around to connect other unrelated parties in a kind of a matchmaking service."[18] Librarians who embrace their *own* role as the "dream match" will stand at the forefront of digital librarianship.

DIGITAL HUMANITIES AND DIGITAL EXHIBIT PLATFORMS / TOOL KITS

Digital humanities scholars might say that because tools are so liable to change, it is more important to teach underlying computational logic, habits of thought, and critical engagement.[19] True though that is, a look back at digital humanities history reveals perhaps a surprising amount of continuity. The majority of the tools, methodologies, and big names that Devin Higgins mentioned in the 2014 version of this guide are still major players today. The year 2014 may seem laughably recent, but the technologies Higgins mentioned were already then several years old, and anything approaching a decade is ancient history in computing terms. Digital humanities tools are demonstrating signs of at least relative maturity.

Table 9.1 lists digital tools that fall into several categories: content management systems that enable media-rich storytelling, software packages for text mining and analysis (often referred to as "distant reading"), programming languages and modules for working with statistical data and creating graphical visualizations, GIS and mapping systems, and software that is a hybrid of multiple tools. The list could be substantially enlarged, but the following chart organizes some of the more popular free / open source tools by rough order of complexity. Descriptions with links are available at https://scholarsgrotto.github.io/lita-2018.html.

TABLE 9.1
Popular systems and tool kits for digital humanities projects.

	Entry-level complexity	Medium-level complexity	High-level complexity
Text mining, cleaning, and analysis	Voyant	OpenRefine	MALLET Stanford NLP Tools
Content management / publishing platforms	Scalar Omeka Wordpress	Drupal	
GIS/mapping	Palladio	ArcGIS Story Maps	
Data visualization / statistical modeling	Palladio	RStudio	Gephi R Shiny
Python programming		Anaconda Google Colaboratory	

One of the major challenges for libraries supporting digital humanities is helping patrons cross from beginner-level, out-of-the-box tools to more advanced DH methods. It stands to reason: the knowledge and experience needed to master (or at least sufficiently engage with) computer programming, database development, server management, statistical analysis, and so forth could hardly be covered in several semesters' worth of coursework, let alone in one-off workshops. Patrons simply may not have the freedom or opportunity to pursue this amount of formal training. Thankfully, tools have been developed in recent years that help people navigate the treacherous intermediate territory between novice and expert for themselves, and libraries can help lead patrons through.

For example, Google's recently announced Python platform, Colaboratory, "requires no setup to use and runs entirely in the cloud."[20] In beta status at the time of writing, the platform allows users to open a Python program in their browser, choose the 2.X or 3.X codebase, and then save programs in their Google Drive. No complicated installations. No rigmarole with installing packages from the command line. A library-based Python workshop could start immediately with Colaboratory, so long as the attendees have Internet-connected computers. The programs one writes on Colaboratory are not "stuck" in the cloud but can be freely copied from the user's Drive account and run as regular Python programs. More advanced knowledge, and the advantages that accrue from working with a text editor and the command line, can be learned in due course, as needed.

Another choke point is the jump to full-service websites. Patrons may become familiar with basic web page development, perhaps by configuring a free Word-Press blog, but more advanced uses of the web are often a stumbling block, especially because university IT departments tend to restrict customized applications of patron web development (they break more easily and can introduce security issues). Can I do server-side programming? Can I install platforms like Drupal on my university webspace? How do I get my own domain name? Often, the answer is "That's not allowed." One solution is Reclaim Hosting, which began as an effort at Mary Washington University to make web development more accessible to students and has expanded to become an education-serving commercial host. Offering advanced server control and domain name registration to students and faculty for a reasonable yearly fee, Reclaim Hosting has partnered with dozens of universities.[21] A pay service is perhaps not the ideal, but at a fraction of the cost of a textbook, Reclaim offers power that would otherwise be hard to come by.

From the patron's perspective, the Reclaim partnership gives remarkable control that IT departments are reluctant to surrender (for good reason). From the IT department's perspective, the outside vendor reduces support overhead and eliminates a layer of middle management between patrons and projects. And the service satisfies data migration needs: though universities may enforce certain policies, patrons retain ownership of their accounts and can back them up.

For a more comprehensive listing of digital humanities tools, the Carolina Digital Humanities Initiative (CDHI) at the University of North Carolina (http://digitalhumanities.unc.edu/resources/tools/), Anthony Sanchez at the University of Arizona Libraries (http://libguides.library.arizona.edu/dighumantools/epub), and Miriam Posner at UCLA (https://docs.google.com/document/d/1Z-14hgZPMIiAzT6vx1mVg5l60zkRVU9EHgZgK9HHdU4/edit) have strong listings of free / open source tools featuring a variety of commentary on options and uses.

Chapter Nine: Digital Exhibits to Digital Humanities

DEVELOPING A DIGITAL COLLECTIONS AND DIGITAL HUMANITIES PLATFORM

As noted previously, the Hesburgh Libraries have also committed to enhancing the value of our service offerings to scholars through innovation. In the fall of 2014, following two decades of supporting stand-alone digital collections applications, the Hesburgh Libraries engaged in an effort to build our own scalable unified digital exhibits and collections platform that we call Honeycomb. To cover several significant unsolved needs for librarians and scholars, our developers created three main tools: (1) Digital Exhibits and Collections (DEC), a visually compelling user interface for digital collection showcases; (2) Collection Discovery, a software layer that provides search and browse functionality for a digital collection; and (3) Collection Analyzer, an interface that provides textual analysis and digital content comparison across a corpus of texts (see figure 9.1).

Our initial objective was to provide online tools for curators to create digital exhibit websites drawing from content in the libraries' online collections. Accessing certain collections might still require some custom development, but most content (70–80 percent) is accessible within this framework without intervention from IT staff. When IT intervention is needed, features can be rolled back into the platform. The functional objectives for the project, then, were to enable curators to manage and organize items in a collection, upload high-resolution images of artifacts, tell a story about specific items or topics, and create web pages highlighting and enhancing particular artifacts while allowing end users to

- zoom and pan high-resolution images of artifacts for closer examination;
- browse through items in the exhibit;
- view the exhibit on modern devices, such as tablets, phones, computers, and large-screen displays;
- navigate through large collections with advanced search functionality and facets defined by the curator; and
- experience a story about a topic via the online display of artifacts with text descriptions, commentary, transcriptions, and so on.

At the time, there were three external applications in various states of maturity that we could have used: Omeka, Google Open Gallery, and the Samvera/Stanford project Spotlight. While these platforms all showed some promise as tools that could support what we were trying to accomplish, Omeka was getting ready to undergo a major application refactor, which would mean waiting; Google Open Gallery was in beta and the long-term stability of the application was

PART III: Repositories and Access

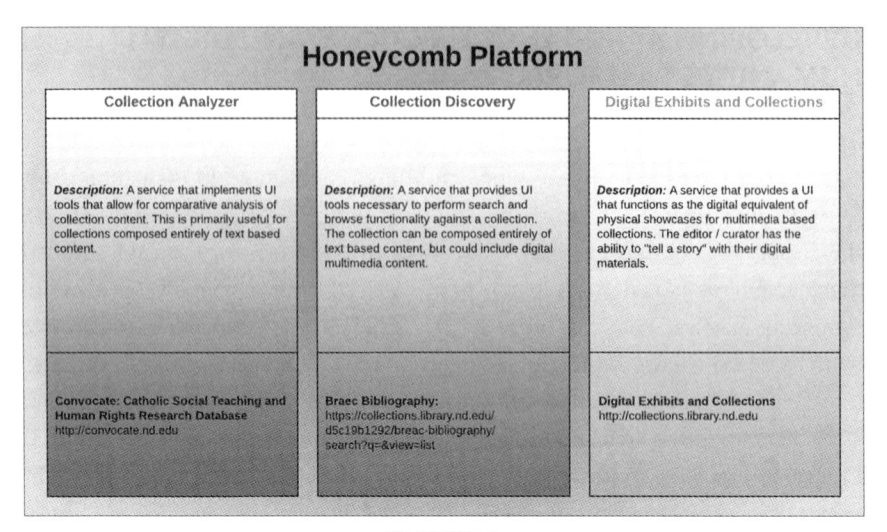

FIGURE 9.1
The Honeycomb platform.

unknown; and Spotlight was very early in its development and required Fedora underneath.

As we were developing DEC, there were several new and legacy projects that required a searchable and faceted discovery interface for bibliographic objects coming both from our internal departments as well as from scholars, particularly in the humanities. These projects were very similar in nature to abstracting and indexing databases one would find through vendor platforms like EBSCOhost and ProQuest. Because discovery and faceted browse were initial requirements for DEC, this functionality became the basis for the Collection Discovery part of the Honeycomb platform.

In early 2015, the libraries were approached by the Notre Dame Center for Civil and Human Rights about a possible partnership. The center wanted to develop a project based on a print collection managed by the center and the libraries that could digitally compare Vatican doctrine and human rights law—a project now called Convocate (https://convocate.nd.edu). The project was a perfect intersection between a discovery interface, text mining, and machine learning and became the foundation for the third segment of the Honeycomb stack, Collection Analyzer.

The future development plan for Honeycomb includes rearchitecting for multitenancy and cloud hosting, development of functionality to support museum digital artifacts, and a broad set of functionalities designed to enhance its handling of digital collections. The long-term goal for Honeycomb is to launch it as "software as a service" that not only supports library-related collections but could become a "what you see is what you get" (WYSIWYG) content management tool designed specifically for working with digital bibliographic, fine art, and manuscript artifacts. Along with our CurateND platform (based on the Hyrax component of the Samvera project), the Honeycomb platform will be another component in a Mellon Foundation–funded project that endeavors to provide digital asset management functionality across museums, libraries, and archives, and one of the core goals is to make the resulting software available to the broader community in 2021.[22]

WHERE DO WE GO FROM HERE?

Digital humanities maintain a tight relationship with digital libraries, but their futures are open-ended. In 2014, Higgins projected a slow normalization of text mining, whereby "the techniques will become easier to integrate into the interpretive approaches we currently do not consider 'new.'" Digital techniques in the humanities do seem to be integrating more and more as simply another viable option for research rather than an exotic experiment, and as a result, the opportunities for libraries to push into new territory are increasing.

Some libraries, for example, are positioning themselves as direct publishers of scholarship rather than simply providers. The Library Coalition, founded in 2014, hosts annual conferences that explore how libraries might host original digital content, either alone or in partnership with university presses.[23] To advance this goal, the University of Michigan Library and Press, in collaboration with others, are developing an open source publishing platform, Fulcrum, and other open source platforms are available in plenty.[24] This model could turn some libraries into a one-stop shop that teaches patrons how to perform digital analysis, solicits publishers to vet the content produced and lend it cachet, and configures the publishing platform to be both code compatible and archive friendly.

But this is only one possibility. Like the digital humanities, library-based digital humanities programs and services cover a multitude of practices. If there is one unifying thread, we would have to say that it is collaboration. Whether the engagement is informal consultation or grant-funded partnership; whether the pedagogy is one-off workshops or library-based, credit-bearing courses; whether the library collects, creates, models, or publishes the data, the need is the same: to bring people together to form a community of practice.

PART III: Repositories and Access

This is scary—especially for humanities scholars. The stereotypical image is the solitary pedant laboring away in the lonely carrel. Yet we think we can safely say that the insight gleaned from deep individual study is in no great danger. Digital humanities are not the enemy of such interpretation, or to quote a recent article by Sarah E. Bond, Hoyt Long, and Ted Underwood, "'Digital' Is Not the Opposite of 'Humanities.'"[25] But as the budding digital humanist John Donne wrote, no one in this world "is an Iland, intire of itselfe" either. If scholars and librarians wish to understand the new kind of evidence being presented—and especially to create it for themselves—they will need to work together, at least for a few moments at a time. The carrel will still be there, ready to receive them after the rejuvenating journey.

Special thanks to Matthew Sisk, GIS librarian and anthropology and archeology subject specialist, and Eric Lease Morgan, digital initiatives librarian, both of the Hesburgh Libraries of the University of Notre Dame, for sharing their insights into the best GIS and text-mining tools.

NOTES

1. For a visual representation and analysis of this thick milieu, see Ted Underwood's 2015 blog post, "Seven Ways Humanists Are Using Computers to Understand Text," *Stone and the Shell* (blog), last modified June 4, 2015, https://web.archive.org/web/20171220200820/https://tedunderwood.com/2015/06/04/seven-ways-humanists-are-using-computers-to-understand-text.

2. See, for example, Devin Higgins's analysis of text mining in the previous LITA *Top Technologies* edition of 2014, "Text Analysis Seems Poised to Shorten the Distance between Interpretation and Classification, between Librarian and Humanist": "Text Mining in Critical Practice," in *Top Technologies Every Librarian Needs to Know: A LITA Guide*, ed. Kenneth J. Varnum (Chicago: American Library Association, 2014), https://ebookcentral-proquest-com/lib/ndlib-ebooks/detail.action?docID=1774127.

3. Hitoshi Kamada, "Digital Humanities: Roles for Libraries?," *College & Research Libraries News* 71, no. 9 (2010): 484–85.

4. Micah Vandegrift, "What Is Digital Humanities and What's It Doing in the Library?," *In the Library with the Lead Pipe*, June 2012, www.inthelibrarywiththeleadpipe.org/2012/dhandthelib/.

5. Christine L. Borgman, "Why Are Online Catalogs Still Hard to Use?," *Journal of the American Society for Information Science* 47, no. 7 (1996): 493–503, https://doi.org/10.1002/(SICI)1097-4571(199607)47:7<493::AID-ASI3>3.0.CO;2-P.

6. Leonardo Candela, Donatella Castelli, and Pasquale Pagano, "History, Evolution and Impact of Digital Libraries," in *E-publishing and Digital Libraries: Legal and*

Organizational Issues, ed. Ioannis Iglezakis, Tatiana-Eleni Synodinou, and Sarantos Kapidakis (New York: Information Science Reference, 2011), 1–30.

7. Calvin Reid, "Columbia Experiment Will Put Library Collection Online," *Publishers Weekly* 240 (February 1993): 13.

8. Raym Crow, "The Case for Institutional Repositories: A SPARC Position Paper," *ARL: A Bimonthly Report on Research Library Issues & Actions* (August 2002): 1–4, www.sparc.arl.org/resources/papers-guides/the-case-for-institutional-repositories.

9. See, for example, Susan Hockey's "The History of Humanities Computing," in *A Companion to Digital Humanities*, edited by Susan Schreibman, Ray Siemens, and John Unsworth (Malden, MA: Blackwell, 2004), 3–19, http://onlinelibrary.wiley.com/book/10.1002/9780470999875; and multiple essays in Matthew K. Gold, ed., *Debates in the Digital Humanities*, part 1 (Minneapolis: University of Minnesota Press, 2012), http://dhdebates.gc.cuny.edu/debates/1, especially Matthew Kirschenbaum's "What Is Digital Humanities and What's It Doing in English Departments?" These venerable practices are still alive and well. A recent example of that most classic of DH activities, concordancing, is on display in Violet Wiegand, Michaela Mahlberg, and Peter Stockwell, "Corpus Linguistics in Action: The Fireplace Pose in 19th Century Fiction," *Programming Historian* (blog), last modified September 21, 2017, https://programminghistorian.org/posts/corpus-linguistics-in-action.

10. See the Library of Congress' "Chronicling America" page at http://chroniclingamerica.loc.gov. See also David A. Smith, Ryan Cordell, and Abby Mullen, "Computational Methods for Uncovering Reprinted Texts in Antebellum Newspapers," *American Literary History* 27, no. 3 (September 2015): E1, https://doi.org/10.1093/alh/ajv029.

11. Smith, Cordell, and Mullen, "Computational Methods," E13.

12. The possibility of data download was mentioned in discussion; publication information on the beta, as of December 2017, is available at https://web.archive.org/web/20171220192456/https://www.gale.com/primary-sources/digital-scholarship.

13. Our sense of information as structured data is a simplification of a larger terminological debate rehearsed, for example, in C. Zins, "Conceptual Approaches for Defining Data, Information, and Knowledge." *Journal of the American Society for Information Science and Technology* 58 (2007): 479–93, https://doi.org/10.1002/asi.20508.

14. "About," Humanities Data, n.d., http://humanitiesdata.com/about.

15. "300,000 Images (and Many More to Digitize before We Sleep)," Beinecke Rare Book & Manuscript Library, May 11, 2011, http://beinecke.library.yale.edu/about/blogs/beinecke-library/2011/05/11/300000-images-and-many-more-digitize-we-sleep.

16. John E. Russell and Merinda Kaye Hensley, "Beyond Buttonology: Digital Humanities, Digital Pedagogy, and the ACRL Framework," *College & Research*

Libraries News 78, no. 11 (December 2017), http://crln.acrl.org/index.php/crlnews/article/view/16833/18427.

17. In Laura Mandell's experience, this digital-cum-intellectual engagement "helped many of what had been 'the worst' students become excellent ones." Mandell, *Breaking the Book: Print Humanities in the Digital Age* (Chichester: Wiley Blackwell, 2015), 181, http://onlinelibrary.wiley.com/book/10.1002/9781118274538.

18. Trevor Munoz, "Recovering a Humanist Librarianship through Digital Humanities," in *Laying the Foundation*, ed. John W. White and Heather Gilbert (West Lafayette, IN: Purdue University Press, 2016), 6, https://doi.org/10.26530/OAPEN_605454.

19. As Sarah Melton remarks in surprise about changing technology, "Preserving something as seemingly straightforward as a web page raises a number of questions. (Even once-ubiquitous web technologies like Flash are no longer supported!)." Melton, "The Center That Holds: Developing Digital Publishing," in *Laying the Foundation*, ed. White and Gilbert, 108.

20. "Colaboratory," Google, n.d., https://colab.research.google.com.

21. At time of writing, $30/year was the most basic plan: https://reclaimhosting.com/shared-hosting/. A list of partnering universities is available here: https://reclaimhosting.com/institutions/.

22. Tara O'Leary, "Notre Dame Receives Mellon Foundation Grant to Develop Software Platform to Help Universities Access Library and Museum Holdings," *Notre Dame News*, March 13, 2018, https://news.nd.edu/news/notre-dame-receives-mellon-foundation-grant-to-develop-software-platform-to-help-universities-access-library-and-museum-holdings/.

23. See https://librarypublishing.org/library-publishing-forum/.

24. See www.fulcrum.org. The Library Coalition's 2018 preconference is offering presentations on Fulcrum and other platforms including Janeway, Open Journal Systems, Manifold, PubSweet, and Vega.

25. Sarah E. Bond, Hoyt Long, and Ted Underwood, "'Digital' Is Not the Opposite of 'Humanities,'" *Chronicle of Higher Education*, November 1, 2017, www.chronicle.com/article/Digital-Is-Not-the/241634.

Chapter Ten

Digital Repositories
A Systems Perspective

*Joshua A. Westgard, Kate Dohe,
David Durden, and Joseph Koivisto*

WHAT ARE DIGITAL REPOSITORIES?

In the context of libraries, digital repositories are software systems for gathering, describing, preserving, and providing access to digital assets. While all digital repository systems share certain core features, they have different emphases depending on their intended purposes and users. Broadly speaking, they can be divided into the following three main types:

1. institutional repositories (IR) and subject-area repositories, which focus on gathering and providing access to preprints and e-prints of the research output, respectively, of an institution's faculty and staff or of a specific field of research or subject area;
2. digital collections repositories that house digital versions of materials held by an institution or consortium—frequently digitized surrogates of

materials in archives or special collections but increasingly also born-digital archival collections; and

3. research data repositories that specialize in the curation of domain- or format-specific data generated in the course of research projects.[1]

REPOSITORY SYSTEMS

Fedora

Flexible and Extensible Digital Object Repository Architecture (Fedora) originated in the late 1990s in a collaborative project between researchers at Cornell University and the Corporation for National Research Initiatives to create an open, interoperable, and extensible system for digital asset management.[2] In the early versions of Fedora, digital objects were composed of two essential elements: data streams, or sequences of either local or remotely referenced bytes, and disseminators, which can be understood as different access methods or transformations that could be applied to an object in response to a request.

In 2003, through development efforts at Cornell and the University of Virginia, these ideas culminated in the 1.0 release of the Fedora Repository software. The Fedora project continued through the 2000s, passing through versions 2 and 3. Starting with version 2, the system used an XML wrapper schema known as Fedora Object XML (FOXML) to store both descriptive metadata and content modeling information.[3] The metadata inside the FOXML wrapper could conform to various other schemas—for example, the Library of Congress' Metadata Object Description Schema (MODS) or a similar hierarchically structured metadata schema. Eventually, stewardship of the Fedora project was assumed by the not-for-profit corporation DuraSpace, which had been formed by the merger of the DSpace and Fedora Commons organizations in 2009.[4] DuraSpace continues to oversee the project today, receiving support in the form of membership pledges and in turn providing staff support, governance, and digital infrastructure for ongoing maintenance and development of the software. In 2014, the community implementation of Fedora was rewritten with the goal of reducing the size and complexity of the code base by making use of other open source software to provide some of its core functionality. Version 4 was released in 2014 and focused on the adoption of semantic web standards and recommendations such as the Linked Data Platform (LDP) and Resource Description Framework (RDF).[5] This was followed by an effort to define a formal HTTP-based application programming interface (API) to codify and clarify the project's use of other standards and fill in some points of ambiguity.[6]

Fedora provides a mechanism for asset preservation, description, and access but does not provide a user interface. Other applications and tools must be layered on top of the repository to facilitate access and administration. There are two primary open source projects that can be used to construct user interfaces on top of a Fedora repository: Samvera (formerly Hydra) and Islandora. Samvera is a Rails-based framework, and Islandora uses the PHP-based Drupal content management system.[7] Since the release of Fedora 4, both the Samvera and Islandora communities have launched their own development efforts to adapt to the new system.

DSpace

In contrast to Fedora, DSpace provides a turnkey solution focused on the IR use case. As such, it has strong support for creating hierarchies of collections and communities and for delegating administrative responsibilities. It also has strong support for self-registration of users and self-deposit, plus configurable workflows for deposited materials. While the IR is one focus of DSpace development, it is not the only use case that can be supported by the platform, particularly with customizations. DSpace is widely used around the world and is also supported by a robust community of commercial service providers who offer hosting, support, and custom development for DSpace adopters.

The DSpace application has a number of attractive features for IR managers who must support both open access and preservation of the research output of an organization. In addition to supporting user submissions and basic workflows for submission approval and item description, DSpace supports embargoes on submitted materials, such as electronic theses and dissertations, and provides analytics data regarding the use and impact of a given item. Application administrators have access to batch-ingest and metadata-export tools for large-scale collection changes. The application supports multiple authentication methods, including Shibboleth, Lightweight Directory Access Protocol (LDAP), and IP authentication. Administrators also have robust user-management tools to control individual and group permissions based on roles and requirements in different communities—for example, a user may be a collection manager of one collection and a submitter to another.

DSpace's user interface has evolved significantly over more than a decade of active development and stewardship. Historically, DSpace adopters have often needed to implement significant interface customizations to match institutional branding and accommodate the needs of individual administrative units. Initial versions of DSpace relied on an interface built with JavaServer Pages (JSP), known as the JSPUI, which required nontrivial development expertise to configure, customize, and maintain. In response to demand for simplified and granular control over public user interfaces, the Manakin framework emerged in 2007.[8] DSpace's Manakin implementation relied on modular XML configuration changes (often referred to as the XMLUI) that were easier to maintain and deploy for specific communities and collections.[9] In practice, this enabled IR managers to offer more customized branding for parts of a repository (e.g., a research institute or a high-profile digital collection).

Over time, the "two-interface problem" meant that DSpace adopters needed to choose their interface carefully, with little ability to move back and forth between the XMLUI and the JSPUI.[10] This decision complicated over time as features were introduced for one interface only, or implemented differently in each interface. In 2014, DuraSpace began working closely with the community to envision, prototype, and eventually select a single new user interface. This interface will be based on AngularJS and is in development at the time of this writing, with release anticipated in 2018. The Angular interface promises to bring increased performance, improved accessibility, search engine optimization (SEO), and the opportunity for greater interface extensibility. Another improvement planned for DSpace 7 is a Representational State Transfer (REST) API that adheres to current best practices. The back end will continue to be Java based.[11]

EPrints

EPrints is a Perl-based repository system managed by the School of Electronics and Computer Science at the University of Southampton. EPrints was created in 2000 and focuses on providing solutions for open-access institutional and data-repository services. Like DSpace, the default configuration of EPrints is focused on the IR use case. It provides a turnkey solution for this use case and does not require additional development work to get started. EPrints differs from other repository systems in key ways, such as its close integration with the Open Archives Initiative and its built-in support for hierarchal subject classification.[12] In contrast to Fedora and DSpace, EPrints has not seen significant development in recent years. At the time of this writing, the current stable release of EPrints is version 3.3, which was first released in 2011.

Hosted Solutions

In addition to the above-mentioned open source repository solutions, several exclusively hosted solutions are available. One widely used solution is ContentDM, a hosted repository solution provided by the Online Computer Library Center (OCLC) that focuses on the digital special collections use case.[13] Another hosted option is the Digital Commons product from the Berkeley Electronic Press (bepress), which focuses on providing a single platform supporting all the electronic output of a college or university, including faculty scholarship, digital collections, and journal publishing. In 2017, bepress was acquired by the academic publisher Elsevier.[14]

EARLY ADOPTERS

At the time of this writing, digital repositories are a well-established and mature technology widely used in academic and research libraries.[15] If anything, the importance and prevalence of digital repositories seem likely to deepen and spread as new domains, such as research data and born-digital archives, become more important and new types of institutions—for example, community colleges and public libraries—seek to provide the services that digital repositories make possible.

Many lessons have been learned from the first wave of digital-repository adoption. For example, even so-called turnkey software requires some amount of dedicated, appropriately skilled staff support to run well. The cycle of updates and patches and cosmetic and functional changes to keep up with stakeholder requirements mean that significant institutional resources need to be brought to bear on supporting the repository. Additionally, because most of these systems are open source, additional resources are required by the wider community to maintain the core software, and generally these resources are acquired by a combination of monetary and in-kind (in the form of developer hours) support from the adopting institutions as well as grant support for major new initiatives.[16] Another important lesson is that in the world of open source software, less can be more. Over the course of the first decade of these major open source repositories, it has become clear that supporting a software project with largely donated labor means that maintenance of a large code base can easily become problematic, and as a result, both the DSpace and Fedora projects have recently undertaken efforts to streamline and simplify their code bases.

Finally, the initial promise of IRs as easy-to-use storehouses for an institution's scholarly output has been difficult to achieve. A lack of participation by faculty and researchers has meant that IR managers often struggled to find individuals or departments willing to undertake the considerable task of identifying eligible versions of published scholarship and preparing them for submission.[17] That said, few institutions are likely to abandon their IRs in the near future. Many emerging scholarly services and initiatives rely on the existing IR infrastructure, including electronic theses and dissertations programs, library publishing services, and open educational resource (OER) initiatives. Ultimately, these programs support the mission of academic libraries to advance access to the intellectual and cultural products of the institution, and they have the potential to have a significant positive impact on both researchers and students.

CURRENT TRENDS AND FUTURE DIRECTIONS

Linked Open Data

Libraries, archives, and museums have not been immune to recent waves of interest and enthusiasm for linked data. With the release of version 4, Fedora shifted from an XML-native metadata serialization to a system based by default on RDF. RDF has many advantages for a web-based repository infrastructure. Its use of globally unique identifiers, when paired with the adoption of well-established schemata and ontologies, can lead to a high level of interoperability—even among datasets from disparate sources.[18] There are also trade-offs: Because it is graph based, RDF does not lend itself to hierarchy or ordering of multivalued elements. And while certain operations with RDF are efficient, a large dataset converted to RDF from a relational layout can easily balloon to thousands or even millions of triples (see chapter 1). In addition, the identification of the correct vocabularies and predicates to use can be time consuming and difficult, which adds to the up-front cost of adopting RDF.

Trends in Metadata and Discovery

Usage Statistics

A primary concern of many IR managers is the ability to demonstrate usage and impact through meaningful statistics that illustrate web traffic, end-user behavior, and content-contributor practices. Not only do analytical measures provide general insight into the use of published content; they also support evidence-based justifications for expenditures, resource allocation, and ongoing support of IR implementations by providing an assessable measure of use and impact. This in turn introduces an important dimension to cost-benefit analysis and discussion of IR approaches to open-access publishing platforms and services.[19]

When considering electronic publications, the breadth and variety of content publishers, metadata formats, and repository platforms can confound parallel data collection. This mélange of data, systems, and methods makes it difficult to generate statistics for one IR that can be accurately compared to the statistics for another. Project COUNTER, a notable protocol developed with the intent to standardize e-resource usage between libraries and publishers, underscores this complexity by establishing a code of practice to be adhered to by distributed parties.[20] Thus far, bepress's Digital Commons product appears to be the only IR platform to have fully adopted COUNTER-compliant methodologies.[21]

For many institutions, the ubiquitous Google Analytics (GA) tool (https://analytics.google.com) has become the primary analytics platform for a variety of IR applications. In addition to providing a free analytics service that tracks page interactions—views, clicks, and traffic flow-through—GA provides a host of pre-packaged report dashboards that make review and assessment accessible to non-technical users.[22] GA is not without shortcomings, however. When coupled with GA, DSpace does not provide reliable usage metrics for all incoming web traffic because direct requests for non-HTML resources (e.g., PDFs, Word or Excel files, etc.) via third-party links—Google Scholar, social media sites, article citations—bypass the obligatory GA code snippet, rendering this traffic invisible.[23] Such a gap hobbles efforts to accurately account for resource use and impact, illustrating the importance of critical assessment of analytics platforms—especially those that are commonly used and widely available. The Repository Analytics and Metrics Portal (RAMP) is currently developing corrective solutions for this issue.[24] This initiative is still in its pilot phase but holds promise for more holistic analytics collection for DSpace users.

In addition to potential gaps in data collection, the ethical implications of using an analytics platform that is part of a larger corporate ecosystem that extracts commercial value from individuals' information behaviors have also become a cause for concern.[25] An alternative solution is the open source analytics platform Matomo, formerly known as Piwik.[26] This tool provides localized control of analytics collection and an increased level of privacy control over third-party platforms. While local, open source implementations of analytics tools such as Matomo do not erase all privacy concerns—user activity is still logged and may be subject to hacking or data leaks—there is less concern over commercial reuse of user data.

Search Engine Optimization

It is increasingly the norm that information seeking begins with web-scale search engines such as Google. This means that the visibility of IRs in search engines is a key aspect of their discoverability and use. Proactive management of SEO and social media optimization (SMO) methodologies helps both increase the use of IR resources and improve search engine indexing and ranking. Practices such as promoting backlinks on external and internal web pages, publishing links to otherwise invisible pages, and increasing web content can lead to an increased number of indexed pages and improved traffic from search engine referral.[27] Similarly, a well-crafted and implemented social media policy that facilitates easy sharing, encourages engagement, and promotes reuse of IR resources can provide dramatic increases in both user traffic and indexing on search engines.[28]

While there are actions that IR administrators can take to enhance their SEO, many common repository practices can hinder automated search engine indexing and ranking. For example, it has been noted that Dublin Core, the de facto metadata standard for several platforms, is insufficient to adequately describe scholarly publications to the satisfaction of Google's indexing algorithms, which helps explain the low rates of IR indexing on Google and Google Scholar.[29] Because they may lack some of the bibliographic metadata traditionally associated with journal articles and preprints, open-access repositories are frequently bypassed by search engine indexing algorithms, a problem that impacts multiple platforms and institutions.[30] While this creates issues for discoverability of IR resources, it also points toward larger impacts: these indexing issues may disproportionately affect institutions that rely heavily on IR platforms for publishing and dissemination of materials that are "outside the academic communications mainstream," further decreasing the web visibility of scholarly output that is underrepresented in global academic discourse.[31]

Trends in Research Data

Data Repositories

Research data curation and archiving in digital repositories has been a common practice for the past decade but dates back to the 1960s.[32] In 2011, the National Science Foundation (NSF) introduced mandatory data management plans directed at ensuring the longevity of publicly funded research.[33] Digital repositories are a common solution to such data preservation requirements. Mandatory data preservation (or more specifically, persistent access) is relatively new, but the concepts of archiving and curating research data are not. Evidence shows that the older a research publication becomes, the greater the risk that supporting data will eventually disappear.[34] As researchers across domains become more inclined to preserving and sharing their research data, libraries increasingly are being tasked with accommodating these emerging data curation and preservation needs. Library-centric data curation may leverage an existing IR or establish a dedicated data repository; examples of each approach are the Digital Repository at the University of Maryland (DRUM) and Deep Blue Data at the University of Michigan.[35]

Data repositories support the emerging idea that data are a primary academic resource that should be accessible, stewarded, and citable. Data citation initiatives such as Force11 and DataCite have made clear that data should be assigned the same level of attribution and credibility as publications.[36] The citation and attribution of research data require the infrastructure of the digital repository to support discoverability and access. Not all data are publicly accessible, and access to data may be restricted for a variety of reasons, including the presence of confidential or personally identifiable information common in the social sciences and biomedical fields. Data repositories can be designed in such a way to support discoverability and attribution of data while maintaining adequate levels of information security.

Data repositories may exist as a set of standards applied to a digital storage infrastructure or as a self-contained software suite. IR platforms like DSpace have been successfully deployed for dedicated data repositories (e.g., https://datadryad.org). Digital repository software and services have been developed specifically for data. Two examples of repository platforms of this nature are Dataverse and Comprehensive Knowledge Archive Network (CKAN).

Dataverse. Dataverse is an open source, Java-based web application developed through Harvard University's Institute for Quantitative Social Science "to share, preserve, cite, explore, and analyze research data."[37] The Dataverse software can be deployed locally and established as an independent repository, or users may choose to deposit data into Harvard University's hosted Dataverse application. A repository built on the Dataverse software may contain structured thematic collections known as dataverses (with a lowercase *d*), which in turn contain dataset records. Each record includes metadata, data, and supplementary files. Dataverse collections can be created for various organizational levels, including projects, individuals, institutions, journals, and research groups.

Each dataverse collection features access controls at the file level that are set by the submitter. This permits documentation, README, or deidentified files to be freely accessible while allowing sensitive or proprietary datasets to remain restricted or only available by request. The Dataverse application allows users to generate private URLs to facilitate access to private data or to share unpublished data. All standard features of the Dataverse software can be tested on a demo instance located at https://demo.dataverse.org. Harvard University's instance of Dataverse currently hosts more than 2,000 dataverse collections, more than 75,000 datasets, and more than 365,000 individual files.[38] An example dataverse collection file structure can be seen using the National Digital Stewardship Alliance (NDSA) dataverse collection,[39] which contains five datasets at the collection level. The first of these, "Replication Data For: Staffing for Effective Digital Preservation 2017: An NDSA Report," contains three individual data files.[40]

CKAN. CKAN is an open source, Python- and JavaScript-based data repository software package designed for institutional or organizational data publishing. CKAN is "a content management system like WordPress—but for data, instead of pages and blog posts" and provides users with advanced browsing and previewing tools, such as "maps, graphs, and tables."[41] The software is open source and highly customizable, and the default "out of the box" software includes social media integrations—including Google+, Facebook, and Twitter—and features the Disqus comments and sharing service. An additional powerful feature of CKAN is the Data API that allows users to create data stores, insert and modify existing data, and query a CKAN repository. CKAN software is used to power several government open-data initiatives, including data.gov in the United States and open.canada.ca in Canada. A demo of CKAN may be found at https://demo.ckan.org.

Hosted Data Environments

Data stewarded and stored in any repository can be thought of as "hosted" in the sense that data are accessible via the web through a server-client model. Repositories serve up data in viewable or downloadable formats with the expectation that the end user will make use of the data locally—on either a personal computer or a local network. Hosted data environments, however, provide access to data in an integrated online-only user interface through which data are accessed, queried, or analyzed remotely. Common technological solutions to supporting hosted data often come in the form of cloud services, such as the Google Cloud Platform or Amazon Web Services S3. Hosting data is especially useful for datasets that are too large to reliably download or have prohibitive technical or legal restrictions. Hosted data environments can be found across commercial, government, and academic sectors; institutions protect the economic value of their assets by limiting access and distribution of data while simultaneously encouraging use of the data. Google, for example, has several "big" datasets that are accessible through a web interface and may be analyzed dynamically.[42]

Data Publishing

Research data are covered by a variety of sharing and access frameworks aimed at protecting public investments (e.g., NSF, NIH) and encouraging scientific advancement (e.g., Human Genome Project). Several journals have implemented either mandatory or recommended data-sharing policies.[43] This has created a reciprocal relationship between digital repositories and data publishing by which a digital repository may function as both a publisher and a provider of research data. Data journals, such as Data (published by the Multidisciplinary Publishing Institute), are hybrid publication repositories focused on engaging the research community, increasing visibility and access to research data, and promoting altmetrics and bibliometrics for data.[44]

Virtual Research Ecosystems and Integrated Systems

The shift to performing research in a purely digital environment—which includes researcher profile pages, electronic lab notebooks, digital repositories, and online publication streams—has resulted in what is known as a "virtual research ecosystem."[45] Researcher profile pages on systems like LinkedIn, ResearchGate, or VIVO link to publications, archived data, and awarded grants, which enables others to discover their work and facilitates collaboration and the exchange of preprints and increases access to data. Digital repository applications, such as Dataverse, integrate with other virtual research systems, including Open Researcher and Contributor ID (ORCID) for author disambiguation, DMPTool for data management planning, Open Journal Systems for open access publishing, and the Open Science Framework (OSF) for project management.[46] As integrations become more common, digital repositories will be expected to provide metadata in exportable, machine-readable formats. Fenner et al. recommend that data repositories should provide citations, accessibility restrictions, and licensing information in auto-generated and machine-readable formats.[47] The data repository Dryad allows users to export citations for both datasets and supporting publications in exportable RIS (a common reference manager file format) and BibTex formats.[48]

CONCLUSION

As platforms for the preservation, description, and access to digital information resources, digital repositories have become, and are likely to remain, an important component of the digital infrastructure of libraries. Particularly for institutions seeking to support an institutional research agenda or the creation or collection of digital surrogates for printed and archival materials, as well as born-digital collections, digital repositories are an important tool for access, management, and preservation of such materials. For digital repositories to be successful, they need to be sustainable, reliable, and interoperable with other digital tools and standards, such as discovery systems, data transmission and storage formats, and unique identifier systems. In short, they must strive to put into practice in the digital realm the long-established values and best practices of librarianship.

NOTES

1. One example of a subject repository is arxiv.org for physics, mathematics, and computer science. On research data repositories, see Katherine McNeill, "Repository Options for Research Data," in *Making Institutional Repositories Work*, ed. Burton B Callicott, David Scherer, and Andrew Wesolek (West Lafayette, IN: Purdue University Press, 2016), 17.
2. Sandra Payette and Carl Lagoze, "Flexible and Extensible Digital Object and Repository Architecture (FEDORA)," in *Research and Advanced Technology for Digital Libraries (ECDL 1998)*, ed. Christos Nikolaou and Constantine Stephanidis, Lecture Notes in Computer Science, vol. 1513 (Berlin: Springer, 1998), 41–59. See also Sandra Payette and Carl Lagoze, "Flexible and Extensible Digital Object Repository Architecture (FEDORA)" (presentation given at the European Conference on Research and Advanced Technology for Digital Libraries, Heraklion, Crete, Greece, September 21–23, 1998), https://arxiv.org/abs/1312.1258.
3. Carl Lagoze, Sandy Payette, Edwin Shin, and Chris Wilper, "Fedora: An Architecture for Complex Objects and Their Relationships," *International Journal on Digital Libraries* 6, no. 2 (April 2006): 124–38.
4. "DuraSpace," duraspace.org, n.d., http://duraspace.org.
5. "Linked Data Platform 1.0," w3.org, n.d., www.w3.org/TR/ldp/; "RDF 1.1 Primer," w3.org, n.d., www.w3.org/TR/rdf11-primer/.
6. "Fedora API Specification," Fedora unofficial draft, October 31, 2018, https://fcrepo.github.io/fcrepo-specification/.
7. For general information, see https://samvera.org and https://islandora.ca.

8. Scott Phillips et al., "Manakin: A New Face for DSpace," *D-Lib Magazine* 13, nos. 11–12 (2007), http://webdoc.sub.gwdg.de/edoc/aw/d-lib/dlib/november07/phillips/11phillips.html.
9. "Manakin Themes," wiki.duraspace, last modified by Tim Donohue on April 5, 2010, https://wiki.duraspace.org/display/DSPACE/Manakin+Themes.
10. Tim Donohue, Art Lowel, and Andrea Bollini, "On the Road to DSpace 7: Angular UI + REST" (presentation at Open Repositories 2017, Brisbane City, Australia, June 26–30, 2017), https://goo.gl/Hrt4Ct.
11. See the presentation slides by Tim Donohue, "Introducing the New DSpace User Interface" (presentation at Open Repositories 2016, Dublin, Ireland, June 13–16, 2016), www.slideshare.net/tdonohue/introducing-the-new-dspace-user-interface.
12. "Home Page," Open Archives Initiative, n.d., www.openarchives.org.
13. "ContentDM," Online Computer Library Center, n.d., www.oclc.org/en/contentdm.html.
14. "Elsevier Acquires bepress," Elsevier, last modified August 2, 2017, www.elsevier.com/about/press-releases/corporate/elsevier-acquires-bepress,-a-leading-service-provider-used-by-academic-institutions-to-showcase-their-research.
15. The Directory of Open Access Repositories provides an overview of digital repository adoption worldwide. "The Directory of Open Access Repositories," OpenDOAR, last modified April 23, 2014, http://opendoar.org.
16. See a recent example at "Hydra-in-a-Box," Samvera Community, n.d., http://hydrainabox.samvera.org.
17. Dorothea Salo, "Innkeeper at the Roach Motel," *Library Trends* 57, no. 2 (Fall 2008), http://digital.library.wisc.edu/1793/22088.
18. A useful resource for identifying relevant vocabularies is the linked open vocabularies website, http://lov.okfn.org/dataset/lov/.
19. C. Sean Burns, Amy Lana, and John M. Budd, "Institutional Repositories: Exploration of Costs and Values," *D-Lib Magazine* 19, nos. 1–2 (2013), www.dlib.org/dlib/january13/burns/01burns.html.
20. "Project COUNTER Home Page," COUNTER, n.d., www.projectcounter.org.
21. Stacy Konkiel and Dave Scherer, "New Opportunities for Repositories in the Age of Altmetrics," *Bulletin of the Association of Information Science and Technology* 39, no. 4 (2013): 22–26, https://doi.org/10.1002/bult.2013.1720390408.
22. Google Analytics 360 is a premium service suite that offers additional features and Salesforce marketing services. Babak Pahlavan, "Google Analytics 360 + Salesforce: A Powerful Combination," *Google Analytics Solutions* (blog), November 6, 2017, https://analytics.googleblog.com/2017/11/google-analytics-360-salesforce.html.

PART III: Repositories and Access

23. Patrick O'Brien et al., "Undercounting File Downloads from Institutional Repositories," *Journal of Library Administration* 56, no. 7 (2016): 854–74, www.tandfonline.com/doi/full/10.1080/01930826.2016.1216224.

24. Patrick O'Brien et al., "RAMP—the Repository Analytics and Metrics Portal: A Prototype Web Service That Accurately Counts Item Downloads from Institutional Repositories," *Library Hi Tech* 35, no. 1 (2017): 144–58, https://doi.org/10.1108/LHT-11-2016-0122; "Repository Analytics and Metrics Portal," RAMP, n.d., http://ramp.montana.edu.

25. Jeff Karlsen, "Is It Ethical to Add Google Analytics to a Library Catalog?," *40 Versions* (blog), July 1, 2011, http://scc.losrios.edu/~karlsej/blog/?x=entry:entry110701-115535; Janis McKenzie, "Ethics of Using Google Analytics" (presentation at the British Columbia User Experience Interest Group, May 4, 2017), http://summit.sfu.ca/item/17107.

26. "Home Page," Matomo Open Analytics Platform, n.d., https://matomo.org.

27. Daniel Onaifo and Diane Rasmussen, "Increasing Libraries' Content Findability on the Web with Search Engine Optimization," *Library Hi Tech* 31, no. 1 (2013): 104–5, https://doi.org/10.1108/07378831311303958.

28. Doralyn Rossmann and Scott W. H. Young, "Social Media Optimization: Making Library Content Shareable and Engaging," *Library Hi Tech* 33, no. 4 (2015): 529, https://doi.org/10.1108/LHT-05-2015-0053.

29. Kenning Arlitsch and Patrick S. O'Brien, "Invisible Institutional Repositories: Addressing the Low Indexing Ratios of IRs in Google Scholar," *Library Hi Tech* 30, no. 1 (2012): 72, https://doi.org/10.1108/07378831211213210.

30. Ibid.

31. Enrique Orduña-Malea and Emilio Delgado López-Cózar, "The Dark Side of Open Access in Google and Google Scholar: The Case of Latin-American Repositories," *Scientometrics* 102, no. 1 (2015): 844–45, https://doi.org/10.1007/s11192-014-1369-5.

32. Peter Doorn and Heiko Tjalsma, "Introduction: Archiving Research Data," *Archival Science* 7, no. 1 (2007): 3, http://dx.doi.org/10.1007/s10502-007-9054-6.

33. "Dissemination and Sharing of Results," Office of Budget Finance and Award Management, National Science Foundation, n.d., www.nsf.gov/bfa/dias/policy/dmp.jsp.

34. Timothy H. Vines et al., "The Availability of Research Data Declines Rapidly with Article Age," *Current Biology* 24, no. 1 (2014): 94–97, http://dx.doi.org/10.1016/j.cub.2013.11.014.

35. "Digital Repository at the University of Maryland," University of Maryland Libraries, n.d., https://drum.lib.umd.edu; "Deep Blue Data," University of Michigan Libraries, n.d., https://deepblue.lib.umich.edu/data.

36. Maryann Martone, ed., *Joint Declaration of Data Citation Principles* (San Diego: FORCE11, 2014), https://doi.org/10.25490/a97f-egyk; "Our Mission," DataCite, n.d., www.datacite.org/mission.html.
37. "About," Dataverse Project, n.d., https://dataverse.org/about.
38. See the Harvard Dataverse website at https://dataverse.harvard.edu.
39. See the NDSA data archive in the Harvard Dataverse. National Digital Stewardship Alliance, "National Digital Stewardship Alliance Dataverse," Harvard Dataverse, n.d., https://dataverse.harvard.edu/dataverse/ndsa.
40. NDSA Staffing Survey Working Group, "Replication Data For: Staffing for Effective Digital Preservation 2017: An NDSA Report," Harvard Dataverse, 2017, http://dx.doi.org/10.7910/DVN/XBMAXP.
41. "About CKAN," Comprehensive Knowledge Archive Network, n.d., https://ckan.org/about/.
42. "Public Datasets," Google Cloud Platform, n.d., https://cloud.google.com/public-datasets/.
43. Timothy H. Vines et al., "Mandated Data Archiving Greatly Improves Access to Research Data," *Federation of American Societies for Experimental Biology Journal* 27, no. 4 (2013): 1307, https://doi.org/10.1096/fj.12-218164.
44. "About *Data*," MDPI AG, n.d., www.mdpi.com/journal/data/about.
45. Tyler Walters, "Assimilating Digital Repositories into the Active Research Process," in *Research Data Management: Practical Strategies for Information Professionals*, ed. Joyce M. Ray (West Lafayette, IN: Purdue University Press, 2014), 191.
46. "Integrations," Dataverse Project, n.d., https://dataverse.org/integrations.
47. Martin Fenner et al., "A Data Citation Roadmap for Scholarly Data Repositories," *BioRxiv*, October 9, 2017, https://doi.org/10.1101/097196.
48. See this landing page in the Dryad Digital Repository. Start Denon and Gilbert Benjamin, "Data From: Plant Sex Alters Allee Effects in Aggregating Plant Parasites," Dryad Digital Repository, November 22, 2017, http://datadryad.org/resource/doi:10.5061/dryad.c6f97/1.

Chapter Eleven

Digital Repositories

Jessica Wagner Webster

Digital repositories are storehouses of digital library or archival content. Currently, many institutions have some flavor of digital repository: a digital asset management system (DAMS), a long-term digital preservation storage solution, or an institutional repository (IR). These all have different purposes, though some software vendors package these systems together.

Most commonly, digital repositories can be designed to focus on either providing access to users or preserving digital content for long-term use. Though many digital repository products offer to do both of those jobs, the requirements for each job differ widely enough that it is often preferable to implement separate products for access and for preservation and ensure both products can work well together. Ideally, an institution can hold a preservation copy of a digital file in a preservation repository and generate access copies of those files to populate the access repository. Digital repositories designed to provide access, like IRs or DAMS, allow libraries to share their content widely, particularly with users unable to visit collections on-site. Repositories specializing in preservation can help libraries store content safely for the long term. Preservation repositories are usually only accessible to key staff members and are designed to work as a sort of vault or lockbox for digital files. Digital content is fragile: it is easy for these items to get destroyed or deleted or suffer bit rot or link rot (see chapters 3 and 4 for more about these topics). If libraries take steps to store archival digital content in a preservation repository, they can protect key digital holdings for use in the future and provide patrons with access copies of these holdings generated from the preservation copies in the repository.

In this chapter, I will provide a broad overview of both institutional and archival digital repositories. Coverage of these topics in scholarly literature elsewhere has been extensive, however, and this overview only attempts to address broad points about the functionality of these systems and shed light on best practices. I will then consider future directions for improving repository software and hardware to both optimize user access to content and streamline workflows on the part of library and archives staff.

INSTITUTIONAL REPOSITORIES

Institutional repositories have been adopted by many universities as a way to showcase the creative and intellectual output of faculty and students alike. Furthermore, they can provide access to this content outside of the paywalls of electronic publishers and databases, which can be prohibitively high and cause patrons difficulty in accessing content they need. Institutional repositories are frequently associated with the open-access movement and the affiliated movement in support of open educational resources (OERs). The benefits are huge: institutional repositories can aggregate content created by an institution and its scholars or staff in one place and, ideally, provide a stable home for organizations to host web content outside of the strictures of journal databases. Further, institutions that support IRs are theoretically able to provide access to content generated by their own scholars without paying for it twice—first, by funding the scholars; second, by funding the databases that serve up the scholars' work. IR can provide long-term hosting for content and establish permanent web links for articles and other scholarly output; this aids researchers in locating and citing articles and removes barriers in the form of paywalls created by fee-based database services. An IR can also increase visibility for scholars and their research by allowing Google and other search engines to index content more easily.

ARCHIVAL DIGITAL REPOSITORIES

Archival digital repositories can provide two key functions: first, they can offer end-user access to digital archival content; second, they can store digital archival content safely for the long term. Some solutions offer to perform both roles, whereas others specialize in one or the other.

Access Repositories

Access repositories are the primary method by which institutions can connect users with digital content, especially digital archival content. Digital archival content can be composed of material that was "born digital" (computer-generated content, such as e-mails, digital photographs, videos, and websites) or material that was digitized (e.g., scanned documents and images). Any material housed in an access repository must be teamed with related metadata to allow users to search and find it. Archivists should also include metadata pertaining to any access restrictions to inform users of their rights when consulting the material. Materials in digital repositories should be in an easily supported format; any larger-size file, in particular, should be in a compressed and lightweight format to allow users to easily download or stream the file (e.g., a digital photograph should be provided in JPEG format rather than TIFF, which is likely to be a much larger file size).

Digital access repositories allow archivists and librarians to make unique, rare, or fragile physical items accessible, which can help in turn with preservation because this strategy limits the handling of these items. Researchers can "leaf through" newspapers in a digital access repository, for example, that would crumble if they were physically touched.

Digital access repositories can significantly aid researchers who may want to access materials that are located far away from where they live and work. In addition, digital access repositories can help unite collections that are intellectually related but situated in different areas. These materials might be related because they are parts of the same collection that ended up being donated to different repositories or because they contain highly related subject matter. Institutions holding related collections must be committed to collaborating and providing consistent, thorough metadata.

Increasingly, digital repositories have become key resources for scholars in the digital humanities. Repositories containing text-based documents that have been made keyword searchable through optical character recognition (OCR) software can provide a rich data source for textual analysis projects of all kinds. Similarly, repositories containing map data or other data sets may provide scholars with content to analyze or build into visualizations, software applications, or websites. In this way, libraries and archives with access repositories can fill an important role for these scholars.

Librarians and archivists must account for several factors when making decisions about which holdings are suitable for sharing in an access repository. First, copyright status and ownership of materials are key; materials whose legal status is in dispute may be subject to takedown notices. An institution should have the authority to place materials in its custody online before doing so. Next, file size should be considered; larger files require more resources (e.g., memory and bandwidth) to support. In terms of intellectual content, librarians must consider either providing access to whole collections or allowing patrons to see a selection of materials along with descriptive information outlining the resources that have not been digitized. Further, accessibility for users with disabilities should also be addressed, such as ensuring that text is easily readable by screen-reader software and attaching descriptive tags and captioning to photographs, audio, and video.

Because access systems can accomplish a variety of goals for an institution, it is essential to weigh priorities and consider the features available when selecting one. The interface functionality is very important; it relates closely to the sorts of materials an institution would like to share in the repository. For example, an organization that has a large number of text-based documents would likely need a repository that supports keyword searching. A collection that is primarily visual in nature, like photographs or pamphlets, may be best served by a system with robust metadata searchability to aid users in exploring descriptive information. A collection with audiovisual material like videos may also require a system with an embedded video player. Institutions should, therefore, thoughtfully select features for their access system with an eye toward how the content will likely be used by researchers.

Preservation Repositories

One of the most important functions a digital repository can perform is to provide long-term, secure storage for digital archival items; however, not all systems advertised as preservation repositories are equally prepared to handle this task. Preservation repositories are the equivalent of a locked vault for analog items, though they can require more hands-on maintenance than a physical vault would need. There are a number of unique challenges associated with long-term digital storage, so digital repositories designed for this purpose should have several key features.

Chapter Eleven: Digital Repositories

Theoretically, content placed in a "dark archive" has been selected to be content "of record"; it may be the only version of a particular file or object that survives. Therefore, digital items chosen for preservation storage should be as "complete" as possible. For example, a digitized copy of a print item should be digitized at a high pixels-per-inch (PPI) rate (three hundred or more), and files should be saved in a format chosen for long-term sustainability, such as TIFF (which is an uncompressed file format, described further below). Either way, archivists should identify formats and procedures that yield the highest-quality, most-complete files possible for preservation.

Preservation copies of digital items should be either uncompressed or losslessly compressed (i.e., compressed by a method that does not remove pixels) to ensure the capture of all the bits in the item. Lossless compression is particularly relevant with respect to audiovisual materials. Compression works by removing pixels in regular intervals from a digital item to reduce file size, so choosing not to compress files in order to preserve the full content leads to collections containing files of very large size. Any preservation-level repository should have an appropriate storage capacity and be able to grow and expand to accommodate more content. Because preservation repositories are designed as long-term homes for files with enduring value, the storage requirements will likely balloon over time.

Two other key components are security and access. In most cases, long-term storage should be in a "dark archive" to which very few people have access. It can be conceived of as a sort of one-way valve; the repository ingests material and locks it away, and only archivists and other trusted staff members can access it. This helps ensure that the material is held safely and that a copy of the record of this content is maintained. Ideally, then, a preservation system should not also provide access to users; there should be a parallel system to provide smaller, compressed copies of the digital items. This also helps alleviate the bandwidth issues and lengthy download times associated with providing web-based access to large uncompressed files.

In order for content placed in any archive to be discoverable and have adequate context, robust, descriptive metadata should be included. One popular solution is to use an archival management system (such as Archivematica) in conjunction with suitable archival storage.[1] Archivematica can work in conjunction with packages of content and metadata generated in compliance with the BagIt specification. BagIt creates an enclosed bundle of digital content and metadata and generates a manifest and a checksum so that content and metadata can be stored and moved together, and users can be sure that the bundle is complete. Bagger, a software program that generates these bags, can also be used on its own as part of a larger preservation strategy.² These products must be used in conjunction with a safe storage location, which I will describe in more depth below.

To ensure that files do not change over time, it is important that a long-term storage solution supports file fixity. In a preservation context, file fixity refers to "the assurance that a digital file has remained unchanged, i.e., fixed," over time.³ As items are moved from one storage solution to another, files can become corrupted and lose data and therefore become unusable. A number of tools exist to perform fixity checks on files; one common solution is to generate a checksum for digital content. A checksum is like a digital fingerprint; to generate a checksum, a mathematical algorithm is applied to a file, and a unique value is generated. After an operation has been performed on a file (e.g., moving it to a different location), another checksum can be generated. If the file is identical to how it was before it was moved, the two files will have the same checksum. Archivists can run checksums on content at regular intervals to ensure it has not degraded over time or after working with it.⁴

Any system designed to support long-term storage of digital content should address file format issues as well. Ideally, preservation archives would store material in supportable formats—that is, formats the archival and information technology communities have selected to be maintained and readable into the future. These tend to be open and nonproprietary, or formats that have been widely adopted, such as PDF, TIFF, and JPEG. However, archivists also must plan for the possibility that these formats may not be supported in perpetuity. It is important to have a plan to identify and migrate formats existing in a preservation solution when necessary. Some preservation software products build in the functionality to batch-migrate formats.

Increasingly, archivists are interested in preserving content that is dynamic or interactive in nature, requiring special file formats or software that can open those files. For example, archivists may want to preserve data sets, web pages, software programs, or web applications. Preserving these digital items can be particularly challenging and demand extra support from the selected storage solution.

Another key feature of preservation systems is protection against weather events, technology failure, and other human-made and natural disasters. All preservation systems should include several redundant copies and generate frequent backups. The best systems should have redundant backups stored in geographically disparate locations. For example, it is unlikely that Chicago, San Diego, and Orlando will all face the same natural disaster at the same time, so storing redundant files in servers in each of these locations would mitigate the risk of total data loss.

It is essential that any digital preservation system be accessible only by those individuals who are authorized to work with it, that system owners have a clear understanding of how long it will take to get access to their material, and that the material's ownership status is explicit. Further, system owners should have a policy in place with their vendors to recover their content if they ever decide to leave the system and move their content somewhere else.

FUTURE DIRECTIONS

As technology develops and changes, and as archives increasingly require the ability to store digital content for the very long term, digital repository software must shift accordingly. The following are several areas in which digital repository systems could improve.

For all digital repositories, streamlined procedures to upload and ingest materials would be of huge benefit. Currently, it can be quite difficult to balance the desire for distributed collecting of materials with the need for security, standardized description, and appropriate metadata. For example, if an archivist would like to collect digital videos from a university department for her repository, she must determine a way to acquire those videos along with any corresponding metadata generated by the creators. One solution would be a software product that allows the university department to upload the videos and metadata to a repository, which the archivist could then access in order to standardize the descriptions, move any preservation copies to a preservation repository, and present access copies in a public-facing portion of the repository. Alternatively, the archivist could do the collecting by visiting the department and loading the material and metadata onto an external drive, accessing the content in a shared network storage location, or doing the upload herself. Clearly, then, a workflow that supports a more streamlined upload procedure, as well as improved technological infrastructure by the host institution (e.g., sufficient bandwidth), would encourage participation by content creators and improve efficiency.

Another area for improvement is smoother integration with other library discovery software. Ideally, all content in a digital repository should be findable through multiple access points. Access to digital objects would be improved if they could be located via a single search across the library catalog, the institutional repository access system, and any other access products. Similarly, archival resources are often described using a descriptive tool called a finding aid and may also be cataloged using archives-oriented description software like ArchivesSpace. Metadata housed in these tools can easily be siloed. However, archivists can improve access to the content if descriptive links are created among archival objects in a digital repository, metadata in a finding aid or archival description database, and records in a library catalog. It is possible to create these links now, but it requires quite a bit of extra work on the part of the archivist, cataloger, or metadata librarian. Digital repositories of the future could very much improve their service if they made it easier to link content across various software products, such as by enabling all products to work with the Open Archives Initiative Protocol for Metadata Harvesting (OAI-PMH), a method of harvesting and transferring metadata from one descriptive product to another.[5]

Future Directions: Institutional Repositories

With respect to institutional repositories, one huge area for improvement is the process for securing permissions to upload publications into a digital repository. Currently, many journal publishers allow an author to retain the right to share his article in an online institutional repository or personal website, but the publishers vary as to whether he may post the preprint, a postprint, or a publisher's PDF. The process for determining the version of an article that a publisher authorizes an author to post can be quite onerous: software tools can help authors check, and authors can contact their journals for clarification, but this procedure often places a lot of the burden on the authors or librarians to perform the necessary legwork.

Even once this process is complete, the workflow can be complex. For example, a librarian has identified which versions of the English professor's articles are authorized to be added to the campus IR. The librarian and professor must track down the correct versions for upload. Some journals will allow the professor to add the final, published version of an article to the campus IR; the professor and librarian can then easily locate and upload the publisher's PDF of the article. But if a journal allows only unpublished drafts to be added to an IR, the librarian must ask the professor to find those earlier versions of her article, which may or may not still exist. Then finally, the librarian might upload the article on behalf of the professor; doing so might require obtaining official permission from the professor, which often necessitates additional steps. The professor could certainly do all of these steps on her own, but even so, she might require help or guidance along the way from the librarian or may find that the labor involved becomes too burdensome and time consuming. IR software, then, could streamline many of these processes. For example, future institutional repositories may want to include tools to address this issue, perhaps by allowing content submitters to natively look up the journal policy via a link to major publishers' policies or websites before uploading their articles.

Several IR products have taken a new direction toward social commenting and collaboration. One initial impetus for digital repositories in the sciences was to share early drafts of research so that authors could solicit comments; many scholars in the sciences and other disciplines continue to use these so-called preprint repositories for this purpose. Increasingly, in our world of digital social networks, it seems obvious that institutional repository pages should include ways for authors to have colleagues read their publications, comment, and add links to related material. Institutional repositories can breed interest by supporting collaboration via enabling commenting tools.[6]

Future Directions: Archival Repositories

In considering the future of archival repositories, archivists and support staff must look for ways to increase the volume of content their repositories can store. As described previously, preservation repositories can require a huge amount of storage for uncompressed video and other sizeable files. Libraries should select vendors that have highly customizable storage packages, thereby encouraging vendors to offer suites with a wide range of storage capacities and the flexibility to increase storage as needed. Further, as storage costs come down generally, archivists should also see their repository prices decrease. In addition, in order to reflect best practices and mitigate disaster risks, any cloud-based repositories should offer the option to have geographically dispersed storage.

Archival digital repositories should also become easier to configure. Software products currently on the market can be challenging to set up. Easier implementation would promote broader adoption by a wider variety of institution types. Archivists and librarians have a wide range of technical abilities, and not every institution has information technology staff available to troubleshoot a digital repository. Vendors should provide options for hosted solutions or solutions an institution can host themselves; they should also provide levels of customization that correspond to the technical skills, needs, and other requirements of library staff and institutions.

Furthermore, archivists should look for ways to improve metadata interoperability. Institutions may use a variety of products and tools to manage their digital collections: one for cataloging and description, one for providing access, one for short-term storage, and one for long-term storage, to name just a few. Different file formats in a collection may call for different systems: an institution may choose System A to provide access to its text files because they need robust keyword search functionality, but it may choose System B to provide access to its video files because they require playback and captioning functionality that System A does not have. Importantly, each of these systems may use a different type of metadata and different file formats for export or import, and this variety and potential incompatibility can cause a lot of problems for the archivist or librarian trying to manage all moving parts. For example, an archive may use a cataloging product that is built on hierarchical Encoded Archival Description (EAD) and supports import and export of metadata in XML format. An access platform for digital photographs may support ingestion of metadata in comma-separated values (CSV) form and may prefer descriptions to be formatted using Dublin Core. EAD and Dublin Core do have fields that overlap, and XML can be converted to CSV, but technical skills and additional steps are required to do so. Therefore, archival digital repository workflows would be streamlined dramatically by supporting transferability of metadata.[7]

Another area of development for digital repositories involves establishing compliance with the Trusted Digital Repository (TDR) standard and other best-practice models. TDR is based on Trustworthy Repositories Audit & Certification: Criteria and Checklist (TRAC), a report published by the National Archives and Records Administration (NARA) and the Research Libraries Group (RLG) in 2003. TDR is an International Standardization Organization ISO standard (16363) that establishes a checklist for digital repositories to "provide reliable, long-term access to managed digital resources to its Designated Community, now and into the future."[8] The TDR checklist works in conjunction with the Open Archival Information System (OAIS) model, which is a conceptual framework for understanding the collection, description, and long-term storage of digital material.[9] Essentially, TDR helps an institution determine whether its digital repository setup, management infrastructure, and information security protocols adequately comply with the OAIS model and are able to do so into the future. Importantly, TDR provides universal guidelines that will allow an impartial group to audit any institution's repository.

Currently, many digital repository software vendors advertise their products' OAIS compliance. However, it would be extremely beneficial for software vendors to address each step in the TDR checklist. This would allow institutions to ensure they are following best practices. For example, TDR requires institutions to have clear procedures about checking digital material for completeness upon ingest and transfer.[10] If a digital repository software product not only complied with these requirements but indicated it clearly to the repository owner, it would allow the owner to have a much clearer sense of what he needed to do to follow best practices.

At present, TDR certification is a rigorous process; few institutions have completed certification, in part because the requirements are resource- and labor-intensive to complete. The TDR checklist represents an ideal, a goal, more than a reality. However, if repository products could help an institution strive toward certification, it would certainly add value and improve outcomes for the institution.

Finally, digital repositories could strive to better support partnerships of various kinds. When institutions are able to share and preserve their digital content, they enable scholars, granting agencies, and partner institutions to interact with the content. Digital access repositories could support scholars doing textual analysis (or other digital humanities work) by allowing them to download content in usable file formats or supporting textual analysis tools.[11] Additionally, software vendors could provide support for accessing collections housed in multiple institutions. For example, two institutions may hold digital materials relating to the same collecting area or theme and may decide that they would like to hold their materials in a shared digital space so that researchers can search across both collections using one interface. Vendors that could support such resource sharing would certainly add value to their product.

CONCLUSION

Many institutions employ some kind of digital repository: they provide access to digital content through a DAMS, they have an institutional repository system to provide a home for scholarly output, or they store digital holdings for long-term preservation in a "dark archive." While many vendors suggest that their products can do more than one of these jobs, it is rare to find software that can multitask according to archival best practices. And even though digital repositories are used relatively frequently, they can be expensive, hard to implement, and difficult to maintain. The suggestions I outlined previously would go a long way toward enhancing the usability of digital repository products, which would in turn encourage archives and libraries to make room in their software setup for these tools.

If a library were able to set up a series of digital repositories following the guidelines I described in this chapter, patrons would be able to benefit fully from the wide array of digital collections maintained by libraries. End users could search the library web discovery tool for content on a particular topic, and their searches would locate records on that topic from archival collections and institutional repository materials as well as from traditional library holdings. Due to robust metadata, users could select limiting criteria for single or specified groups of collections. If a patron wanted to use digital archival content, her search would look through the institution's archival access repository. Any content that was suitable to be accessed via the open web would be shown in an appropriate native player, such as a video viewer or keyword-searchable PDF display. All players would be designed to accommodate screen readers and other assistive technologies for disabled patrons. End users would be able to access articles and other content from the institutional repository in a similar way. All users would have streamlined, seamless access to content.

For the archivist or librarian and other institutional colleagues, setup and maintenance of these repositories would be improved if the products complied with international standards and best practices, including OAI-PMH and TDR requirements. This would make it much easier for metadata to be transported from one software product to another. Archivists would have two repositories for archival content, the access repository and the preservation repository, and there would be a streamlined way to move content off of network storage and into the respective repositories. Further, archivists would have a simple way to manage metadata and versioning across these repository locations. A setup like this would enable archivists to provide users with a public-facing access copy of digital content while storing a preservation copy in a dark archive built on geographically disparate servers. Storage would grow to accommodate increasing file volumes, and pricing would reflect the overall decrease of storage costs. Archivists would be able to ingest content simply from constituent groups, such as academic departments. Similarly, the institutional repository software would allow submitters to easily check the appropriate version of a published article within the IR user interface, avoiding the legwork involved by the submitter or librarian. The IR product would provide for social commenting and collaboration.

The ideal digital repository system for libraries and archives should favor interoperability, metadata portability, and ease of use for both staff and patrons, with separate systems for access and preservation of archival materials. Institutions that adopt these best practices will be able to highlight their unique and specialty materials, including archival collections and faculty scholarship. In this way, libraries can provide high-quality user services for their distinctive holdings and indicate that they are safe custodians of these holdings, thereby showcasing their value to their institutions and securing ongoing support.

NOTES

1. See www.archivematica.org/en/.
2. J. Kunze et al., "The BagIt File Packaging Format (V0.97)," 2016, https://tools.ietf.org/html/draft-kunze-bagit-14; Library of Congress GitHub page, Bagger, https://github.com/LibraryOfCongress/bagger.
3. Jefferson Bailey, "Protect Your Data: File Fixity and Data Integrity," *The Signal* (blog), Library of Congress, April 7, 2014, https://blogs.loc.gov/thesignal/2014/04/protect-your-data-file-fixity-and-data-integrity/.
4. Ibid.
5. Carl Lagoze, Herbert Van de Sompel, Michael Nelson, and Simeon Warner, eds., "The Open Archives Initiative Protocol for Metadata Harvesting," Open Archives, 2015, www.openarchives.org/OAI/openarchivesprotocol.html.
6. Mary Wu, "The Future of Institutional Repositories at Small Academic Institutions: Analysis and Insights," *D-Lib Magazine* 21, nos. 9–10 (September–October 2015), www.dlib.org/dlib/september15/wu/09wu.html.
7. Kari R. Smith's presentation, "Stop Looking for the Quarter under the Light" (Radcliffe Workshop on Technology and Archival Processing, Harvard University, April 4–5, 2016), https://libraries.mit.edu/digital-archives/files/2016/07/StopLooking4Quarter_RadcliffeWkShp_2016v3_withNotes.pdf, has some good information about the complexity of the landscape of tools used in digital collections, including a diagram of the Massachusetts Institute of Technology Archives and Special Collections tool set on page 20.
8. "Audit and Certification of Trustworthy Digital Repositories," Consultative Committee for Space Data Systems, 2011, https://public.ccsds.org/pubs/652x0m1.pdf.
9. Brian Lavoie, "Meeting the Challenges of Digital Preservation: The OAIS Reference Model," OCLC Research, 2000, www.oclc.org/research/publications/library/2000/lavoie-oais.html.
10. "Audit and Certification," 4-4, 4-5.
11. HathiTrust is already providing innovative services in this area. HathiTrust Research Center Analytics, https://analytics.hathitrust.org.

Chapter Twelve

Maximizing Assets and Access through Digital Publishing
Opportunities and Implications for Special Collections

Ellen Engseth and Marguerite Ragnow

The future is now. Technology is driving us forward into new ways of thinking about how we interact with our constituents and how we surface content. New opportunities to maximize our institutional assets, such as collections of distinction, present themselves every day. How we respond to these opportunities is one measure of our flexibility and adaptability—in effect, our prospects for successfully traversing an ever-changing technological landscape.

Long recognized as important to libraries of all types, high-impact holdings are often central to our scholarly and cultural contributions, and libraries have a strong tradition of both sharing and making institutional use of these collections. Archivists and librarians are building on this strong tradition by capitalizing on new technologies and innovative forms of teaching and learning tools that facilitate scholarly communication and quick global reach. One option for realizing this reach is to publish and license library materials through third-party digital publishers. Already viable for many libraries, this will become an increasingly possible and technologically transformative option that will, among other things, extend the digital life of special collections. Digital outreach and user accessibility through digital products is the future for special collections.

The prominent "inside-out" model for today's library features, in part, archives and special collections. In this model, the library distributes institutional assets and research expertise to both local and global audiences, juxtaposed with a traditional "outside-in" model wherein a collection is bought and gathered in primarily for a local user community. For example, Dempsey et al. assert that for academic libraries, the "inside-out orientation will become more important as universities focus attention on distinctive institutional assets and libraries direct increased curatorial attention toward special collections, new scholarly products, research preprints, and pedagogical resources."[1] Concurrently, archives and special collections are receiving more attention from those outside of special collections for their distinctive roles in teaching, learning, and research—something long known to those who daily work with these materials. This wider interest drives demand for more curated digital materials, which supports and often directs the process of scholarship. In the inside-out model, curatorial expertise is required and "turned 'outward' to help contextualize and characterize the value of institutional holdings."[2] However, the necessary staff, time, and technical resources to effectively curate and host the digital scholarly conversation, though certainly developing on the academic campus and in the nonprofit environment, are limited.

The greater attention generally enjoyed by special collections in the recent era will continue, in part due to the increase in the number of libraries adopting the inside-out model. The current digital age presents striking opportunities for these special collections: for digital preservation and access; in outreach, branding, and revenue streams; and for more public roles in knowledge production and the evolving research ecosystem. This environment "requires new ways of thinking"—both now and in the future.[3]

Publishing digital content through a third party to reach goals of outreach and asset building demonstrates a new way of thinking. Third-party vendors and ventures now present libraries with options for digitizing, licensing, and sharing high-value or high-impact holdings. They also provide opportunities for realizing revenue streams, reaching new or wider audiences, and relieving libraries of some of the technically prohibitive or difficult tasks associated with digital projects. The resulting digitized special collection is a next-generation institutional asset, one that is useful for preservation, sharing, and reuse; building reputation; and providing rationale for digital infrastructure. This chapter shares our experience and analysis of partnering with a nonlibrary vendor for digitizing and publishing as one example for building institutional assets and enhancing access.

Further, although libraries are seen generally to operate with different values than those of profit-driven organizations, and there may be an aversion to intentional asset building inherent in library culture, strategic use of our collections falls squarely within the framework of library entrepreneurship. The continuing era of funding shortages demands additional and alternative sources of funding. While challenging, this environment clearly presents opportunities for innovation. Third-party partners or commercial enterprises have long proved useful to other cultural heritage institutions and will increase in value and usefulness to libraries interested in pursuing innovation in the future.[4]

The technical arena adds crucial layers to today's already complex and multifaceted library environment. At the University of Minnesota (UMN) Libraries, the Archives and Special Collections Department utilizes a complicated matrix of digital delivery modes, platforms, and products all to extend access and reach. Some components were developed or provided by internal skills, staff, and resources. Others are collaborative at some group level or interact with non- and for-profit third parties. Table 12.1 reveals the array of our practices at the time of the digital publishing project described in this chapter.

TABLE 12.1
A partial high-level view of digital platforms and discovery/delivery tools for archives and special collections. The third-party commercial publishing platform discussed in this chapter is italicized.

Audience	Scale		
	Institutional	*Group/noncommercial*	*Commercial third-party*
Local	Shared network drives		Sharing software (e.g., Google Drive) FTP servers
Group	Shared network drives		Sharing software
Web/global	Curated exhibits (e.g., Omeka, bespoke platforms) Digital collections and research data repositories Web-based collection management and access systems (e.g., ArchivesSpace, legacy tools)	Catalog records (OCLC) Specialized portals (e.g., Minnesota Digital Library, DPLA)	*Platform provided by third-party vendor*

*The concept for this table was adapted from Lorcan Dempsey, Constance Malpas, and Brian Lavoie, "Collection Directions: The Evolution of Library Collections and Collecting," *Portal: Libraries and the Academy* 14, no. 3 (2014): 416.

We reached our decision to digitize, license, and publish our materials through a third-party digital publisher in light of the environment sketched above and only after much consideration.

The authors of this chapter are the curators who head two repositories within the Archives and Special Collections Department: the Immigration History Research Center Archives (IHRCA) and the James Ford Bell Library (Bell Library). The IHRCA is an archive and library for the study of immigration, ethnicity, and race; the Bell Library documents the history and impact of international trade and cultural exchange prior to circa 1800 CE. Both strive to preserve collections and make them accessible and discoverable locally and globally, with an emphasis on research and learning. As our discussion of the inside-out library affirms, it is increasingly important to find innovative and cost-effective ways to share our materials digitally. The UMN Libraries plays an integral role in campus life and is a significant contributor of resources and programs to the academic community and the general public. We and our colleagues provide a highly collaborative environment that is distinguished by new models for teaching and learning, research support, and scholarly communication. As the UMN Libraries is known for advanced web services, significant collaborative digital library development, and a record of innovative partnerships, it had the infrastructure to consider the third-party vendor projects we were interested in pursuing: the IHRCA's "Migration to New Worlds" and the Bell Library's "Age of Exploration."

TECHNOLOGY

Digital projects come in all shapes and sizes, and each one may require different technological parameters. They all have these requirements in common, however: (1) technology necessary to convert analog material to digital format, along with a computer and software to ensure quality control; (2) a platform and software through which to make the digitized material available to the target audience; and (3) storage for the digital objects both in the short term and for the long term.

All digital conversion projects, regardless of the technology used, have multiple phases. Once the items for conversion have been selected and prepared for digitization, most projects will include the following steps:[5]

- scanning text or image files or the conversion of video or audio files
- creating digital master files
- digitally processing the captured data and producing derivative files

- collecting and recording metadata for each digital object or set of objects
- ingesting the digitized objects and their associated metadata into a digital management system
- preserving and storing the digital objects created
- creating a user interface for making the digital objects accessible

As this list suggests, multiple technologies, many working in concert, are required to successfully mount a curated digital primary source database with an effective public interface. This is true whether the project is small, featuring a single collection, or large, bringing together multiple collections. For the projects discussed in this chapter, many of these steps were the responsibility of our publishing partner, Adam Matthew Digital (AMD), which is an imprint of SAGE Publishing and an award-winning commercial publisher of digital primary source collections for the humanities and social sciences. Sourced from leading libraries and archives around the world, their unique research and teaching collections cover a wide range of subject areas, from medieval family life to twentieth-century history, literature, and culture. The investment AMD has made in developing attractive and very user-friendly public interfaces for their products was one reason we were drawn to them as partners.

While the IHRCA project did include the conversion, translation, and transcription of some audio sources, we'll focus here on the technology used for the conversion of paper-based analog objects that were common to both projects: books and bound and unbound documents and maps. Key to the success of many digitization projects is the use of a rapid-capture process for quickly digitizing materials. Raw rapid capture was first created specifically for the National Archives and Records Administration. Rapid capture refers to the speed of workflow and was initially used primarily for flat single-sheet documents. New technology, however, enables even rare book digitization to be accomplished more rapidly. Some projects have resulted in 1,000 to 1,500 scans per day for unbound documents, whereas others have scanned from 150 to 300 pages per day of bound material. Bound material presents more of a challenge than unbound material. The tightness of the binding may require images to be photographed from particular angles, for example, or page size within a single binding may vary. Each of these conditions may require frequent camera adjustments.[6]

We reached an agreement with AMD that the digital conversion would be outsourced but that it had to take place at the UMN. We weren't comfortable sending our materials off-site; on-site conversion also would enable us to more closely monitor progress and deal with special handling issues as they arose. AMD

PART III: Repositories and Access

contracted with LUNA Imaging Inc. to undertake the conversion. In consultation with LUNA, AMD, and the UMN Libraries' digital experts, we agreed that it made sense to use the same rapid-capture system for both projects. Despite the format differences, both collections were best suited to planetary, overhead image capture rather than a sheet-fed system. LUNA hired an experienced local digital photographer to do the image capture using a proprietary rapid-capture system with components integrated and configured by LUNA. The basic components were a vertical copy stand, a full-frame camera as the capture device, and UV-filtered light fixtures containing high-intensity discharge lamps. The camera height on this system is adjustable, and the cameras can be switched out based on the requirements of the individual objects. Bound items were captured by also employing a LUNA-designed ninety-degree book cradle. LUNA shipped all of its equipment to the UMN Libraries for the project.

There are other vendors as well as similar equipment, less the proprietary elements developed by LUNA, that are available for both internal and outsourced projects. For example, other types of planetary scanning systems, such as the i2S Copibook HD with freestanding fluorescent lights, have been used at the UMN for a variety of projects; we also have used a Fujitsu fi-6230 Color Duplex Flatbed scanner for materials that can be placed in a high-speed sheet feeder.[7]

Both of our AMD projects included a variety of types of analog formats: single-sheet documents; documents held together by metal clasps, staples, and paper clips; bound documents; rare books; vellum manuscript documents; oversized flat maps; and books and scrapbooks with inset images or maps that also were often folded, in addition to the audio files noted above. The LUNA technician worked closely with the project manager on the IHRCA project to prepare the documents for scanning, including the removal of clasps, staples, and other temporary bindings. He also worked with the Bell Library curator to ensure the proper handling of rare materials, foldouts, and vellum manuscripts that had to be photographed through clear Mylar sleeves.

LUNA staff worked closely with AMD staff to run quality checks and create master and derivative files. Master files were captured as 300 dpi TIFF files and processed to produce 300 dpi JPEG files for display.[8] As curators, we participated in image checks and file-name convention development, but the balance of the digitization process was handled by AMD for ingesting into their proprietary data management system.

AMD partners with federated platform providers such as Ex Libris, ProQuest, EBSCO, and OCLC to ensure discoverability within their products, including

Chapter Twelve: Maximizing Assets and Access through Digital Publishing

through Primo Central, Metalib, SFX Knowledge Base, Summon, EBSCOHost, WorldCat, and WorldCat Local. Their curated and contextualized online databases also utilize 360-degree object viewers, interactive maps, and a proprietary federated searching tool (a widget) that can be added to a library's website to facilitate searches. Metadata in MARC 21 format is fully downloadable.

Short- and long-term storage issues for the digital assets were faced by both the publisher and our library. The publisher uses a storage vendor, Portico, and its D-collection preservation service for long-term dark storage and data preservation. The master files supplied to our library under the contract with the publisher will be stored on our storage area network (SAN) storage servers, which provide for both redundancy and tape backup as well as off-site storage for all files.

CASE STUDY

Our goals in undertaking these projects were to expand global reach and increase access to support teaching and research. For this chapter, however, we will concentrate on our decision-making process and the technological aspects of the projects.

Adam Matthew Digital representatives first approached each of us separately about contributing to "Migration to New Worlds" and "Age of Exploration" products, and independently of one another, we were intrigued by the opportunities their proposals presented. When we discovered a shared perspective on both potential benefits and concerns regarding subscription-based products, we determined that it would be ideal to work together to (a) evaluate the benefits of participating in such projects, (b) explore issues of access and cost, and (c) steer the proposals through the contract development and negotiation phases. The UMN Libraries had not yet participated in any such projects. Our strategy was to work together as copilots for the libraries' first foray into a royalty-producing digital publication of primary sources. This strategy proved fruitful. For example, together we consulted with our internal copyright specialist on contractual issues related to access. Although much of the IHRCA materials required rights considerations whereas the Bell Library materials are public domain, we were both concerned about licensing and subscription access.

As librarians generally committed to the ideal of open access, we were initially resistant to participation in subscription-based products. As we learned more about how this public-private partnership would work, we also had serious concerns about a paywall, which would be part of the license agreements. The materials we contributed could not be used in other large-scale digitization projects until a certain number of years elapsed; in other words, they would remain behind a paywall for the duration of the licenses. Additionally, only people who had access to the products through an institutional subscription would have digital access to our contributed content. However, through more discussions with AMD and with other UMN Libraries staff, we realized that these issues were not the insurmountable obstacles they initially seemed to be.

We came to understand that the investment in technology made by AMD to create these products could not be matched by our institution at this time. Nor did the content to be included in these products fall within the existing parameters of our internal strategic digitization plans. We realized that if we did not contribute our materials, then only those people who could physically visit our collections would have access to them—a much more limiting prospect. Moreover, the paywall would in no way interfere with our ability to make the materials available to our researchers on the same basis as we always had. Individual researchers, regardless of their ability to access the AMD online products, would still be able to use and exploit the analog items, including requesting digital copies on an individual basis.

The time embargo imposed by the paywall[9] also became a nonissue, as we had no plans for including the materials in other large-scale projects during the term covered by our licenses. Once this license expires, we will be free to provide open access to this content through our institutional repository or any other avenue. The paywall was likewise a concern of UMN Libraries administrators, but they agreed that limited digital access was better than no digital access, and they were willing to commit to long-term maintenance of the digital assets created through these projects both during the paywall period and once released to us.

Another issue when using a third-party provider is what happens should that company be sold or go out of business. Fortunately, AMD provides for a dark storage and data recovery service (referenced above) that also ensures continued subscriber services for the life of each existing subscription. When we understood how the recovery process worked, we were satisfied that this did not pose a significant risk.

Once we made the decision to license our content with a third-party publisher, there were staffing and logistical issues to consider. We hired a part-time temporary project manager. This staff person led collection management, document preparation, and communications with the outside providers. As noted, this included working with the digital technician brought on-site by LUNA Imaging as well as liaising with AMD staff. Hosting an outside digital-service provider also necessitated finding adequate space on campus. In order to provide this space, the UMN

Chapter Twelve: Maximizing Assets and Access through Digital Publishing

required an addendum to our licensing agreement that addressed the use of university real estate by an outside party. In addition to work space, we needed to provide storage for the scanning equipment shipping containers. To accommodate the digitization operation, we had to displace student staff and relocate them elsewhere for the duration of the project. Furthermore, we provided the digital photographer with a UMN e-mail account to support rapid and robust digital content delivery.

Our decision to participate in these particular projects with this particular vendor was based on numerous factors. One of the benefits we identified early in the process was the attractive and easy-to-use public interface and the user support provided with all AMD products. We and our faculty and students were already familiar with these benefits through our own institutional subscriptions to some of their existing products. Also, because some of our content had either minimal or no MARC records, AMD offered improved and original MARC records for the digital surrogates ingested into the database, representing a significant cost savings to us. Additionally, the IHRCA project would result in fully searchable digital versions of increasingly obsolete and degrading audio tapes.

As librarians, we are always interested in access and reach, and user-friendly, high-quality educational publications that are well placed in the global information landscape will help us reach these goals. When they came to us with their proposals, AMD's team had already conceived of the project themes and found institutional partners that ensured a broad array of primary source materials, which would result in multi-institution cross-searchability. They also surveyed our collection content to narrow down the proposed selections for inclusion in the projects. These actions represented significant cost savings to us when compared to undertaking such projects in-house. Perhaps the most important savings was the digitization of our material at no direct cost to us. The resulting 68,000 images and nearly twenty hours of audio recordings would have cost us approximately $35,000 had we digitized them ourselves. These benefits are in addition to the marketing and user-support services our publication partner will provide for the duration of the license. Moreover, our entire university community—composed of students, staff, and faculty at five campuses around the state—now enjoys access to these publications. Additionally, both of our collections will realize royalties from the licensed materials, income streams that may have a significant impact on our ability to create our own digital assets and curated products in the future.

For all of the benefits and cost savings these projects afforded, we realized that the UMN Libraries would incur some costs. Each curator had to determine if she had the time to take on the project. Meetings with staff and libraries administration, meetings with the third-party vendors, and hiring and supervising additional project-specific staff would be time consuming. For us, the benefits we foresaw compensated for the time we anticipated spending on the projects. In retrospect, we underestimated that time. Contract reviews with legal counsel, evaluating space and equipment needs, and negotiating with both libraries administration and the vendor was time that was either unanticipated or took longer than expected. Ingesting the metadata created and provided by AMD as well as rights information also absorbed staff time. Going forward, the libraries will invest time and funds in managing the digital surrogates, including providing for dark storage of master files. These were projects that we did not have the internal capacity to undertake ourselves, and therefore, this represents a time and funding commitment not anticipated by the UMN Libraries in its long-term planning.

Overall, we are pleased with how the process unfolded and anticipate reaching all of the project goals. We now have digital assets that we are sharing with the wider community, which both extends our reach and contributes to the research and learning ecosystem. Our experience working with a commercial vendor in this way will, we believe, pave the way for other such partnerships in the future.

CONCLUSION

It is time to begin thinking about outreach and access as part of an investment strategy for building user communities on a global stage. The combination of continuously evolving technology and library administrators' increasing focus on reducing costs makes the inside-out model viable now and a future standard for special collections. Creating digital assets and making them accessible on a broad scale is part of that model. Our experience with a commercial digital publisher demonstrates that partnering with such a third-party vendor can provide a level of access and discoverability that many libraries cannot afford to provide for themselves, as the cost of developing and managing similar projects in-house is beyond their capacity. Third-party publishers often will sustain those costs while at the same time provide a new revenue stream for their library partners that might help ease the tension between preservation and access with respect to the allocation of institutional resources.

Strategic digitization of library assets can be beneficial no matter the size or nature of a particular collection or library, whether academic, public, or private. And these benefits do not have to be realized with a third-party commercial vendor.

Chapter Twelve: Maximizing Assets and Access through Digital Publishing

Many libraries use digital images of collection materials to promote their collections on social media platforms such as Facebook, Instagram, and Tumblr or as part of online exhibitions, courses, or other projects. New technologies can also assist librarians to innovate teaching and learning and enhance scholarly communication. For most librarians, providing access to our materials is a key motivator, and finding partners for digitization projects, whether commercial vendors or other institutions with similar interests, may help improve access and broaden reach more affordably than attempting to undertake a large digital project on one's own.

The advances in image capture and other types of digital conversion technologies—as well as improvements in data management systems, international standards for output and display such as IIIF (http://iiif.io; see chapter 13 for more about this standard), options for long-term digital preservation, and access and discoverability tools—are already changing the ways librarians work and think about their collections. The inside-out model supports the adoption of these technologies and provides a rationale for this type of partnership with third-party publishers. The future of the outward-facing special collections library is entrepreneurial; as we continue to explore improved access and discoverability and extend reach on a global scale, digital publishing technologies offer one option for realizing this future now.

NOTES

1. Lorcan Dempsey, Constance Malpas, and Brian Lavoie, "Collection Directions: The Evolution of Library Collections and Collecting," *Portal: Libraries and the Academy* 14, no. 3 (2014): 420, https://doi.org/10.1353/pla.2014.0013.
2. Lorcan Dempsey, "Library Collections in the Life of the User: Two Directions," *LIBER Quarterly* 26, no. 4 (2016), https://doi.org/10.18352/lq.10170.
3. Dempsey, Malpas, and Lavoie, "Collection Directions," 394.
4. See, for example, Elizabeth Kirk, "The Entrepreneurial Library: Creating Revenue in the Age of E-commerce," in *Crossing the Divide: Proceedings of the Tenth National Conference of the Association of College and Research Libraries*, ed. Hugh A. Thompson (Chicago: Association of College and Research Libraries, 2001). See also Peter Hirtle, "Archives or Assets?," *American Archivist* 66, no. 2 (Fall–Winter 2003): 236, https://doi.org/10.17723/aarc.66.2.h0mn427675783n51: "In short, archives and manuscript repositories control and manage assets worth hundreds of billions, if not trillions, of dollars. . . . The sale of reproductions of archival materials and the licensing of material for commercial use are becoming ever more important as possible sources of income for archives. Archives, in seeking to draw revenue from the content that they own, are following in the footsteps of museums, which have long used licensing programs to augment their income."

PART III: Repositories and Access

5. Allison Zhang and Don Gourley, *Creating Digital Collections: A Practical Guide*, Chandos Information Professional Series (Oxford: Chandos, 2009).

6. See, for example, the variety of results discussed in Ricky Erway, *Rapid Capture: Faster Throughput in Digitization of Special Collections* (Dublin, OH: OCLC Research, 2011), www.oclc.org/research/publications/library/2011/2011-04.pdf.

7. Erway, 12–14.

8. There have been numerous standards used for digital projects. See Iris Xie and Krystyna K. Matusiak, *Discover Digital Libraries: Theory and Practice* (Oxford: Elsevier, 2016), 69–71, for a summary of best practices.

9. This multiyear embargo varies from institution to institution based on a variety of factors. Our contract requires that we not disclose specific terms.

PART IV

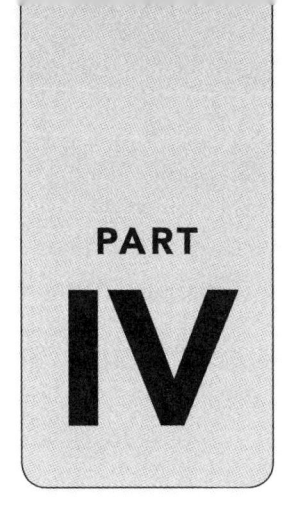

Interoperability

Chapter Thirteen

Impact of International Image Interoperability Framework (IIIF) on Digital Repositories

Kelli Babcock and Rachel Di Cresce

Over the last decade, many libraries and memory institutions have increased investments in digital special collections.[1] The institutional goals driving this increase likely vary from library to library or even collection to collection—whether for access, preservation, promotion, or a combination of these reasons. Whatever the motivation behind increased investments in digital special collections, access to these digital objects is often made possible through digital repository platforms such as Fedora (with front ends including Samvera and Islandora), CONTENTdm, DSpace, EPrints, or online exhibit tools such as Omeka (see chapter 10 for more information on this tool).

As libraries continue to invest in acquiring and creating digital special collections and making them accessible, it is prudent to recognize that each library's repository platform may actually be limiting the efficiency of image-based research. Each repository is a siloed "site" that researchers must visit to find the images they are

PART IV: Interoperability

seeking. Imagine a graduate student in art history studying the depiction of cats in early printed eighteenth-century manuscripts. An exhaustive search for images online would currently include visiting many rare book libraries' online repository websites as a first stage of research. In our roles at the University of Toronto Libraries (UTL), we have investigated a piece of technology (a standard, actually) that has the potential to make our digital special collections more easily discoverable by enabling image interoperability—namely, the ability to share images across many repositories at once. The standard could also inform how we build sustainable repository frameworks to make these collections accessible while meeting the current needs of our patrons and research community by offering new ways for users to interact with digital special collections. This standard is the International Image Interoperability Framework (IIIF, pronounced "triple-I F").

In this chapter, we will define IIIF, describe IIIF projects at UTL and beyond, and discuss how IIIF has impacted our digital special collections repository, Collections U of T.[2] We will also address future trends in IIIF and how the standard could affect the library community of the future. We hope this chapter provides readers with a foundational knowledge of IIIF and generates ideas of how IIIF may fit into your library's digital repository framework to increase your return on investments in digital special collections.

WHAT IS IIIF?

IIIF is a set of standards and guidelines aimed at providing worldwide uniform access to image-based resources with the goal of enhancing the research of digital images. IIIF is not the end result of a process but rather the instructions that can enable libraries to create new ways to use their digital special collections. Think of it as more of the recipe for a cake—a global, interoperable cake made of digital images but potentially other digital media—rather than the finished cake itself.

IIIF is a set of application programming interfaces (APIs), which define the ingredients and instructions that enable interoperability between repositories, along with the integration of other technologies. It is a way to structure and deliver data consistently across platforms—from one repository, web viewer, or image tool to another—without imposing specific platforms or tools on a library or individual making use of the images. Its aim is true open access for digital images, in which a user from anywhere can look at and employ any digital image resources within a single interface. In practice, this means a user can compare two or more

Chapter Thirteen: Impact of IIIF on Digital Repositories

IIIF-enabled manuscripts, maps, artworks, and so on in one image viewer.[3] Figure 13.1 demonstrates how researchers might use IIIF to evaluate manuscripts from separate libraries.

The major benefit of the IIIF specification is that it enables libraries to separate the presentation of the image from the repository storing the content. Through IIIF, a digital collection can be shared across institutions and consortiums without transferring large TIFF files between repositories.[4] IIIF images can be reused across platforms, across users, and across tools. IIIF is also flexible, as it can work well with other World Wide Web Consortium (W3C) recommendations such as web annotation and Webmention. Both are powerful ways to create and share information about digital resources through crowdsourcing and distributed metadata.

Although IIIF is at its core a technical specification, it would not be as powerful or successful without the thriving community supporting it. Those active in the IIIF community include librarians, technologists, system administrators, developers, and researchers. All work together to find solutions to common problems, develop new tools, offer advice and guidance, and push IIIF forward.[5]

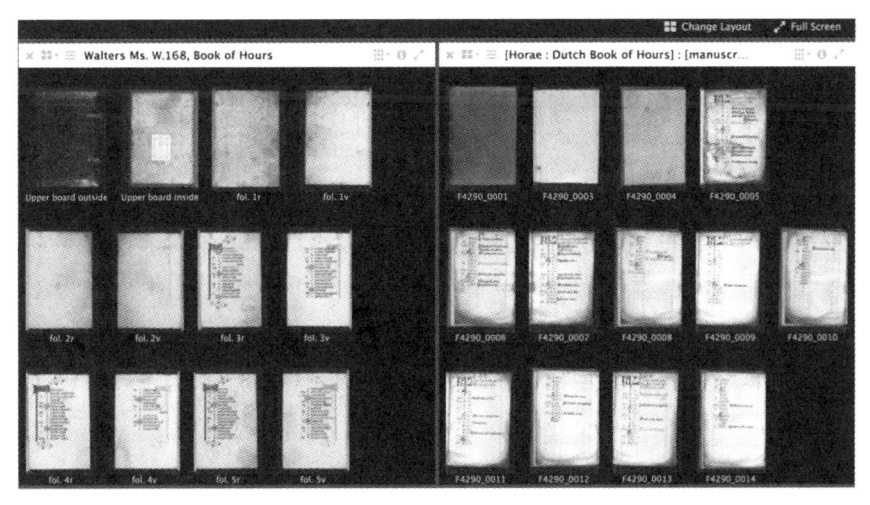

FIGURE 13.1
The comparison of two different *Book of Hours* manuscripts, from two separate digital repositories, displayed together in the Mirador viewer. On the left is a page view of a Walters Art Museum manuscript. On the right is a Thomas Fisher Rare Book Library manuscript.

IIIF manifest URL: https://purl.stanford.edu/qm670kv1873/iiif/manifest and https://iiif.library.utoronto.ca/presentation/v2/fisher2:137/manifest.json.

PART IV: Interoperability

HOW DOES IIIF WORK?

IIIF starts with the implementation of the Image API, which simply specifies a web service that returns an image to a standard HTTP(S) request. The Uniform Resource Identifier (URI) can specify the region, size, rotation, quality characteristics, and format of the requested image and can also be constructed to request basic technical information about the image to support client applications.[6] Essentially, the Image API defines a standard way of creating URIs for your digital images and how they can be requested. See figure 13.2 for a breakdown of a IIIF Image API URI.

The URI request in figure 13.2 returns the full image (6,000 × 3,960 pixels) of page 1 from the *De humani corporis fabrica libri septum* manuscript from the Thomas Fisher Rare Book Library with no rotation at the default quality available (color). See figure 13.3 for the image this URI will return.

The Image API allows you to modify the image in various ways. Perhaps you only want to focus in on the center area of the image with the main subject. Your URI request would then instead indicate the pixel region you desire to view. For example, the URI https://iiif.library.utoronto.ca/image/v2/anatomia:RBAI035_0001/900,3000,2000,1200/full/0/default.jpg would return a selected region of the image in figure 13.3, as seen in figure 13.4.

Anyone using the IIIF Image API to call an image can stop here, view the images as he wishes, and use the IIIF Image API to implement useful technology, such as image zooming and annotation, while being IIIF-compliant. But institutions can take their IIIF implementation one step further by making use of the IIIF Presentation API,[7] which opens digital special collections to wider and more interactive use. It provides a standard layout for how a IIIF object should be structured and presented along with basic information for the user (e.g., table of contents, title, date, and rights information). The Presentation API ensures that no matter where that item may be accessed, it will look the same and provide the same contextual information to the end user.

SERVER	PREFIX	IDENTIFIER	REGION	SIZE	ROTATION	QUALITY
https://iiif.library.utoronto.ca/	image/v2/	anatomia:RBAI035_0001/	full/	full/	0/	default.jpg

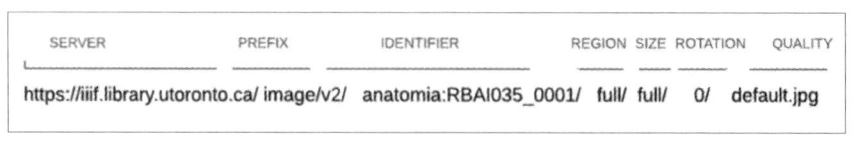

FIGURE 13.2
A breakdown of a IIIF Image API URI.

FIGURE 13.3
The image returned by the IIIF Image API URI for https://iiif.library.utoronto.ca/image/v2/anatomia:RBAI035_0001/full/full/0/default.jpg.

PART IV: Interoperability

FIGURE 13.4
Updating the IIIF Image API URI for https://iiif.library.utoronto.ca/image/v2/anatomia:RBAI035_0001/full/full/0/default.jpg to https://iiif.library.utoronto.ca/image/v2/anatomia:RBAI035_0001/900,3000,2000,1200/full/0/default.jpg will result in delivering a specific region of the image.

The Presentation API layout results in something called a *manifest,* or the representation of the digital object in the form of a JavaScript Object Notation (JSON) file. The manifest is the overall description of the structure and properties of the digital representation of an object. For example, the manifest for a book would indicate the order of each page image so that a user can move through the object in its intended sequence. However, a manifest for digital images of a 3-D sculpture may include multiple images from many angles, for which the manifest would also indicate the desired order of the images. Presentation API manifests are intended to be very easy to read. See figure 13.5 for a rendering of a manifest created by UTL.

So far, what we have described is how the APIs work to enable IIIF use. But what does all of this mean and look like at a server level? What actually happens when a user from outside of UTL wants to look at the manifest described in figure 13.5 and calls the manifest from an external IIIF viewer? What systems are at play that make this happen?

When a user wishes to view a digital image from a web client in an image viewer, she sends a request to the server. The server acts as the intermediary to get the IIIF manifest and send it back to the web client (see figure 13.6). The web client

```
{
    "@context":"http://iiif.io/api/presentation/2/context.json",
    "@id":"https://iiif.library.utoronto.ca/presentation/v2/anatomia:RB
AI035/manifest",
    "@type":"sc:Manifest",
    "label":"De humani corporis fabrica libri septem.",
```
Metadata about Manifest

```
"metadata" : [
    {
        "label": "Title",
        "value": " De humani corporis fabrica libri septem."
    },
    {
        "label": "attribution"
        "value":"For rights and reproduction information please cont
act collections@library.utoronto.ca"
    }
```
Metadata about the Object

```
"sequences":[
    {
        "@type":"sc:Sequence",
        "label":"De humani corporis fabrica libri septem., in order",
        "canvases":[
            {
                "@id":"https://iiif.library.utoronto.ca/presentation/v2
/anatomia:RBAI035/canvas/anatomia:RBAI035_0001",
                "@type":"sc:Canvas",
                "label":"RBAI035_0001",
                "thumbnail":{
                    "@type":"dctypes:Image",
                    "format":"image/jpg",
                    "height":6000,
                    "width":3960,
```
Order of Images

FIGURE 13.5

The Presentation API JSON view for the Thomas Fisher Rare Book Library's *De humani corporis fabrica libri septum* manuscript, which contains the image identified in figures 13.3 and 13.4.

The manifest is available at https://iiif.library.utoronto.ca/presentation/v2/anatomia:RBAI035/manifest.json.

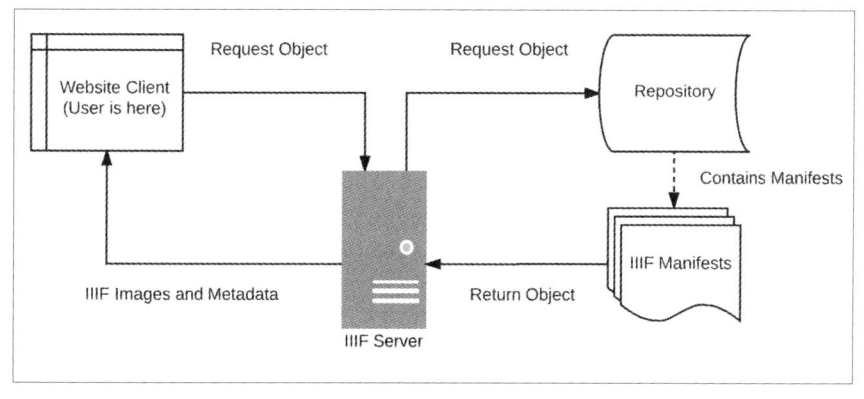

FIGURE 13.6

A diagram displaying a user's request to access a IIIF manifest.

presents the images found in the manifest, which in turn point to the image files sitting in the repository and served by the server.

IIIF USE CASES

By creating IIIF-compliant digital repositories, a single IIIF URI for a given digital object (whether it be archival images, manuscripts, newspapers, etc.) has great potential for use and reuse of that image. A researcher or archivist could then

- annotate, transcribe, translate, or perform optical character recognition (OCR);
- make side-by-side comparisons;
- manipulate images (crop, zoom, color inversion, etc.);
- simply cite and easily share images;
- engage in storytelling;
- reassemble libraries, books, items, and so on; and
- make use of different imaging techniques (photogrammetry, X-ray, etc.) and provide multiple images per page that a user can click through.

THE IMPACT OF IIIF ON DIGITAL SPECIAL COLLECTION REPOSITORIES

There are many potential use cases for IIIF, but for UTL's Information Technology Services Department, the focus is currently on exploring how IIIF will impact our digital special collections as well as the support we provide to faculty and researchers working in this area. UTL's first project incorporating IIIF began with a collaboration called French Renaissance Paleography.[8] The project was developed and launched in January 2016 in partnership with the Newberry Library, Iter, and St. Louis University. The purpose of the project was to enable the study of writing systems and deciphering paleography, the study of handwriting, through online pedagogical resources and an annotation tool, T-PEN, using a repository of more than one hundred French manuscripts from the 1300s to the 1700s.[9] IIIF allowed for the project's digital manuscripts, stored in UTL's Fedora repository but displayed through a Mirador viewer embedded and presented in Islandora, to be pulled in to Saint Louis's T-PEN annotation tool.

Chapter Thirteen: Impact of IIIF on Digital Repositories

In mid-2016, UTL embarked on the creation of modular, interoperable tools integrated with IIIF under another project called Digital Tools for Manuscript Study.[10] These tools apply IIIF to existing digital scholarship tools to enhance the use of images in research and teaching in both manuscript studies and the wider digital humanities community. The project makes use of popular tools (Omeka, Mirador, and Viscoll) but is also focused on producing new methods for IIIF integration with various repository platforms while considering how these tools could be used by an individual researcher or small institution looking to employ IIIF.

The work conducted in these two projects informed how UTL could incorporate IIIF into Collections U of T, which is composed of a single Fedora repository with multiple Islandora sites acting as the point of access for each top-level collection. After development was completed for French Renaissance Paleography, we made a portion of our Collections U of T objects IIIF compliant. The IIIF manifests for objects within Collections U of T are available at https://iiif.library.utoronto.ca/presentation/v2/collections, with updates occurring regularly. By enabling IIIF for Collections U of T digital special collections, the images within our collections are now "free" from a single point of access (i.e., their Islandora sites).

We are currently exploring possibilities for exposing our digital special collections in multiple places: not just our Collections U of T sites but also IIIF-enabled consortial image repositories; through an embedded Mirador viewer for corresponding library catalog records; other IIIF community–related initiatives; or within associated archival descriptions for archival image content.[11] There appear to be endless opportunities and "places" to provide access to the rich resources available within Collections U of T. The work now is to pursue this exposure.

As more institutions adopt IIIF, we can see its potential to impact how libraries maintain and provide access to digital special collections—both individually and collaboratively. While there are a few puzzle pieces to be fleshed out—for example, library websites containing IIIF viewers will have to support researchers in understanding how to find the manifests they want to view—IIIF alters what was once one of the primary functions of our digital repository platforms: access. Because IIIF enables us to provide users access to our digital special collections in any IIIF-enabled viewer *anywhere*, the repository platform is now just one of many locations where patrons can interact with these digital images.

The IIIF-enabled interoperability of our collection images, and how our patrons and researchers view them, has many benefits. Digital repository platforms can, in some perspectives, be barriers to researchers. With so many repository platforms in use across institutions, every image within each repository is locked into that specific institutional repository due to "differences in the handling of storage, management, and delivery of digital material across repositories, which frequently use separate frameworks, formats, and applications."[12] While repository frameworks such as DSpace and Islandora have been successful at integrating interoperability standards for metadata (e.g., Open Archives Initiative Protocol for Metadata Harvesting [OAI-PMH]) this same interoperability treatment has not been applied to images.

IIIF also has the potential to impact how we build sustainable repository infrastructure in our libraries. When discussing repository platforms at Open Repositories 2017, Tom Cramer noted, "Monolithic systems tend to serve poorly. . . . If you have a huge, expensive system, you're going to need to refresh that."[13] For many libraries, the implementation of a complex content management system (CMS)—such as stand-alone Drupal, Drupal with Islandora "atop" a Fedora repository, or Samvera—has been the access solution to digital special collections. These types of solutions will inevitably require migration. Adopting IIIF made us question what our migration path will be; access now becomes a question of creating a CMS- or platform-*independent* model. With IIIF, "there is no more need to download and upload images into different CMS' for different use cases, and no need for endless copies in different systems."[14]

Of course, IIIF will not perform every function currently fulfilled by our powerful repository platforms, such as preservation. For UTL, search and discovery through IIIF-enabled viewers also require more investigation. Inspiration can be found in institutions that have incorporated Blacklight or other indexing tools alongside their IIIF viewers.[15] The suggestion is not that IIIF will replace our digital repository platforms. It can, however, be adopted as an alternative or supplement to how libraries currently provide access to digital special collections or be incorporated into our current repository frameworks to improve image interoperability.

IIIF INITIATIVES: EARLY ADOPTERS

UTL has been fortunate enough to follow the path of many of IIIF's early adopters and its large and expanding community. IIIF was created to address a growing need in the education and heritage sectors for greater freedom and access to digital resources. As such, from its inception, the IIIF community has placed this use case at the center of its tool development and API refinement decisions.

The IIIF Image API was published in 2012 and was followed shortly after by the Presentation API in 2013. IIIF was initiated by Stanford University and included the National Library of France, British Library, National Library of Norway, Cornell University, and Oxford University. Since then, the APIs have undergone several refinements and have been steadily adopted by more than one hundred institutions worldwide, totaling more than 355 million IIIF images.[16] The newest additions at the time of this writing come from the National Library of Israel and the Kyoto University Rare Materials Digital Archive.[17] The initial use case for the Image API was to allow a viewing client to request an image in low-resolution tiles (to reduce server load) for deep zoom and panning tools.[18] These functionalities are particularly useful, for example, for researchers who desire an extremely close analysis of art and map objects without losing image clarity.

At this point, IIIF performs its basic functions, but what else can be done with the images? Early adopters crowdsourced use cases and began work on IIIF tool development, integrating IIIF into existing tools and refining the APIs to work more efficiently. Due to this, what someone can do with IIIF images is always changing and growing. As an example, scholars often wish to compare two manuscripts of the same work, two maps of a certain region, a finished painting with its study, and so on. With IIIF technology, users are free to do this with objects from different institutions; they can reunite books or collections that exist in separate digital repositories in a single digital space.

These cases offer only snapshots of what can be done with IIIF. As development continues and new institutions join, IIIF is being used to address all sorts of research and nonresearch needs. Other recent developments include annotation; storytelling; map and image overlay from Reflectance Transformation Imaging (RTI) and photogrammetry methods; gaming; scientific data representation; machine-learning integration; and more.[19]

IIIF FUTURE TRENDS: AUDIO, STEM, 3-D

What's next for IIIF? As its name suggests, IIIF has its roots firmly in the image resource world. It also grew out of the arts and humanities sphere and has maintained a focus in this area. However, community members are now expanding the application of IIIF principles and APIs to audiovisual materials and science, technology, engineering, and mathematics (STEM).

In 2017, the IIIF community issued a charter to define the scope and timeline for an initiative to make audiovisual materials comply with IIIF specifications.[20] As of spring 2018, IIIF Presentation API 3.0, which will include changes to incorporate audiovisual materials, will be ready by the end of 2018.[21] More materials of this type brought into the IIIF space will mean more opportunities for new tool development and a greater ability for institutions to address researcher needs and use cases.

In addition, the past year saw the development of STEM and 3-D community interest groups within IIIF. The STEM group is working at consolidating use cases and experiments for how IIIF can be used in researching, teaching, and publishing in STEM fields. To date, Harvard University has had great success with their Mirador image viewer in biology classes, making use of IIIF images and web-annotation capabilities.[22] Similarly, a community of 3-D enthusiasts has very recently begun to take shape with an aim to investigate how IIIF might be applicable to 3-D object research.

Finally, the IIIF community will continue its outreach to different parts of the world and new types of institutions. In particular, IIIF has been gaining traction in Japan and China and seeks to continue this trend toward a true global presence. Outreach events, workshops, and conferences are all under way for the coming year with an aim to garner new support for IIIF, new users, content providers, and community members.

A FUTURE COMMUNITY OF IIIF-ENABLED INSTITUTIONS

As more library and memory institutions adopt IIIF, their patrons and researchers stand to benefit. Making our digital objects interoperable will improve how they are discovered and interacted with. This has already been demonstrated through IIIF-enabled image-based research. Emmanuelle Delmas-Glass of the Yale Centre for British Art has stated that a "main obstacle to efficient and scalable image-based research has been the lack of interoperability between image silos."[23] She goes on to add that IIIF's annotation functionality within a IIIF viewer such as Mirador offers efficiency for "researchers to bring forth their arguments and document their reasoning while consulting the image-based evidences that they have brought together." She notes, "The value added of IIIF is that it is supported by two data models that adopt the principles of Linked Open Data and the Architecture of the World Wide Web: SharedCanvas and Open Annotation." Many other adopters have also demonstrated the positive impact IIIF has on image-based scholarship. Biblissima enables scholars to reunite pieces of a manuscript scattered across several institutions.[24] The virtual reconstruction project Reconstructing Ege Fol 47 brings together dispersed materials from the personal collection of Otto F. Ege.[25]

Chapter Thirteen: Impact of IIIF on Digital Repositories

There are other impacts on research that must be considered. For example, IIIF has the potential to remove digital special collections from their original context. Lauren Magnuson has noted that "injecting objects from other collections might skew the authentic representation of some collections, even if the objects are directly related to each other," but the benefit is that "this approach might work well to help represent provenance for collections that have been broken up across multiple institutions."[26]

Researchers who are inspired by IIIF functionality might request that libraries respond with new reference and support services. In an academic library setting, IIIF could be a tool for aggregating reference materials in response to a faculty or student research query. It may also require our library community to present new opportunities for staff training, such as "data representation with JSON/JSON-LD [and] understanding Web Annotations," which are "crucial to understanding the general direction of web-based document transcription and annotation."[27]

The standard is itself a community. Increased adoption of IIIF will lead to the growth of that community over the years, from which consortial and cross-institutional projects can be facilitated.[28] In a future of IIIF-enabled institutions, the community may have more capacity to increase its support for smaller institutions grappling with the resources required to adopt IIIF. For example, integration with legacy repository platforms may be a barrier to smaller institutions that don't have information technology infrastructure or those institutions that rely on vendor solutions for their digital repository needs. Lauren Magnuson notes, "It may be some time before legacy digital asset management applications integrate IIIF easily and seamlessly. Apart from these applications *serving* up content for use with IIIF viewers, embedding IIIF viewer capabilities into existing applications would be another challenge."[29] From this perspective, widespread IIIF adoption risks leaving some institutions behind. However, conversations about ease of implementation are ongoing. Resources such as online and standardized in-person IIIF training are on the community's radar as items to address in the years to come.[30]

By engaging in IIIF now and in the future, librarians can expect to join an active community of peers who are committed to building a specification that will allow institutions to share digital objects through sustainable, interoperable, and future-focused methods. As our institutions continue to invest in building digital special collections, applying IIIF should become our new best practice—or, at least, one of our top seventeen.

PART IV: Interoperability

NOTES

1. We adopt the "digitized special collections" definition outlined by Nancy L. Maron and Sara Pickle in the 2013 Ithaka S+R and Association of Research Libraries report *Appraising Our Digital Investment: Sustainability of Digitized Special Collections in ARL Libraries*: "Collections of rare or archival content that would ordinarily be kept in a secure special collections or archives facility that your institution has either digitized itself, chosen to have someone else digitize, or taken on the responsibility for managing (i.e., a collection created elsewhere that your institution now hosts and manages)."
2. "Collections U of T," University of Toronto Libraries, last modified January 29, 2018, https://collections.library.utoronto.ca.
3. Visit www.projectmirador.org/demo to test how IIIF works.
4. William Ying and James Shulman, "'Bottled or Tap?' A Map for Integrating International Image Interoperability Framework (IIIF) into Shared Shelf and Artstor," *D-Lib Magazine* 21 (July–August 2015), www.dlib.org/dlib/july15/ying/07ying.html.
5. For more details about the IIIF community, see the Biblissima's introduction to IIIF page, http://doc.biblissima-condorcet.fr/introduction-iiif.
6. Taken from http://iiif.io/api/image/2.1/#status-of-this-document. Visit http://iiif.harvard.edu/about-iiif/ to try out the API and learn more in this video by Jon Stroop, "IIIF DC—the IIIF Image API by Jon Stroop," YouTube, uploaded July 24, 2015, www.youtube.com/watch?v=Hv_Wh51c5Aw.
7. See http://iiif.io/api/presentation/2.1/#objectives-and-scope for full documentation. The following video by Rob Sanderson offers a great exploration as well, "IIIF DC—Introduction to the Presentation API," YouTube, uploaded July 24, 2015, www.youtube.com/watch?v=fdWzwDc85EU.
8. "French Renaissance Paleography," Newberry, last modified January 28, 2018, https://paleography.library.utoronto.ca.
9. "T-PEN," T-PEN, n.d., http://t-pen.org/TPEN.
10. "Digital Tools for Manuscript Study," University of Toronto, last modified 2018, https://digitaltoolsmss.library.utoronto.ca.
11. IIIF community–related initiatives such as http://universalviewer.io/#showcase and https://graph.global/universes/iiif. UTL currently uses the AtoM archival description platform, https://discoverarchives.library.utoronto.ca.
12. Jeffrey P. Emanuel, Christopher M. Morse, and Luke Hollis, "The New Interactive: Reimagining Visual Collections as Immersive Environments," *VRA Bulletin*, December 2016, www.academia.edu/30544005/The_New_Interactive_Reimagining_Visual_Collections_as_Immersive_Environments.
13. Tom Cramer, "An Uncomfortable Truth: Digital Preservation and Open Repositories" (paper presented at Open Repositories 2017, Brisbane, University of Queensland, 2017).

14. John B. Howard, "Letter from the Editors," Europeana Pro, 2017, https://pro.euro peana.eu/page/issue-6-iiif.
15. For example, see the North Carolina State University Libraries Digital Collections catalog, https://d.lib.ncsu.edu/collections/catalog.
16. Explore some of the IIIF manifests currently available at https://graph.global/universes/iiif.
17. For information about the National Library of Israel, see http://web.nli.org.il/sites/NLI/English/digitallibrary/Pages/default.aspx. More information for the Kyoto University of Rare Material is available at https://rmda.kulib.kyoto-u.ac.jp/en.
18. Try out the OpenSeadragon viewer at https://openseadragon.github.io.
19. For further exploration and details on a host of IIIF applications, please refer to https://github.com/IIIF/awesome-iiif.
20. Read the charter at https://gist.github.com/azaroth42/2d6204e5c6932a4da56efba38c5be86d.
21. Howard, "Letter from the Editors."
22. HarvardX, "Cell Biology: Mitochondria," edX, n.d., https://courses.edx.org/courses/course-v1:HarvardX+MCB64.1x+2T2016/d16e07a5cec442eeb7cd9dfcb695dce0/.
23. Emmanuelle Delmas-Glass, "Yale Center for British Art's Reformation to Restoration Project: Applying IIIF Mirador Technology to Support Digital Scholarly Collaboration and Research" (paper presented at MW2016: Museums and the Web 2016, Los Angeles, Millennium Biltmore Hotel, 2016).
24. For more information, see http://demos.biblissima-condorcet.fr/chateauroux/demo.
25. To test out this project, visit http://lis464.omeka.net/exhibits/show/about-this-project/a-treasure-rediscovered.
26. Lauren Magnuson, "Store and Display High Resolution Images with the International Image Interoperability Framework (IIIF)," ACRL TechConnect, 2016, http://acrl.ala.org/techconnect/post/store-and-display-high-resolution-images-with-the-international-image-interoperability-framework-iiif.
27. Howard, "Letter from the Editors."
28. For example, Parker Library on the Web 2.0 is a collaboration between Corpus Christi College in Cambridge and Stanford University Libraries. See Gabrielle Karampelas, "Parker Library on the Web Celebrates 10th Anniversary with a New Service," Stanford Libraries, July 14, 2015, https://library.stanford.edu/news/2015/07/parker-library-web-celebrates-10th-anniversary-new-service.
29. Magnuson, "Store and Display."
30. The community is making great steps to make training resources, such as https://iiif.github.io/training/intro-to-iiif/, publicly available.

PART IV: Interoperability

BIBLIOGRAPHY

An extended bibliography can be found at http://hdl.handle.net/1807/82481.

Cramer, Tom. "An Uncomfortable Truth: Digital Preservation and Open Repositories." Paper presented at Open Repositories 2017, Brisbane, University of Queensland, 2017.

Delmas-Glass, Emmanuelle. "Yale Center for British Art's Reformation to Restoration Project: Applying IIIF Mirador Technology to Support Digital Scholarly Collaboration and Research." Paper presented at MW2016: Museums and the Web 2016, Los Angeles, Millennium Biltmore Hotel, 2016. http://mw2016.museumsandtheweb.com/paper/yale-center-for-british-arts-reformation-to-restoration-project-applying-iiif-mirador-technology-to-support-digital-scholarly-collaboration-and-research/.

Emanuel, Jeffrey P., Christopher M. Morse, and Luke Hollis. "The New Interactive: Reimagining Visual Collections as Immersive Environments." *VRA Bulletin,* December 2016. www.academia.edu/30544005/The_New_Interactive_Reimagining_Visual_Collections_as_Immersive_Environments?auto=download.

Howard, John B. "Letter from the Editors." Europeana Pro, 2017. https://pro.europeana.eu/page/issue-6-iiif.

Magnuson, Lauren. "Store and Display High Resolution Images with the International Image Interoperability Framework (IIIF)." ACRL TechConnect, 2016. http://acrl.ala.org/techconnect/post/store-and-display-high-resolution-images-with-the-international-image-interoperability-framework-iiif.

Maron, Nancy L., and Sara Pickle. *Appraising Our Digital Investment: Sustainability of Digitized Special Collections in ARL Libraries.* Washington, DC: Association of Research Libraries, 2013.

Ying, William, and James Shulman. "'Bottled or Tap?' A Map for Integrating International Image Interoperability Framework (IIIF) into Shared Shelf and Artstor." *D-Lib Magazine* 21 (July–August 2015). www.dlib.org/dlib/july15/ying/07ying.html.

Chapter Fourteen

Embracing Embeddedness with Learning Tools Interoperability (LTI)

Lauren Magnuson

Learning Tools Interoperability (LTI) is an open standard maintained by the IMS Global Learning Consortium (www.imsglobal.org/aboutims.html) that is used to build external tools or plug-ins for learning management systems (LMS). A common use case of LTI is to build an application that can be accessed from within the LMS to perform searches and import resources into a course. For example, the Wikipedia LTI application (www.edu-apps.org/edu_apps/index.html?tool=wikipedia) enables instructors to search Wikipedia and embed links to articles directly into their courses without ever leaving their LMS interface. Academic libraries frequently struggle to integrate library resources in LMS, and LTI can provide functionality to make library resources more easily accessible to students and instructors at the point of need.

PART IV: Interoperability

LTI USE CASES FOR LIBRARIES

LTI tools enable users to access third-party resources, instructional modules, or other data seamlessly from within their LMS courses without having to authenticate with the third-party tool directly or navigate away from the LMS. Students increasingly expect that all essential or recommended course materials, including library materials, will be linked or integrated directly into the corresponding LMS courses, and students report that such integrations are useful.[1] At the same time, academic librarians have strongly embraced becoming "embedded" in courses in the subject areas to which they serve as liaisons.[2] Embeddedness extends traditional librarian bibliographic and information literacy instructional roles to facilitate active pedagogical collaboration with instructors in designing instruction, offering supplemental instruction (particularly relating to information literacy and research methods), and participating in online learning forums and discussions. The ubiquitous adoption of flexible learning management system platforms, such as Moodle and Canvas, as well as the widespread adoption of embedded librarian services has positioned the campus LMS as a natural collaborative nexus for librarians, instructors, and students to interact and share resources. There are three areas in particular where LTI applications can support embedded library services and collaboration: facilitating access to library materials, personalization, and learning analytics.

FACILITATING ACCESS TO LIBRARY MATERIALS

While instructors are accustomed to adding materials to their LMS courses from freely available websites, adding library resources, which require permanent URLs (permalinks) and may have confusing IP-based authentication requirements (e.g., an EZProxy base URL), creates a significant barrier to successful linking of library materials in LMSs. As Waugh and Frank note, students attempting to access links to library materials within their courses often encounter broken links, as instructors used URLs from URL address bars rather than permalinks often found in item records within library discovery systems or electronic databases.[3] The frustration this causes for students and educators alike may lead instructors to download library materials (e.g., as a PDF) and upload those copies into the LMS. While this avoids the problem of confusing or broken URLs, the library can no longer track the usage of the downloaded material. Libraries seeking to cancel low-use resources may then inadvertently cancel a highly used resource because its statistics do not track copies uploaded directly to the LMS.

PERSONALIZATION

The LTI standard supports integrations that leverage authentication from an LMS system itself to establish personalized sessions for third-party tools without presenting additional log-in screens to users. As Waugh and Frank report, students searching EBSCO Discovery System linked from the LMS would attempt to save materials they were interested in but lose access after their session ended, not realizing they needed to also log in to a second personalized "My EBSCOHost" account.[4] The LTI protocol can alleviate this kind of confusion by communicating information that identifies individual users from a particular institution and links activities done in the LTI tool to that personalized account. In the case of Curriculum Builder, a profile is set up in an institution's EBSCOHost administrative interface to enable interaction with the EBSCOHost application programming interface (API) used with Curriculum Builder. Credentials set up in the EBSCOHost administrative interface are then used when configuring an instance of Curriculum Builder, thus identifying that particular instance of Curriculum Builder with the institutional EBSCOHost profile. Information about users can be anonymized in the LTI application, but the user can be confident that work done organizing or interacting with material in the LTI application will be associated with and saved for her personal use across multiple distinct sessions.

LEARNING ANALYTICS

As Andrews notes, "Academic librarians are increasingly being held accountable for the academic success of students," and responding to this requires librarians to work directly with educators to develop effective pedagogical strategies in information literacy and research instruction.[5] It also requires strategies to understand the impact of library resource usage on learning outcomes. LTI integrations offer significant advantages to libraries seeking to report on the return on investment (ROI) of library collections. LTI applications not only can track and report analytics about usage within the LTI application itself but can also report on usage of materials directly to the LMS. Student actions such as clicking a link can be reported back to the LMS grade book or other usage and assessment mechanisms. Instructors and librarians can create reports and analytics to better understand how materials are being used by their students at both an individual and aggregate level from within the LMS. Of course, tracking user clicks does not necessarily translate into engagement with material or learning outcomes; LTI analytics may show that a student clicked on all required readings, but that does not necessarily mean that he read them.

LTI TECHNICAL ARCHITECTURE

There are four concepts essential to understanding LTI technical architecture (see figure 14.1):

1. The **LTI tool provider (TP):** The tool provider is the resource the user sees when she accesses an application from within the LMS. The Wikipedia LTI app linked above is an example of a tool provider.
2. The **LTI tool consumer (TC):** This is the learning management system (e.g., Blackboard, Moodle, Canvas) from which the user accesses the tool provider application.
3. The **LTI launch:** When a user accesses a tool provider from the tool consumer, this is called "launching" the LTI application. Parameters are passed from the tool consumer to the tool provider, including authorization parameters that ensure the user is permitted to access the application as well as information about the user's identity, his roles within the tool consumer, and the type of request he is sending (e.g., a "content item message" is sent to the tool to indicate that the user is expecting to import a link back to the tool consumer).
4. **OAuth:** LTI applications use OAuth signatures for validating messages between the tool consumer and the tool provider. LTI applications require that the tool consumer and the tool provider have each configured a shared key and secret, which are used to build an OAuth access token to enable communication between the two systems.

LTI applications can be written in a variety of programming languages (for PHP, see https://github.com/IMSGlobal/LTI-Tool-Provider-Library-PHP; for Ruby, see https://github.com/instructure/ims-lti). Most modern LMSs, including Blackboard, Moodle, and Canvas, support the basic LTI protocol while also supporting extensions of that protocol for additional functionality specific to the LMS.

While information about users (including name, e-mail address, what role is in the course, and the class where the link is found) can be exchanged using the protocol, this information does not need to be stored in the LTI tool provider and can be anonymized within the provider as needed to protect user privacy.

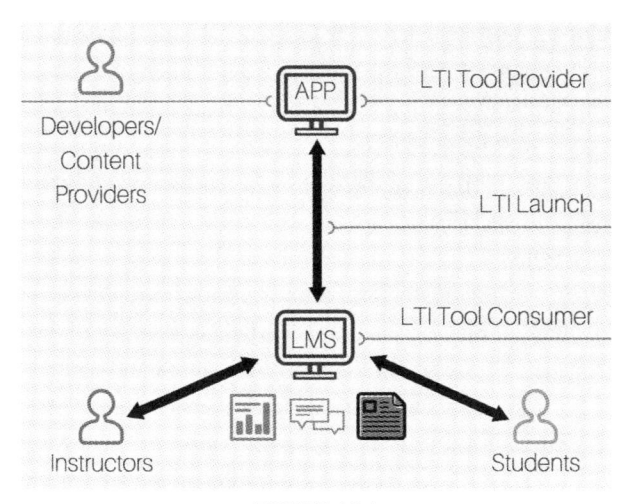

FIGURE 14.1
Technical architecture of LTI applications and LMS integrations.

EXAMPLE LTI TOOLS AND IMPLEMENTATIONS

EBSCO Curriculum Builder at Louisiana State University

Waugh and Frank describe the implementation of EBSCO Curriculum Builder LTI tool at Louisiana State University (LSU), which enables instructors to search EBSCO's Discovery Service (EDS) directly from within the LMS—Moodle, in LSU's use case.[6] EBSCO offers a hosted version of Curriculum Builder, but the code is freely available (https://github.com/ebsco/curriculum_builder), and institutions can install, host, and modify the application to suit their needs. As Waugh and Frank note, the application was built to interact with the EDS API, but similar functionality could be developed with any discovery service API (e.g., Primo or Summon).[7]

EBSCO Curriculum Builder is a PHP/MySQL application. Once installed on a server, the application must be enabled as an authorized external tool in the LMS by an administrator in order for instructors to access it from within their course shells. Educators can then search for materials in an institutionally customizable EDS interface and select materials, which are permalinked for full-text access, access via link resolver, or catalog item availability (for print materials). Instructors can either add a single item or create and save reusable reading lists that contain multiple items. They can also add notes to annotate the items for display in the LMS, providing additional instructions or questions for discussion or reflection.[8]

PART IV: Interoperability

After configuring and launching EBSCO Curriculum Builder at LSU, promotional and training materials for the tool were distributed to all interested library subject liaisons and staff, particularly public services staff and reference librarians. The library also trained staff at a faculty technology support center to help promote and support adoption of the tool by instructors campus wide. Feedback from users was positive, with ease of use and potential cost savings for students cited as primary benefits.[9]

This feedback is consistent with instructor feedback from other implementations of EBSCO's Curriculum Builder, including the first application of the tool at Santa Rosa Junior College.[10] However, instructors at LSU also cited confusion regarding the display of licensing terms and digital rights management (DRM) restrictions in e-books. Download and virtual "checkout" options also caused confusion among instructors and students, as the use of e-book material over the course of a semester is not conducive to built-in digital loan options present on many e-book platforms, which typically represent a short period and require special reading and DRM-management software. In response to confusion over these restrictions, the authors note that LSU began purchasing more DRM-free e-books and university press materials. A prior collection development policy had indicated that the library does not purchase "textbooks," and as Waugh and Frank note, "This systematic approach to disassociating library materials from course materials may partially explain the low adoption rate of the reading list tool."[11]

One significant takeaway from this case study is the importance of repositioning the library not only as a provider of supplementary or research-related resources but as a provider and facilitator of tools and resources that are essential to teaching and learning, including required course materials. This refocusing does not require the library to spend collection funds on traditional, high-cost textbooks (which many library collection development policies, like LSU's, prohibit); instead, the library can partner with instructors to position existing library-licensed resources, open educational resources (OERs), and other scholarly materials as replacements for high-cost materials. Whereas academic libraries have long provided support for both physical and digital course reserves, many academic libraries successfully provide leadership on their campuses for encouraging OER adoption to lower costs for students.[12] LTI enables libraries to curate resources suitable for integration in learning management systems, including OER, digital course reserve material, and other licensed assets. Libraries can build LTI integrations that enable instructors to easily find and organize resources that are suitable for use as required course material (e.g., e-books with unlimited user licenses, perpetual ownership, and

DRM-free titles), which can be transformative in positioning the library as a supplier of essential information that has the potential to dramatically and directly lower costs and facilitate student learning.

Ex Libris Leganto at University of New South Wales

Leganto is Ex Libris's commercial product for course-reading list management, with interfaces both within and outside an LMS, and is designed to work with Ex Libris's Alma library service platform. Leganto features similar functionality to the EBSCO Curriculum Builder in its integration of library resources and permalinks into an LMS, with added features that enable library staff to process materials instructors wish to include on their reading lists that may require copyright clearance, licensing/acquisition, digitization, or other library mediation through Alma. Leganto is a proprietary hosted service, but documentation and configuration requirements for its LTI components are available through the Ex Libris Knowledge Center (https://knowledge.exlibrisgroup.com/Leganto/Product_Documentation/Leganto_Administration_Guide/Configuring_Leganto_Integration_Profiles/Configuring_Learning_Tools_Interoperability_(LTI)).

Neil described the Leganto implementation at the University of New South Wales (UNSW) as driven by four factors: advocacy by instructors, renewed interest in student engagement and the "flipped classroom" model, desire for deeper learning analytics, and the future-oriented strategic plan of the institution.[13] Leganto was employed primarily to support a "self-service" model that would be sustainable

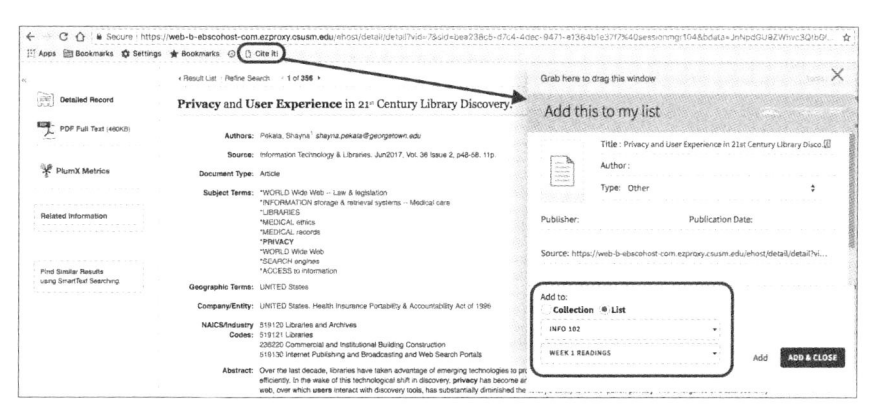

FIGURE 14.2
Leganto's "Cite It!" button enables users to add items to reading lists from within library databases or other compatible websites.

and scalable, benefiting instructors by facilitating easy-to-prepare reading lists, feedback from students, collaboration, copyright and licensing, and analytics. Students benefit from ease of use and access to scholarly materials while being able to organize content interactively with educators. In addition to enabling instructors to create reading lists via the Leganto interface with library content, Leganto features a "Cite It!" bookmarklet (see figure 14.2) that enables users to add freely available web resources or OER to their reading lists.

In 2016, UNSW initiated a staged implementation pilot project of Leganto with nineteen courses in Moodle and fourteen instructors.[14] Feedback from instructors identified issues with authentication and navigation, both of which were resolved by opening Leganto into a new window in Moodle (rather than opening it in an embedded, iframe-like view, which many LTI applications use). Educators also indicated a preference for being able to link to a particular area of a reading list from within their courses, functionality that was not present at the time of the UNSW pilot. Library staff commented on the significant amount of request mediation involved in processing reading lists; at the time of UNSW's pilot, copyright clearance for each individual item required staff intervention, and automation options were limited.

At the conclusion of the pilot implementation, Neil noted that in the short time since learning about Leganto a year earlier, the tool had improved significantly, but integrations between Leganto's LTI component and Alma staff workflows still required additional development.[15] Neil also made the point that Leganto will not necessarily facilitate student engagement on its own; easy-to-find and simplistic course materials must be paired with engaging, effective instructional design to optimize their use.[16] At the time of the pilot, UNSW found that Leganto's features did not accommodate all of the diverse methods instructors use to develop, manage, and display their reading lists, and additional flexibility is needed in the LTI tool to adapt to different pedagogical approaches and methods of engaging students, such as the ability to link dynamically to different parts of an available reading list throughout the course.

While there are many similarities between the EBSCO Curriculum Builder and Leganto, one of the key differences in functionality between the products involves the extent to which Leganto is intertwined with copyright clearance and licensing. These are issues that staff at academic libraries are deeply familiar with, but they still require significant training, resources, and constantly evolving workflows to handle effectively at scale.[17] The implementation of an LTI tool that not only enables integration of library resources with an LMS but also includes the ability to manage copyright compliance and licensing represents an opportunity to engage more directly with users and provide services that patrons may not be accustomed to approaching the library about. UNSW's experiences also illustrate how important detailed, microlevel analytics about usage are; in particular, instructors noted an interest in accessing data about how students engage with a multipage or multichapter resource. (Are students actually reading the whole thing or just clicking the link and exiting without going beyond the first page? How much time are they spending on a resource?) This functionality was not present in Leganto at the time of UNSW's pilot, but it represents the kind of engagement impact metrics instructors expect to be able to use to assess the effectiveness of their course materials.[18]

Springshare LibGuides at Utah State University

Library subject guides are another ubiquitous feature in the landscape of academic libraries, and Springshare's LibGuides system is widely used.[19] Fagerheim et al. discuss how librarians and developers at Utah State University (USU) created and implemented an LTI integration with Springshare's LibGuide system to pull the most relevant research guide directly into courses in the Canvas LMS.[20] The LTI integration matches metadata about the Canvas course with metadata published in the guide to retrieve a relevant subject or course guide. The LTI tool retrieves metadata about course guides via Springshare's API. When a user accesses a "Research Help" link in her guide, the LTI tool performs the lookup to show her the relevant guide based on matching metadata between her current Canvas course and the Springshare API.

Developers at USU also created an interface that used Canvas' built-in analytics functionality, Canvalytics, to track and analyze interactions with the "Research Help" LTI tool.[21] Preliminary quantitative data gathered on LibGuides usage within Canvas indicate that heavy use of research guides from within the CMS generally corresponds to those colleges and disciplines that have the most library instruction activity (at USU, this includes the Colleges of Education and Human Services and Humanities and Social Sciences). Though a "Research Help" LTI link appears by default in all courses, review of analytics data available in Canvas revealed that some instructors had chosen to hide the link. Anecdotal evidence indicated that at least some instructors hid the link not knowing it was a link to library resources, indicating to the authors that subject librarians could play a role in marketing and facilitating promotion of the tool to the instructors with whom they collaborate.[22]

While USU's LTI integration was developed in-house, customers who subscribe to Springshare's LibGuides CMS service have access to an included LTI tool that enables a similar integration, embedding subject and course guides within any

LTI-compliant LMS platform. Springshare's CMS LTI tool also includes analytics within the LTI application itself and can integrate additional Springshare point-of-need services, such as LibChat, LibAnswers FAQs, or room reservations and consultation scheduling through LibCal.[23] After implementing an integration of Springshare's LTI tool at Indiana University, librarians found that referrals to Lib-Guides from their campus LMS (Canvas) increased dramatically despite minimal advertising of the integration by librarians.[24] While this increase was attributed to promotion of the tool by instructors, Lee et al. also found that the overwhelming majority of educators at campuses where the tool was available were not aware of library services embedded into Canvas. At the same time, once informed of the services available, the majority of instructors surveyed indicated they agreed or strongly agreed that they would recommend it to their students. As the authors note, "Faculty mention of Canvas resources may be one of the most important drivers of student use" of embedded library services.[25]

DISCUSSION AND IMPLICATIONS FOR THE FUTURE

Although LTI tools are designed to facilitate self-service and discovery from within an LMS through customization and personalization, training for users and deep integration of existing library services is necessary to maximize engagement with and impact on learning. The correlation of usage of USU's LTI "Research Help" tool with the disciplines that receive the most library instruction is further evidence that the cliché "If you build it, they will come" is not true of passively embedded digital library services, even when those resources are required or recommended by instructors and customized to specific user needs. LTI tools become most useful when required reading materials are organized in a way that motivates student engagement with the materials, such as structuring required reading or resources around focused, explicit homework assignments with extensive instructor feedback;[26] priming students prior to assigning reading with questions or considerations they should keep in mind while doing the reading;[27] and clearly explaining to students the advantages of using the resources.

LTI applications also present academic libraries with an opportunity to lower costs to students and reshape the landscape and workflows of textbook adoption and use of required course materials. Many libraries have taken significant action in facilitating OER adoption and affordable learning initiatives, but that work is often seen as separate from or not directly impacting library collection development. Libraries wishing to further cement their role as campus leaders in lowering textbook costs must actively market the library as a provider of required course materials through its available licensed electronic materials. As Waugh and Frank report, LSU's implementation of EBSCO Curriculum Builder is only a first step in greater collaboration between instructors and the library, and they cite plans for exciting new projects such as facilitating the ability of instructors to search for nonlibrary, DRM-free materials as well as request materials for purchase directly through the reading list management workflow.[28] In order for other libraries to follow LSU's groundbreaking work in this area, many institutions will have to rethink their collection development policies. Improved metadata and display of licensing terms and restrictions can also facilitate instructor adoption of library materials as required course materials, and library liaisons may play a more direct role in instructional design and helping educators integrate library resources effectively into their curriculum.

LTI integrations also have the potential to generate rich analytics about user behavior and engagement with library materials embedded in an LMS. The technical infrastructure and data necessary to create meaningful analytics reporting on this subject are available in LTI applications, but effectively operationalizing this data and identifying actionable strategies from them are still on the horizon. Connecting data about usage of library materials with learning-assessment metrics available from the LMS is an area that could hold a significant amount of promise for librarians who are interested in understanding the ROI of library collections and research guides.

LTI facilitates the kind of flexible personalization and analytics that EDUCAUSE has described as essential to "Next Generation Digital Learning Environments" (NGDLE).[29] However, in order for LTI integrations to be successful and transformative to both library services and student learning, implementation must be thoughtfully coordinated with instructor outreach and training, embedded library instruction, and existing course reserve services and library collection development. Merely because a student has the opportunity to discover required course materials or subject guides in his LMS doesn't mean that he will use them or that he will take full advantage of those materials to enhance his learning. Libraries interested in LTI integrations must continue to work with vendors or develop in-house improvements to LTI-enabled user interfaces and information organization, ensure that instructors have the knowledge and ability to effectively embed resources in their curriculum, and make sure that personalized features closely meet the research and instruction needs of users through continual assessment of LTI implementations.

PART IV: Interoperability

NOTES

1. Raj Kishor Kampa, "Bridging the Gap: Integrating the Library into Moodle Learning Management System: A Study," *Library Hi Tech News* 34, no. 4 (2017): 16–21, https://doi.org/10.1108/LHTN-11-2016-0055.
2. Carl R. Andrews, "Embedded Librarianship: Best Practices Explored and Redefined," *International Journal of Educational Organization and Leadership* 22, no. 2 (2015): 1–14, https://academicworks.cuny.edu/bx_pubs/3/.
3. Mike Waugh and Emily Frank, "Integrating the Library and E-learning: Implementing a Library Reading List Tool in the Learning Management System," in *E-learning and the Academic Library: Essays on Innovative Initiatives,* ed. Scott Rice and Margaret Gregor (Jefferson, NC: McFarland, 2016), 103–14.
4. Waugh and Frank, 105.
5. Carl R. Andrews, "An Examination of Embedded Librarian Ideas and Practices: A Critical Bibliography," *Codex* 3, no. 1 (2014): 69–87.
6. Waugh and Frank, "Integrating the Library," 105–11.
7. Waugh and Frank, 103.
8. Waugh and Frank, 108.
9. Waugh and Frank, 112.
10. Eric Frierson and Alicia Virtue, "Integrating Academic Library Services Directly into Classroom Instruction through Discovery Tools," *Computers in Libraries* 33, no. 7 (2013): 4–9.
11. Waugh and Frank, "Integrating the Library," 113.
12. Joseph Salem, "Open Pathways to Student Success: Academic Library Partnerships for Open Educational Resource and Affordable Course Content Creation and Adoption," *Journal of Academic Librarianship* 43, no. 1 (2017): 34–38, https://doi.org/10.1016/j.acalib.2016.10.003; Laurie Borchard and Lauren Magnuson, "Library Leadership in Open Educational Resource Adoption and Affordable Learning Initiatives," *Urban Library Journal* 23, no. 1 (2017), https://academicworks.cuny.edu/ulj/v0123/iss1/1.
13. Alison Neil, "A Semester with Leganto at UNSW Australia: Measuring Impact and Experiences" (paper presented at the ELUNA 2016 annual meeting, Oklahoma City, OK, May 3–6, 2016).
14. Neil.
15. Neil.
16. Neil.
17. Neil.
18. Deborah H. Charbonneau and Michael Priehs, "Copyright Awareness, Partnerships, and Training Issues in Academic Libraries," *Journal of Academic Librarianship* 40, nos. 3–4 (2014): 228–33, https://doi.org/10.1016/j.acalib.2014.03.009.

19. Michelle Dalton and Rosalind Pan, "Snakes or Ladders? Evaluating a LibGuides Pilot at UCD Library," *Journal of Academic Librarianship* 40, no. 5 (2014): 515–20, https://doi.org/10.1016/j.acalib.2014.05.006.

20. Britt Fagerheim, Kacy Lundstrom, Erin Davis, and Dory Cochran, "Extending Our Reach: Automatic Integration of Course and Subject Guides," *Reference & User Services Quarterly* 56, no. 3 (2017): 180–88, https://doi.org/10.5860/rusq.56n3.180.

21. Fagerheim et al., 184.

22. Fagerheim et al., 188.

23. "LTI: Take a Tour of LibGuides & Courseware Integration," SpringyNews, 2016, https://buzz.springshare.com/springynews/news-31/lti.

24. Yoo Young Lee, Sara Lowe, Courtney McDonald, and Meg Meiman, "Embedding Research Guides at Point of Need Using LibGuides LTI," *InULA Notes* 29, no. 1 (2017): 14–18, https://scholarworks.iu.edu/journals/index.php/inula/article/view/23560.

25. Lee et al., 16.

26. Tracey E. Ryan, "Motivating Novice Students to Read Their Textbooks," *Journal of Instructional Psychology* 33, no. 2 (2006): 135–40.

27. David Gooblar, "They Haven't Done the Reading. Again," *Pedagogy Unbound* (blog), *Chronicle Vitae*, September 24, 2014, https://chroniclevitae.com/news/719-they-haven-t-done-the-reading-again.

28. Waugh and Frank, "Integrating the Library," 113.

29. Malcolm Brown, Joanne Dehoney, and Nancy Millichap, "What's Next for the LMS?," *EDUCAUSE Review* 50, no. 4 (2015), https://er.educause.edu/articles/2015/6/whats-next-for-the-lms.

BIBLIOGRAPHY

Andrews, Carl R. "Embedded Librarianship: Best Practices Explored and Redefined." *International Journal of Educational Organization and Leadership* 22, no. 2 (2015): 1–14. https://academicworks.cuny.edu/bx_pubs/3/.

———. "An Examination of Embedded Librarian Ideas and Practices: A Critical Bibliography." *Codex* 3, no. 1 (2014): 69–87.

Borchard, Laurie, and Lauren Magnuson. "Library Leadership in Open Educational Resource Adoption and Affordable Learning Initiatives." *Urban Library Journal* 23, no. 1 (2017). https://academicworks.cuny.edu/ulj/v0123/iss1/1.

Brown, Malcolm, Joanne Dehoney, and Nancy Millichap. "What's Next for the LMS?" *EDUCAUSE Review* 50, no. 4 (2015). https://er.educause.edu/articles/2015/6/whats-next-for-the-lms.

Charbonneau, Deborah, and Michael Priehs. "Copyright Awareness, Partnerships, and Training Issues in Academic Libraries." *Journal of Academic Librarianship* 40, nos. 3–4 (2014): 228–33. http://digitalcommons.wayne.edu/slisfrp/123.

Dalton, Michelle, and Rosalind Pan. "Snakes or Ladders? Evaluating a LibGuides Pilot at UCD Library." *Journal of Academic Librarianship* 40, no. 5 (2014): 515–20.

Fagerheim, Britt, Kacy Lundstrom, Erin Davis, and Dory Cochran. "Extending Our Reach: Automatic Integration of Course and Subject Guides." *Reference & User Services Quarterly* 56, no. 3 (2017): 180–88.

Frierson, Eric, and Alicia Virtue. "Integrating Academic Library Services Directly into Classroom Instruction through Discovery Tools." *Computers in Libraries* 33, no. 7 (2013): 4–9.

Gooblar, David. "They Haven't Done the Reading. Again." *Pedagogy Unbound* (blog), *Chronicle Vitae*, September 24, 2014. https://chroniclevitae.com/news/719-they-haven-t-done-the-reading-again.

Kampa, Raj Kishor. "Bridging the Gap: Integrating the Library into Moodle Learning Management System: A Study." *Library Hi Tech News* 34, no. 4 (2017): 16–21.

Lee, Yoo Young, Sara Lowe, Courtney McDonald, and Meg Meiman. "Embedding Research Guides at Point of Need Using LibGuides LTI." *InULA Notes* 29, no. 1 (2017). https://scholarworks.iu.edu/journals/index.php/inula/article/view/23560.

Neil, Alison. "A Semester with Leganto at UNSW Australia: Measuring Impact and Experiences." Paper presented at the ELUNA 2016 annual meeting, Oklahoma City, OK, May 3–6, 2016.

Ryan, Tracey E. "Motivating Novice Students to Read Their Textbooks." *Journal of Instructional Psychology* 33, no. 2 (2006): 135–40.

Salem, Joseph. "Open Pathways to Student Success: Academic Library Partnerships for Open Educational Resource and Affordable Course Content Creation and Adoption." *Journal of Academic Librarianship* 43, no. 1 (2017): 34–38.

Waugh, Mike, and Emily Frank. "Integrating the Library and E-learning: Implementing a Library Reading List Tool in the Learning Management System." In *E-learning and the Academic Library: Essays on Innovative Initiatives,* edited by Scott Rice and Margaret Gregor, 103–14. Jefferson, NC: McFarland, 2016.

Chapter Fifteen

Bots and the Library
Exploring New Possibilities for Automation and Engagement

Jeanette Claire Sewell

"Hello, how can I help you?" is a common phrase that has become a universal library standard and a cornerstone value for why librarians enter the field. Whether greeting patrons at the reference desk or making resources available behind the scenes, librarians have a ubiquitous drive to help. Libraries have also continuously automated many processes and adapted to the rapidly evolving digital information landscape. Internet bots (referred to generally as bots going forward) are a popular software resource that can be added easily to any library's existing collection of services.

You and your patrons probably already interact with bots on a daily basis. We wear them to track our physical activity, chat with them to navigate around town, and use them to order takeout from nearby restaurants. You may also be wary of bots due to news stories of those created with malicious intent, but the truth is that libraries have been using bot-like processes for some time now. From a technical services perspective, cataloging staff have utilized macros within the Online

PART IV: Interoperability

Computer Library Center (OCLC) and other applications to automate classification tasks, and MarcEdit is now widely used to batch edit MARC files via task lists. Libraries also use automated services to notify patrons of things such as due dates and overdue notices with text messages and phone calls. Further, IT staff, systems librarians, and web developers are increasingly involved in writing application programming interfaces (APIs) to improve data access in integrated library systems (ILS), the online public access catalog (OPAC), and other functions. The widespread use of existing automation tasks like these enable libraries to implement bots in ways that can benefit both staff and the community.

Bots can be written in a wide variety of coding languages and often have specific, targeted purposes. This makes bot creation ideal for both librarians who understand macros and task lists and those who may not be as experienced with more advanced code-writing practices. Integrating bots within library services can help increase the value of libraries as leaders in new technology adoption and user-centered services.

This chapter will define and discuss various types of bots and their uses and applications and explore ways that libraries can incorporate bot technology to enhance existing services.

WHAT ARE BOTS?

Bot is a shortened form of the term *robot* (coined by Karel Čapek in his 1920 play *R.U.R.*), which usually describes programmed, automatic machines with a larger physical presence. According to the Botwiki website (https://botwiki.org), "in essence, an online bot is a program that does something a human would otherwise do, like post pictures on Tumblr or retweet Tweets that talk about cats." While this definition makes light of one type of Internet bot, "specifically, a bot is an application that performs an automated task, such as setting an alarm, telling you the weather or searching online," among many other possible tasks.[1] Many types of bots operate solely on the Internet, whereas others are connected to a physical device. Wikipedia is also well known for using bots to handle quality control and editing tasks of its community-created entries. Some bots even interact with each other across devices and websites, but the key phrase that ties all types of bots together is *automated task*.

A type of bot that most people are familiar with is the chat bot. Early, basic chat bots have roots in text-based computer games in which gameplay progresses

Chapter Fifteen: Bots and the Library

through command phrases or sentences.[2] The first chat bot to incorporate features such as natural-language processing that are used by many chat bots today was ELIZA. Invented in the mid-1960s, ELIZA was designed to interact with people by answering questions in a manner resembling psychotherapy. The appearance of intelligent conversation fooled many people at the time into thinking ELIZA was human, but like most bots even today, the system relied on scripted responses triggered by keywords. As the Internet grew to include websites that function as marketplaces, chat bots then began to find a home as virtual customer service representatives.

Throughout the 1990s and early 2000s, bots also became popular tools for searching the Internet, blocking pop-up windows and spam, and managing e-mail, among other task-oriented functions. Today, many of these functions have become subsumed by browser extensions, but the BotSpot website (earlier versions are accessible via the Internet Archive's Wayback Machine) provides a fascinating glimpse into the evolution of bots.[3] These earlier bots also point to more sophisticated web scraping that can be accomplished today using Python and a variety of methods to create unique datasets.[4]

Depending on the specific tasks that bots perform, they may also be referred to as voice-activated bots, intelligent personal assistants, or some combination thereof. As smartphones and apps gained widespread use, particularly Apple's iPhone, one of the first voice-activated intelligent personal assistants that people interacted with was Siri. Functioning within the iPhone's operating system, Siri combines a variety of bot processes, from making phone calls and dictating text messages to searching apps and the Internet. The resulting popularity of Siri led to the implementation of other voice-activated personal assistants across the competitive cell phone provider market. Devices such as Amazon's Alexa–enabled Dot and Echo and the Google Home have also expanded these abilities to the home environment. Although all of these assistants can perform similar tasks, a significant recent development is the ability to control other smart-enabled home objects, such as light bulbs, speakers, or thermostats. They can also interact with other virtual assistants. For instance, Microsoft announced in August 2017 that its virtual assistant for the Windows operating system, Cortana, would be interoperable with Alexa-enabled devices.[5]

Bots also now occupy extensive space within the universe of social media and other collaborative websites. The Botwiki also notes that "bots can be funny, useful, artistic—but also annoying and spammy." That last type of bot is one that has attracted a great deal of press and attention in recent years, particularly on social media, for helping spread misinformation. It is important to be aware of

PART IV: Interoperability

the existence of malicious bots and acknowledge concerns that libraries may have about them, but history shows that creators have primarily been dedicated to designing helpful bots. In 2016, Facebook opened its Messenger platform to developers to create chat bots.[6] The service is primarily used by businesses for customer service engagement, but other uses include news updates and games. Twitter is also a popular social media platform for bots and one that is particularly fascinating due to the variety of bots that exist there. Many Twitter bot accounts post automated tweets of news updates and other aggregated content, but there are also more creative bots that tweet everything from generative art to self-care reminders. You can even tweet an emoji to the New York Public Library's NYPL Emoji Bot (https://twitter.com/NYPLEmoji), and it will respond with an image from their digital collections based on the emoji's text character representation.

Collaboration-focused websites such as Slack (https://slack.com) have also implemented bots for task automation. Slack "is a cloud-based set of proprietary team collaboration tools and services" launched in 2013 and is now widely used by technology development companies.[7] On the surface, Slack has the appearance of a chat room, where users start discussions and ask questions in a scrolling, threaded format; however, Slack is unique in that it offers team work spaces with channels and workflows that can be individually customized with bots. Within Slack, bots can perform tasks as simple as moving a post from one channel to another within a work space to more complex actions like time tracking and project management or even assistance with management of Gmail, Office 365, or Dropbox accounts. The relative ease with which bots can be developed and integrated across websites and devices has made them very popular. As Microsoft's CEO, Satya Nadella, noted, "bots are the new apps," and companies are actively working to incorporate them into their existing software to reduce the number of steps between tasks and increase productivity.[8] Companies are also increasingly using chat bots on social media for marketing purposes and to increase sales. Of course, it is important to discern that libraries will have different needs and goals for bots than those of profit-driven companies, but common ground is found in the focus on user-centered task automation.

HOW DO BOTS WORK?

Bots can be simple or complex, but they generally share the following characteristics:

- tasks, processes, statements, or responses to automate

Chapter Fifteen: Bots and the Library

- a stored or hosted script that tells the bot what to do
- interaction with an API or other software system

The impetus to create a bot is often driven by the need to simplify some order of operations or procedures through automation. A series of tasks, processes, statements, or responses is usually identified as the first step. Many bots operate within one platform to perform specific tasks, but increasingly, bots interact with multiple platforms and even with other bots to automate a variety of actions. Bots such as chat bots and voice-activated assistants also include statements and responses to create conversational experiences with users.

One of the biggest advantages to designing bots is that they can be written in a variety of coding languages. If there is a language that you are already familiar with, chances are you can use it to create a bot. Python and JavaScript are two popular languages frequently used for writing bot scripts. JavaScript Object Notation (JSON) is often added "to represent data in a simple, human-readable format" that will become the bot's automated content.[9] Bot devices like the Amazon Echo also usually require a specialized script that is directly related to a company's proprietary interface.

In order to deliver content, a bot also needs to interact with an API or other software system. This typically involves setting up a developer account with the website on which a bot will run to gain access to user-specific keys and tokens. These necessary elements of the script allow a bot to perform its automated tasks. At this point in the process, it is a good idea to become familiar with any policies or restrictions with which your bot must comply. The most important of these are rate and activity limits, or how often your bot is allowed to interact with external servers or software systems. For instance, Twitter has an API rate limit of three hundred posts per one-minute window.[10] Anything beyond this limit will likely result in account suspension. Different APIs and software systems will each have their own limits, and it is necessary to account for them in any bot script. Some free options for making bots, such as Zach Whalen's "How to Make a Twitter Bot with Google Spreadsheets" (www.zachwhalen.net/posts/how-to-make-a-twitter-bot-with-google-spreadsheets-version-04/), include built-in options for post timing; however, scripts written from scratch will need to utilize a scheduling file such as Crontab to manage the timing of posts or other bot actions.[11] Although there are many free or low-cost options for building bots, costs can occur depending on factors such as the use of specific platforms, where the script for a bot is hosted, and data allowances. Thorough investigation and planning are vital with any bot project so that potential costs—including staff time and labor—are effectively managed. More information about the Google spreadsheet method and other tools for creating bots can be found in the "Bot Tool Kit" text box.

Moving forward, bots are well positioned to continue to evolve alongside new websites and devices. They will become more sophisticated as developers and creators incorporate elements like artificial intelligence (AI) and machine learning along with enhanced voice recognition.

BOTS IN LIBRARIES

While libraries are continuously engaged in automation processes, bots are still an emerging technology in most library environments. Cataloging and technical services staff members who work in the OCLC Connexion Client or with MarcEdit may be more familiar with how bots operate than they initially realize if they have worked with macros. Macros "are short programs you write to automate routine tasks."[12] Within Connexion, librarians can install preexisting macros or write their own as needed to perform essential tasks, such as inserting Resource Description and Access (RDA) 33X MARC fields or supplying the Cutter figure in a call number. Additionally, in MarcEdit, librarians can create specialized task lists to batch edit and process record sets. While these processes are confined to the software in which they operate and do not interact with the Internet, they do share similarities in task automation with bots.

Some of the first Internet bots created by libraries were chat bots attempting to serve as reference assistants. In 2002, librarians at Robert Morris College (now Robert Morris University) created Sylvie, a humorously scripted chat bot "who handled ready-reference and directional questions to free up staff for more challenging questions."[13] Following budget cuts in 2009, the Mentor Public Library of Ohio launched a similar chat bot named Emma.[14] In 2010, the University of Nebraska–Lincoln also developed a reference assistant chat bot, Pixel, using Artificial Intelligence Markup Language (AIML) with "metadata [that] supports the ability to 'chain' a conversation" with users.[15] This is the process in which users query a chat bot, and it responds with answers or additional questions based on the information in the bot's database. Interestingly, these chat bots each employed a virtual avatar resembling a person (or, in the case of the Mentor Public Library, a cat), a feature that is largely absent from the bot landscape today, as the trend has migrated more toward text-based conversations and voice-activated assistants. As the focus in bot development has shifted to making conversational experiences more natural, users (especially digital natives) now seem to innately understand these types of interactions without the need for an avatar.

Chapter Fifteen: Bots and the Library

Bots have also been cited following the 2016 US presidential election for spreading misinformation and fake news. It is important to note that bots, in those instances, function on a much broader scale by interacting with many other bots and devices (often referred to as a botnet) to spread malicious content across the Internet and social media websites. Despite this, bots are generally perceived as good if they are operated by an already trustworthy source, such as the *New York Times's* Facebook Messenger bot, NYT Politics Bot, which provided real-time election updates in 2016, or the *Los Angeles Times's* LA QuakeBot (https://twitter.com/earthquakesLA), which tweets updates from the US Geological Survey Earthquake Hazards Program.[16] Similarly, bots can be used to promote library services and engage patrons in positive interactions. According to a 2016 study by the Pew Research Center, "a large majority of Millennials (87%) say the library helps them find information that is trustworthy and reliable."[17] In fact, although there are frequent news reports and a growing body of research focused on bots that spread misinformation on social media, many libraries, archives, and digital repositories already allow bot accounts to use their publicly available data and APIs to promote their unique resources on Twitter. The DPLA Bot (https://twitter.com/DPLAbot) and NYPL Postcard Bot (https://twitter.com/NYPLpostcards) are two examples. These types of Twitter bots passively post tweets that include an image and a corresponding link to the associated digital repository according to a preset schedule, usually three to four times a day. Both institutions also publish information about their public domain datasets and APIs on GitHub. Fondren Library at Rice University created Ted, the Fondren Bot (https://twitter.com/Ted_Fondren_bot), as an experiment in using a Twitter bot to promote general library services, research tips, and links to other campus activities. The Woodson Research Center Special Collections and Archives also created its Woodson Research Center (https://twitter.com/WoodsonRC_bot) Twitter bot to promote historical images from the Fondren Library digital repository. As Scott Carlson, creator of the Woodson Research Center bot, states, "The general public doesn't understand what cool things can be found in digital repositories and archives, much less know they exist. We can work to change that by putting our collections out there in a public setting for people to discover."[18] Twitter bots are especially useful to libraries and archives because they help automate the promotion of resources to audiences who might otherwise be unlikely to interact with content directly on an institution's website.

In September 2017, the Library of Congress launched its Labs website (https://labs.loc.gov) as "a place to encourage innovation with Library of Congress digital collections." It features the "LC for Robots" page that provides links to its APIs and other open data sets that are freely available for anyone to use. This is a big step toward legitimizing bot services and usage in libraries because the Library of Congress is a trusted and well-established institution. As an emerging and evolving technology, bot usage has great potential across platforms to impact and improve libraries.

IDEAS AND POSSIBILITIES

With so many websites, platforms, and devices to use with bots, it can be overwhelming to know where to begin. There are exciting possibilities for creative and useful implementation of bots in all areas of the library.

Bots for Library Instruction and Outreach

Two things libraries do exceptionally well are teach classes and provide outreach that fits the needs of the communities they serve. Bots are perfect projects for coding classes because they accomplish specific tasks rather than something conceptual on a larger scale, such as building a website. Students can approach bots from whichever platform they find most comfortable, whether it is their cell phone or Twitter. Libraries have embraced makerspaces in recent years and created other exclusively tech-focused spaces with more innovative computer equipment such as audio recording and editing software. Bot-focused coding classes can enable patrons to create or modify bots that are uniquely helpful to their own lives. In the same way that the makerspace at Harris County Public Library's Freeman Branch created a 3-D printed prosthetic hand for a five-year-old girl, so might a user attend a coding class to build an Alexa skill for their family or a Facebook chat bot for their start-up business.[19]

As another option, libraries could offer classes that teach patrons how to connect voice-activated assistants to other smart devices through the If This Then That (IFTTT) platform (https://ifttt.com) to accomplish tasks such as turning on the lights or even brewing coffee. Additionally, libraries could collaborate with existing organizations such as the Front Porch Center for Innovation and Wellbeing to provide technology outreach for senior citizens and create more accessibility options.[20] The Central Library branch of the Austin Public Library, for instance, added a Technology Petting Zoo in 2018 that includes a Google Home device, among others, that patrons can explore.[21]

Bot Tool Kit

Whether you are interested in chat bots, Twitter bots, or just want to learn more, the following resources will guide you in creating a range of bots for your library.

The Botwiki is a one-stop shop for information, tools, and tutorials about bots. On the "Explore" page, you can browse bots by category or network to get ideas for what might work best for your library or project. The Botwiki also links to bot directories and a page of essays and articles for further research. Additionally, the team behind the wiki also runs the Botmakers group on Slack, where you can ask questions, get feedback, and see what other creators are up to. Go to https://botwiki.org.

Codecademy offers free, interactive courses in Python, JavaScript, Ruby, and other programming languages that are frequently used for coding bots. You can even learn how to build an Alexa Skill to work with Amazon devices. Codecademy is great for visual and kinesthetic learners because you work through the steps in a code editor as you navigate through courses at your own pace. Go to www.codecademy.com.

Zach Whalen's Google spreadsheet for Twitter bots is a great place to start if you are interested in creating a Twitter bot but have less experience with coding and programming. If you can work with a spreadsheet in Google Drive, then you can make a Twitter bot using this free and straightforward method. Simply copy the spreadsheet into your own Drive account, add content and Twitter app information, and choose from preset timing options. Go to www.zachwhalen.net/posts/how-to-make-a-twitter-bot-with-google-spreadsheets-version-04/.

Cheap Bots Done Quick is another resource for Twitter bots, but this time you will use a JavaScript library called Tracery to combine text with generative grammar rules. Tracery's creator, Kate Compton, also provides interactive tutorials on her Crystal Code Palace website. You can then host and run your Tracery script from the Cheap Bots Done Quick website for free. This is a fun method to use alongside text mining projects to create bots that tell inventive stories. Go to https://cheapbotsdonequick.com and www.crystalcodepalace.com/traceryTut.html.

Glitch is a free website that lets you copy, remix, and host code to create your own applications. It has become popular with bot makers because it includes a built-in code editor that allows you to easily modify existing creative projects for a variety of platforms, including Slack and Facebook. Some features are also similar to GitHub. Go to https://glitch.com.

Pandorabots offers a free web service for creating chat bots using AIML. The website provides a straightforward tutorial and a sandbox environment to help you get started. Pandorabots is used by Twitter and Slack, among others. Go to www.pandorabots.com.

Designing Bots: Creating Conversational Experiences by Amir Shevat. Shevat is the current head of developer relations at Slack, and his book is a great resource if you are interested in creating chat bots. This book can help you get started with the principles of designing effective conversational models to create a chat bot that will be engaging and helpful to library patrons. Go to your local library or http://shop.oreilly.com/product/0636920057741.do.

Bots for Internal Library Communication

While bots can do many things, they cannot replace the valuable human-centered services provided by librarians. However, certain types of bots could be very useful in assisting frontline staff to better serve patrons. Although we have seen that earlier chat bots did not catch on in the long term, this type of reference assistance could be utilized within Facebook Messenger to provide answers to frequently asked questions faster and more efficiently. Bots could also be used to streamline workflows and increase communication and collaboration between departments, particularly with Slack. As libraries integrate new processes, update standards, and migrate data, libraries could incorporate Slack in more diverse ways to increase productivity and facilitate teamwork.

Bots for Fun Library Services and Events

The popularity of websites like Goodreads combined with book clubs and readers' advisories could lead to the creation of a chat bot like And Chill (www.andchill.io/) that would suggest books and other materials to check out. Further, Botnik Studios (www.botnik.org) is a new "community of writers, artists and developers collaborating with machines to create strange new things" by combining text with live-performance art events. A similar initiative could add a fun, interactive element to a bot-coding class, especially for teens. Open mic or slam bot poetry night, anyone?

Bots for Civic Causes beyond the Library

Bots like DoNotPay (https://donotpay-search-master.herokuapp.com) "help users tackle issues in 1,000 legal areas entirely for free." Resistbot (https://resistbot.io/) is a text messaging bot that helps users contact their elected officials. These bots work to bring people together around a common cause. Twitter bots like the @BikeDTLABot could also be developed by patrons to encourage the use of local civic services such as bike shares.

CONCLUSION

Integrating bots within library services can increase the value of libraries as leaders in new technology adoption and user-centered services. As patrons continue to integrate bot devices into their everyday lives and STEM programs inspire the next generation of technologically focused students, libraries can follow the trend by offering free coding classes and discovery spaces. Many bots and apps are created because a developer identifies a specific need, and it makes sense to envision future libraries as places where patrons can learn coding skills to create customized bots for their individual needs. As libraries continue to experiment with including new technologies, such as virtual reality headsets, it is also important to consider how bots may interact with these services. Further, implementation of linked open data when combined with APIs could create the need for bots to help with automation of data structures.

While it is unlikely that librarians or library services will be replaced by bots soon (or ever), it is reasonable to expect that, as in many other industries, librarians will increasingly be working alongside bots in the years to come. Bot creation and usage in libraries offer the unique opportunity to bring groups together: coders, creators, teachers, learners, activists, and customers. Anybody can benefit from some type of bot through the agency of the library.

The world of bots is a fascinating and rapidly evolving place. Creators will continue to respond to demand for convenience and accessibility across devices and the Internet, and bots will also evolve as more sophisticated AI and natural-language processing abilities are incorporated.

NOTES

1. Sarah Mitroff, "What Is a Bot?," *CNET,* May 5, 2016, www.cnet.com/how-to/what-is-a-bot/.
2. Andrew Leonard, "A Plague of Barneys," in *Bots: The Origin of New Species* (San Francisco: HardWired, 1997), 1–13.
3. "Summary of Botspot.com," Internet Archive Wayback Machine, accessed February 5, 2018, https://web.archive.org/web/*/http://botspot.com.
4. Jonathan E. Germann, "Approaching the Largest 'API': Extracting Information from the Internet with Python," *Code4Lib Journal,* no. 39 (February 2018), http://journal.code4lib.org/articles/13197.
5. Andrew Shuman, "Hey Cortana, Open Alexa: Microsoft and Amazon's First-of-Its-Kind Collaboration," *Official Microsoft Blog,* August 30, 2017, https://blogs.microsoft.com/blog/2017/08/30/hey-cortana-open-alexa-microsoft-amazons-first-kind-collaboration/.
6. Seth Rosenberg, "How to Build Bots for Messenger," *Facebook for Developers* (blog), April 12, 2016, https://developers.facebook.com/blog/post/2016/04/12/bots-for-messenger/.
7. "Slack (Software)," Wikipedia, last modified January 27, 2018, https://en.wikipedia.org/wiki/Slack_(software).

PART IV: Interoperability

8. Matthew Reynolds, "Microsoft Is Betting That Bots 'Are the New Apps,'" *Wired,* October 4, 2017, www.wired.co.uk/article/microsoft-build-bots-ai-cortana-keynote-conference.
9. Fasih Khatib, "Non-techie's Guide to Building Bots. Part 1," *Chatbots Magazine,* April 28, 2016, https://chatbotsmagazine.com/non-techies-guide-to-building-bots-part-1-286bc93c92f9.
10. "Rate Limiting," Twitter Developer, n.d., https://developer.twitter.com/en/docs/ads/general/guides/rate-limiting.
11. Paul Vixie, "Crontab(5)," Crontab, January 24, 1994, http://crontab.org.
12. "Basics: Use Macros," Online Computer Library Center (OCLC), last modified June 2016, www.oclc.org/content/dam/support/connexion/documentation/client/basics/macros/macros.pdf.
13. Brian C. Smith, "In Search of Blessed Bots," *School Library Journal* (Spring 2002): 34–35.
14. Michele McNeal and David Newyear, "Chatbots: Automating Reference in Public Libraries," in *Robots in Academic Libraries: Advancements in Automation* (Hershey: Information Science Reference, 2013), 101–14.
15. DeeAnn Allison, "Chatbots in the Library: Is It Time?," *Library Hi Tech* 30, no. 1 (2012): 95–107, https://doi.org/10.1108/07378831211213238.
16. Joseph Lichterman, "The New York Times Is Using a Facebook Messenger Bot to Send Out Election Updates," *NiemanLab,* October 20, 2016, www.niemanlab.org/2016/10/the-new-york-times-is-using-a-facebook-messenger-bot-to-send-out-election-updates/.
17. Abigail Geiger, "Most Americans—Especially Millennials—Say Libraries Can Help Them Find Reliable, Trustworthy Information," Pew Research Center, August 30, 2017, www.pewresearch.org/fact-tank/2017/08/30/most-americans-especially-millennials-say-libraries-can-help-them-find-reliable-trustworthy-information/.
18. Scott Carlson, "You Should Make a Twitter Bot for Your Digital Collection(s)," *Scott Carlson* (blog), n.d., www.scottcarlson.info/you-should-make-a-twitter-bot/.
19. Robert Arnold, "Clear Lake Library 3D Printing Lab Helps 5-Year-Old-Girl Get New Hand," last modified August 19, 2016, www.click2houston.com/news/investigates/parents-search-to-find-prosthetic-hand-for-daughter-ends-at-library.
20. Elizabeth Woyke, "The Octogenarians Who Love Amazon's Alexa," *MIT Technology Review,* June 9, 2017, www.technologyreview.com/s/608047/the-octogenarians-who-love-amazons-alexa/.
21. Omar L. Gallaga, "At Austin Central Library, Hands-On Gadget Time Drives the Tech Petting Zoo," *Statesman,* last modified September 24, 2018, www.512tech.com/technology/austin-central-library-hands-gadget-time-drives-the-tech-petting-zoo/mBU2Ik9qSJM6D7ATXNhjKO/.

Chapter Sixteen

Machine Learning for Libraries

Alan Darnell

As humans, we have an intuitive idea of what it means to learn. It is something we do throughout our lives, from the time we are born until the day we die. We learn as infants to walk and talk, as children to read and write, and as adults to perform the day-to-day but complex tasks required of living and making a living. Underlying these learned skills are capabilities for memorization, rational thinking, interpreting what our senses are telling us, and making judgments about the possible risks and benefits of our actions. Learning is an aspect of what we think about when we think about what it is to be an intelligent being. And intelligence is an important part of what we mean when we talk about consciousness.[1]

What do we mean, then, when we talk about machines—specifically computers—that can learn? Machines are neither conscious nor intelligent. We know that computers can be programmed to perform many functions that were once thought to be solely in the domain of humans: playing chess, for example, or vacuuming the floor. But the instructions to perform those functions are created by programmers. Any learning or understanding is embedded in the code they create. If machine learning (ML) is something different than programming, how is it different, and how does it compare to the way humans learn?

The most-cited formal definition of ML was proposed by Tom M. Mitchell of Carnegie Mellon University: "A computer is said to learn from experience E with respect to some class of tasks T and performance measure P, if its performance at tasks in T, as measured by P, improves with experience E."[2] As with most formal definitions, this encapsulates everything but explains little. In this chapter, my first goal is to provide an operational understanding of what ML is by looking at its development as a field of study within the broader discipline of artificial intelligence (AI). This will involve a high-level overview of its methods and algorithms (no math required). I will focus on the applications of ML to problems that have occupied AI research for decades—speech recognition, natural-language processing, machine translation, and image recognition—the so-called hard problems of AI, and I will try to explain what is so different about the approaches of ML, in particular the use of artificial neural networks, from methods used in "Good Old-Fashioned Artificial Intelligence," or GOFAI.[3]

Understanding how technology works, at least at an abstract level, is fundamental to being able to assess its value and its implications. I think that it is important for every socially engaged librarian to learn enough about ML to be able to assess the debates that surround it, the literature about which is extensive and growing. My second goal in this chapter, in keeping with the theme of the book as a whole, will be to explore the use of ML for solving practical problems of interest to libraries and to speculate on what effects it might have on the future of library practice and our profession. How might machine learning shape the nature of work in our profession and the kinds of services we are able to provide to our communities? And what actions can librarians take to ensure that machine learning promotes the values that we share as a professional community: the importance of openness and equitable access to information in the support of a democratic society and the vital importance of preserving our shared cultural heritage for future generations?

TEACHING MACHINES USING SYMBOLS

As soon as scientists and engineers began constructing digital computers in the middle of the last century, they also began speculating on the possibility of computers becoming intelligent. Alan Turing published a seminal paper in 1950 in which he describes a testable measure of intelligence called the "imitation game," a simple experimental tool that has come to be known as the Turing test.[4] Turing's idea of machine intelligence focused on outward behavior as assessed by acknowledged intelligent beings (humans, in this case) rather than exploring the intent or self-awareness of the system being measured. If it walks and talks like a human, then it is fair to say that it operates with human intelligence. This has had a profound influence on thinking about what it means for a computer to be intelligent, and the Turing test has not been displaced as the measure for assessing artificial intelligence in machines. It is, in fact, built in to the way we assess the results of ML.

Early approaches to AI were concerned with developing logical structures, encoded in programs, to help machines perform tasks that were universally acknowledged as evidence of high intelligence: playing checkers or chess or deducing proofs of theorems.[5] These were structured activities with defined rules and goals. The emphasis on solving these kinds of problems is a consequence of the practical limitations of early computers (they were powerful enough only to support well-bounded "toy" applications that lived in labs) and also perhaps a result of bias among the first generation of AI researchers, who favored high-level rational functions as marks of human intelligence rather than more commonplace activities, such as recognizing shapes.

Many of the hardest problems in AI cannot be expressed in terms of rules because humans are not always conscious of how we perform the functions that we want to code: "In doing common sense reasoning, people are drawing on reasoning processes largely unavailable to introspection."[6] The toughest problems of intelligence cannot easily be encoded in programs: solutions to these problems have to be learned.[7]

HOW DO YOU INCORPORATE UNCERTAINTY AND EXPERIENCE IN TEACHING MACHINES?

This question is at the heart of the field of ML, which emerged as a subdiscipline of AI in the 1950s. Assessing uncertainty is the domain of statistics and probability, and ML leans on those disciplines for its algorithms. Experience, from the perspective of a computer, is nothing more than data. Data stands in for experience, and it is the ability to analyze data and create probabilistic models based on that data that defines ML. A couple of simple examples will help explain how this works.

PART IV: Interoperability

Imagine that you are in the business of buying used cars. You know that the price of a car varies with its mileage, age, make, model, and a number of other factors. What you want to be able to do is predict the selling price of a vehicle based on these features, and to do that, you need to know what influence each feature has on the selling price. You may have hunches about the weight to assign to each feature, but there are too many features and too many cases to rely on intuition. By taking all your data points and using a statistical process of regression, you can come up with a function that weights each feature in such a way as to produce the closest match with your historical pricing data. This function is your model, and the learning algorithm works by adjusting the weights assigned to features of the model so that it matches the expected output values in your dataset. When the model has been optimized in this way, it can then be used for prediction.

The linear model (as illustrated in figure 16.1) is probably the simplest and the most commonly used model in ML, employed to solve a range of prediction problems. Other algorithms are suited for solving other kinds of learning problems. Classification, for instance, is another classic learning problem. Going back to our car example, imagine now that you are an insurance broker and you have evidence that the kind of car that a person purchases affects the number of insurance claims he ends up making. You want to group these cars into two categories: high risk and low risk. This is a "discrete value" solution, unlike the "continuous value" solution of the pricing example: you are interested in how your data fit into one or more

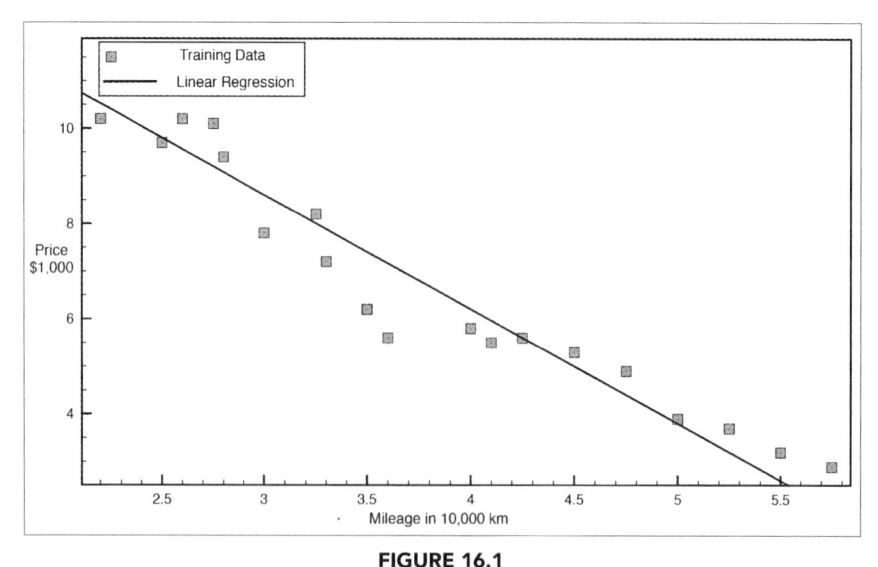

FIGURE 16.1
Simple linear model in two dimensions (mileage and price).

distinct categories and not where they fit along a continuum of prices. Your data in this case include the same features as in the car selling model described above, but the output data now are about claims made and not selling price. By employing a different statistical model, you can group the cars into two categories separated by a line or (in the case of multiple features) a hyperplane, defined again as a function, that describes a boundary between the two classes. Using this function (as illustrated in figure 16.2), you can then categorize any new car you come across into one of these classes.[8]

These are simple implementations of ML, with prediction or classification as a goal. They are also examples of supervised learning. In supervised learning, a model is trained on a set of data that associates features of various input objects with labeled outcomes: in our examples, automobile features with a selling price in one case and an insurance risk category in the other. The training process involves adjusting the weights applied to each feature using an algorithmic process so that the model produces outputs that best match the labeled outcomes. The model is then said to be optimized or trained. Once a model is trained, it can be used with new unlabeled data to predict outcomes.

Often, however, you will be working with unlabeled data, where your goal is not to optimize the weighting of features to match a known output but to explore

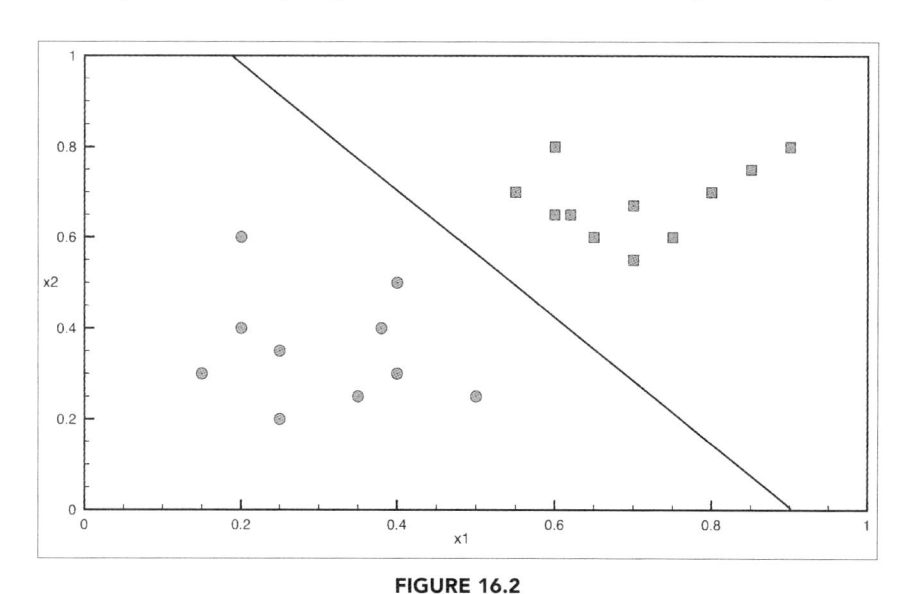

FIGURE 16.2
Simple classification example. Data points in the lower-left half of the chart represent vehicles with a high risk of claims, and data points in the upper-right half of the chart represent those with low risk.

PART IV: Interoperability

hidden regularities and patterns that exist within the data. This is called unsupervised learning and is used for clustering. Examples of clustering include grouping documents with common subjects or segmenting customers based on shared consumption patterns. Clustering is a fundamental application in data mining, and there is a close association between ML and data mining.[9]

Supervised and unsupervised learning methods share the same approach: the use of input data as examples, a process for adjusting weights to apply to features of the data, and the creation of models that can be used to analyze new data and make predictions. The computer is said to learn through the process of adjusting internal weights in a way that is analogous to how humans adjust their intuitive sense of probabilities of outcomes based on experience. And while some of the simplest examples—like those described above—could be solved as pencil-and-paper exercises, by combining statistical approaches with computer processing, we can work with feature sets with large numbers of dimensions and large numbers of example objects. That is the power of ML. The more data, the better the learning outcome. We will return to issues of data selection later in the chapter when we look at some of the limitations and issues of ML.

These learning strategies have a long history not only in ML but in statistics and probability. And while they have been useful for solving many problems in science, medicine, economics, and other fields, they have not been powerful enough to solve fundamental problems of learning—image recognition, speech recognition, and translation, for example. For this reason, from the 1950s until the 1980s, ML existed as a kind of unglamorous subdiscipline of AI, solving a range of narrow AI problems but making little progress on AI's hard problems. Breakthroughs in the 1980s and 1990s in the design of neural networks, however, gave ML a new significance and put it at the center of AI research.

MODELING THE BRAIN WITH NEURAL NETWORKS

Neural networks have become so important in ML that when people speak about ML, they are often speaking exclusively about ML with neural networks. Artificial neural networks (ANNs) are inspired by research into the functioning of the animal brain. Interest in modeling the brain in computers comes from a couple of directions: first, to better understand how the brain works (the interest of psychologists and neuroscientists); second, to use the brain as inspiration for designing algorithms that can learn (the interest of AI researchers). It is often difficult to keep these two perspectives apart when reading about ANN research, but it is important

Chapter Sixteen: Machine Learning for Libraries

to remember that biological plausibility is not a concern from the AI perspective. In other words, the goal of ANN research from an AI perspective is not to rebuild the human brain in silicon but to engineer more capable computer systems using brain-inspired models that can achieve human-level performance in multiple tasks.

The human brain consists of about one hundred billion neurons, each connected to a thousand or more other neurons. Electrochemical signals are transmitted between neurons across synapses. If enough of these signals arrive at a neuron, it reaches a threshold and then "fires," sending a signal to all the neurons it is connected with. Neural pathways are strengthened when pairs of neurons fire together, meaning that some connections between neurons grow stronger than others—a feature expressed in the phrase "Neurons that fire together wire together."[10] Within these connections of neurons, the brain performs computations and stores data. And though signals in the brain are slower than in a computer, neurons work in parallel, giving the brain the power to perform tasks related to sensing and perception at a speed and with an accuracy that has been out of reach of computers until recently.

Artificial neural networks are composed of interconnected nodes, structured in layers, working in parallel. If we think of neurons as nodes and synaptic connections as links, we can represent these as vertices and edges in a directed weighted graph, a common data structure used in computer science. In any ANN, there is an input layer and an output layer, with many "hidden layers" in between (see figure 16.3). Information is passed from input to output through these hidden layers

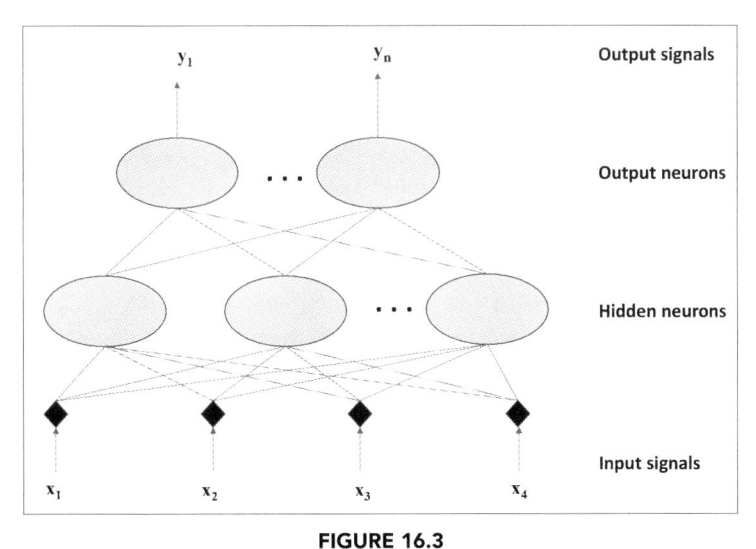

FIGURE 16.3
Diagram of a simple neural network as represented by a directed weighted graph.

and analyzed and transformed at each layer. The connections between nodes in one layer and another have different strengths, as represented by numeric weights associated with links. These weights create pathways through the nodes. Weights between nodes in an ANN change as the network processes new data. An ANN learns in the same way as any ML model: it uses labeled training data to compare its inputs with known correct outputs and then adjusts the weights in its model so that the inputs and outputs align. The algorithm used to adjust weights in an ANN is called back-propagation.[11]

WHAT HAPPENS INSIDE THE HIDDEN LAYERS OF AN ANN?

One way to understand this is to look at a common use case: pattern recognition. As training input for this learning task, we will use a selection of photos of people with their names provided as labels. Imagine that we have lots of photos of John, Joan, and Bill, and we want to build a learner that can recognize these individuals in new photographs. The data we feed to the learner at the input layer is interpreted as a collection of pixels, with a value for each pixel representing its color. The first thing we want to do is identify boundary areas in the training photos where colors change. This might be the task we assign to the first hidden layer of our ANN. At the next level, we may want to assess where these boundary divisions are vertical or horizontal in orientation and represent these as lines. We might then pass the information to another layer that associates those lines with shapes—squares and circles, for example. Shapes are then associated with physical features like eyes, ears, and mouths. The distance between these features is then assessed to help identify the outline of individual faces and so on until, at the end of the process, we pull all that information together to come up with a guess about who is represented in the photo and express that in the output layer. If our guess is wrong—that is, if it does not match the labeled value for the input—then we iterate through the layers and adjust weights at each node so that we associate the combination of features identified in the learning process with the correct label. Each new image passes through the same set of layers and causes the same kind of adjustment in weights—making the connections stronger if we guess correctly and weaker if we do not. In this way, we build up a statistical model that allows us to assess new images to see if the features are characteristic of John, Joan, or Bill. If we analyze a lot of images and build a good statistical model, we can achieve a level of accuracy better than a person making the same assessment in a controlled experiment. That is what has happened with ML, where ANN-based statistical models have recently come to perform better at feature recognition of standard image sets than human beings, pushing standard error rates down below 5 percent, a historical limit for human performance of this task.

Over the last two decades, ANNs have been applied to areas such as drug discovery, speech recognition, machine translation, image recognition, natural-language processing, and cybersecurity. In each case, the performance of these systems has reached or exceeded that of human-level performance. Meanwhile, popular imagination has been captivated by the spectacle of computers beating human beings in showcase events such as IBM's Watson appearance on Jeopardy in 2011 and DeepMind's AlphaGo defeat of Lee Sedol, a world-class Go champion, in March 2016.

What explains this explosion in ML research and performance over the last twenty years? First, the emergence of parallel processing computer architectures in the 1980s and 1990s allowed ANNs to scale up to handle large problems requiring multiple layers, with some ANNs now supporting more than one hundred hidden layers and billions of connections.[12] Second, the development of commercial cloud computing platforms in the early part of this century, services such as Amazon's Web Services Cloud (AWS) and Google's Cloud Platform, has given researchers access to the scalability needed for complex ML tasks without the high costs of developing in-house high-performance computing platforms. And third, the emergence of ML as a dominant research paradigm for AI over the last two decades has been fueled by the availability of very large datasets for training ANNs. Indeed, without the availability of vast quantities of data drawn from a wide range of domains, ML might never have escaped from the AI labs where it was born.

IT'S ALL ABOUT THE DATA

I want to focus on the issue of data in ML because the creation, management, and preservation of data has become a central concern of librarianship in the "age of big data."[13] Since the nineteenth century, governments have played a dominant role in creating large datasets by issuing census surveys and collecting information in day-to-day interactions with individuals as citizens.[14] Likewise, science and medicine have a long history of creating data, collecting them from instruments and generating them from clinical experiments. Today, however, web-based corporations such as Facebook and Google have created platforms that encourage individuals to share information about themselves while also allowing those corporations to repurpose that information as data. We interact with these systems as customers and in relationships where rules regarding privacy and data ownership, governed by user agreements, are very different from practices and policies that have evolved over the years in domains like government, science, and medicine. Questions related to the ownership of data and their reuse have become more urgent in an era of ubiquitous computing, when individuals are generating and sharing personal data at an increasing rate. The ownership of those data and the possibilities for their exploitation as a capital resource through technologies like ML has resulted in an increase in funding for ML research from venture capital funds while also raising troubling questions about who is benefiting from the technology and under what rules.

Similar to the way that algorithms are not always value neutral and may embed "inductive bias," training data can also encapsulate prejudice.[15] This is particularly true of data derived from social interactions on the web, where humans rather than instruments are creating the data. In these circumstances, the data inevitably will reflect the biases of the people who create them. If the outcomes recorded in a training dataset are structurally biased, then the trained model will reflect those biases. This is called teacher noise in ML, and it is an area of increasing concern to researchers in the field. Recommender systems, another domain of ML, seem particularly vulnerable to the effects of data bias, creating "filter bubbles" in news, music, and movie sites that rely on previous user selections to suggest new content.[16]

AN AI APOCALYPSE?

Dystopic visions of technology controlling humanity are as old as technology itself. So, however, are utopian visions of technology saving us from our own failings. The philosopher Nick Bostrom, in his book *Superintelligence: Paths, Dangers, Strategies,* explores the possibility of the emergence in this century of an artificial general intelligence (*AGI*).[17] ML has pushed computer intelligence to new levels in a number of narrow tasks, but many people are alarmed at (or excited by) the prospect of the emergence of a more general form of AI—a strong rather than a weak or narrow AI—that might allow computers to redesign themselves and achieve beyond-human levels of intelligence.

Chapter Sixteen: Machine Learning for Libraries

A less philosophical and more immediate issue raised by recent advances in ML concerns its economic consequences. Discussions of this topic often conflate ML with robotics, but the argument presented is that ML represents a growing risk, not to traditional blue-collar jobs, but to white-collar jobs, which have remained largely immune to earlier waves of computer automation. Any profession, the argument goes, that involves an element of routine mental work—law, medicine, and even librarianship—is vulnerable to automation when computers can learn from data.[18]

AUGMENTED INTELLIGENCE: A GENTLER AI

Given the history in AI of high expectations followed by dashed hopes, as each new generation of researchers has stumbled on the complexities of the field, it seems likely that our future experience of ML will be neither apocalyptic nor ecstatic: the robots won't kill us, nor will they save us from ourselves. It seems clear, though, that over the coming decades, individuals will continue to experience higher levels of interaction with ML at work and at home. We will notice wider use of speech recognition and speech-to-text services as we interact with computers. We will experience ML in machine translation and the automated production of routine documents. We will experience it in the form of assisted and autonomous driving, faster medical diagnostic technologies, and new drug treatments.

MACHINES IN THE LIBRARY: THE THIRD TECHNOLOGY WAVE

It is from this perspective of an augmented AI—a technology, like any other, with mixed benefits—that I want to look at the implications of ML for libraries and librarianship. David Lewis describes two waves of technology that have washed over libraries in the last half decade.[19] The first wave supported the automation of library processes, and though this changed how we worked, it didn't undermine the established model of what a library is and what purposes it was meant to serve. The second wave of technology, Lewis argues, has been more disruptive, moving libraries away from building local collections of published materials to facilitating access to these resources on the web for library users. Librarians are just now coming to terms with the implications of that change.

If ML emerges as the next major disruptive technology in the short sixty-year history of computing, what will this mean for libraries and librarianship and related professions like archival science? Collection management in libraries and archives is an area in which there seem to be many opportunities to use ML. Advances in machine translation, for example, could be applied to enhance access to the rich collections of non-English-language books held by libraries by making them more visible in search engines and simplifying the difficult and slow task of cataloging these resources. ML classification tools could also assist in organizing collections that are costly to categorize using manual processes—collections of music recordings and images, for instance. Speech-to-text tools will open up opportunities for video captioning, making moving-image resources more accessible for audiences with hearing impairments. And image-recognition tools may allow for the automated extraction of scene descriptions in photographs and videos. ML should also greatly improve the performance of optical character recognition software, even into handwritten text and manuscripts. This will be a critical aid in the transcription and the study of these sources and could open up large archival collections for indexing without the cost of manual transcription. Natural-language processing will help with semantic analysis of texts and will become an important tool for digital scholarship while providing new approaches to information retrieval beyond simple full-text indexing, using parts of speech and semantic meaning instead of simple word matching. ML may also allow new approaches to the study of bibliometrics by moving away from current citation and impact-factor analysis and using sentiment analysis or other more powerful algorithms to identify measures of influence and credit in the published scholarly record. Cautions about the limitations of recommender systems and the potential for narrowing choice will need to be observed in cases like this.

HOW WILL LIBRARIANS INTERACT WITH ML SYSTEMS?

The need for network-untethered ML systems will grow as they become embedded in autonomous systems (e.g., self-driving cars and robots), where learning algorithms will need to run independently of the network. Tools will become simpler and more functional, available on desktop and mobile platforms. But because of its dependence on large training datasets, most ML takes place now in the cloud, and in the near term, librarians who work with ML will be using cloud-based services. Specifically, we will make use of application programming interfaces (APIs) offered by commercial cloud services to apply ML models against datasets of interest, including the kinds of digital texts, images, videos, and web archives that many libraries now routinely collect and preserve. The Google Cloud Platform, for instance, offers image-feature recognition and machine translation as online services as well as access to clusters of computers running their own ML framework called Tensorflow. Amazon and Azure offer similar services. The desire to expose data for processing by ML algorithms will accelerate the trend toward storing digital library resources in the cloud.

In this context, however, it will be critical for librarians to also engage with alternative ML technologies. There are dozens of open source frameworks, projects, and institutes devoted to promoting open principles in AI and ML. These OpenAI and OpenML movements are part of the larger trend toward openness in scientific research and are concerned with issues of transparency and accountability in ML algorithm design and in the construction of datasets used to train learning systems. These concerns align with the goals of our profession, including equitable access to information and transparency about the sources of that information. Just as the movements for open source, open access, open data, and open learning have been embraced by librarianship, so too should OpenML.

The social concerns of OpenML are also the domain of a new research discipline called data science.[20] There is a strong engineering element to current conceptions of data science and also a strong emphasis on statistics and computer science. What is becoming clear, however, as ML moves out of the research lab is that more attention needs to be paid to the social benefits and risks of this new technology. The librarian profession has a long-standing interest in information literacy and data literacy. It seems inevitable that data science will be a force that will expand the horizon of our professional concerns. This should also encourage us to welcome data science as an important new dimension of our practice of librarianship and data scientists as important new colleagues in our institutions. Not every librarian needs to be an expert in ML or to become a data scientist, but it will be in our interests, I believe, to domesticate the "feral librarians" of data science (as James Neal has referred to those drawn to librarianship by heart and calling if not training) into our professional community and, once again, expand the scope of our professional practice.[21]

PART IV: Interoperability

CONCLUSION

Historians of science are cautious about narratives that focus on discontinuity: the metaphor of progress is still so strong in science studies that heroic stories about individual breakthroughs solving long-standing theoretical or engineering problems are still popular and too common. There is an element of that in the narrative of this chapter: the rise and fall of symbolic AI, the rebirth of research into neural networks in the 1980s and 1990s, the discovery of critical algorithms at critical times to advance research in the field. A longer work with more depth would focus more on the continuities in this history. But it is legitimate to remark that for the first time in history, AI, because of the contributions of ML, has broken out of the research laboratory and is becoming a feature of life for ordinary people. The early "toy" applications of the AI lab are being superseded by applications that will affect the lives of billions. Turing's test might not be within reach of this new generation of AI technology. But the accomplishments of ML in solving some long-standing problems in AI and reaching human-level competence in many tasks make it a technology worth watching in the coming decade.

NOTES

1. The literature about the nature of human consciousness and the functioning of the human brain is vast. Accessible introductions include Steven Pinker, *How the Mind Works* (New York: W. W. Norton, 1997); and Daniel C. Dennett, *Consciousness Explained* (New York: Back Bay Books, 1991).
2. See Tom Mitchell, *Machine Learning* (New York: McGraw Hill, 1997).
3. John Haugeland gave the name GOFAI (Good Old-Fashioned Artificial Intelligence) to symbolic AI in Haugeland, *Artificial Intelligence: The Very Idea* (Cambridge, MA: MIT Press, 1985), 112.
4. A. M. Turing, "Computing Machinery and Intelligence," *Mind: A Quarterly Review of Psychology and Philosophy* 59, no. 236 (October 1950): 433–60.
5. The program that Allen Newell and Herbert Simon devised for this task was called the Logic Theorist, and it is a wonderful example of the focus of early AI researchers and GOFAI. Turing, 53.
6. See Ernest Davis and Gary Marcus, "Commonsense Reasoning and Commonsense Knowledge in Artificial Intelligence," *Communications of the ACM* 58, no. 9 (September 2015): 92–103, https://doi.org/10.1145/2701413.
7. In Michael Polanyi, *The Tacit Dimension,* rev. ed. (Chicago: University of Chicago Press, 2009), the author argued that "we know more than we can tell." This has become known as Polyani's paradox. Similarly, Hans Moravec, a professor at

Carnegie Mellon University, has noted the oddity in the fact that while high-level reasoning takes relatively few computational resources to replicate, low-level sensorimotor skills take far more.

8. There are dozens of textbooks on ML that describe the range of algorithms currently in use. Three of the more accessible are Ethem Alpaydin, *Introduction to Machine Learning* (Cambridge, MA: MIT Press, 2014); Shai Shalev-Shwartz and Shai Ben-David, *Understanding Machine Learning: From Theory to Algorithms* (Cambridge: Cambridge University Press, 2014); and Jeremy Watt, Reza Borhani, and Aggelos Katsaggelos, *Machine Learning Refined* (Cambridge: Cambridge University Press, 2016).

9. Ian Witten, Eibe Frank, and Mark A. Hall, *Data Mining: Practical Machine Learning Tools and Techniques,* 3rd ed. (New York: Elsevier, 2011).

10. A phrase coined by the Canadian psychologist Donald O. Hebb in *Organization of Behavior: A Neuropsychological Theory* (New York: John Wiley and Sons, 1949).

11. See David E. Rumelhart, Geoffrey E. Hinton, and Ronald J. Williams, "Learning Representations by Back-Propagating Error," *Nature* 323 (1986): 533–36, https://doi.org/10.1038/323533a0. Geoffrey E. Hinton provides a simplified explanation of the algorithm in his "How Neural Networks Learn from Experience," *Scientific American,* September 1992, 145–51. There is also a good description in Nils J. Nilsson, *The Quest for Artificial Intelligence: A History of Ideas and Achievements* (New York: Cambridge University Press, 2010), 409.

12. Building a learner is also a simpler engineering task than designing software to work well in large parallel computing systems, and so ML was able to take advantage of the new architectures sooner than other software systems.

13. See this *New York Times* article for a study of the origin of the term *big data.* Steve Lohr, "The Origins of 'Big Data': An Etymological Detective Story," *New York Times,* February 1, 2013, https://bits.blogs.nytimes.com/2013/02/01/the-origins-of-big-data-an-etymological-detective-story/.

14. See Ian Hacking, *The Emergence of Probability: A Philosophical Study of Early Ideas about Probability, Induction, and Statistical Inference,* 2nd ed. (Cambridge: Cambridge University Press, 2006), for a fascinating philosophical and historical exploration of the emergence of statistical thinking in modern societies.

15. On bias in algorithms, see Cathy O'Neil, *Weapons of Math Destruction: How Big Data Increases Inequality and Threatens Democracy* (New York: Crown, 2016); O'Neil, "How Algorithms Rule Our Working Lives," *Guardian,* September 1, 2016, www.theguardian.com/science/2016/sep/01/how-algorithms-rule-our-working-lives.

16. Tien T. Nguyen, Pik-Mail Hui, F. Maxwell Harper, Loren Terveen, and Joseph A. Konstan, *Exploring the Filter Bubble: The Effect of Using Recommender Systems on Content Diversity* (Seoul: IW3C2, 2014), https://doi.org/10.1145/2566486.2568012.

17. Nick Bostrom, *Superintelligence: Paths, Dangers, Strategies* (Oxford: Oxford University Press, 2014).

PART IV: Interoperability

18. The literature on the topic of the possibility of economic dislocation being created by ML is extensive and growing. See, for example, Jerry Kaplan, *Humans Need Not Apply: A Guide to Wealth and Work in the Age of Artificial Intelligence* (New Haven, CT: Yale University Press, 2015); Andrew McAfee and Erik Brynjolfsson, *Machine, Platform, Crowd: Harnessing Our Digital Future* (New York: W. W. Norton, 2017); James Barrat, *Our Final Invention: Artificial Intelligence and the End of the Human Era* (New York: Thomas Dunne Books, 2013); and Martin Ford, *Rise of the Robots: Technology and the Threat of a Jobless Future* (New York: Basic Books, 2015).

19. David Lewis, *Reimagining the Academic Library* (Lanham, MD: Rowman & Littlefield, 2016).

20. Turing Award winner Jim Gray imagined data science as a "fourth paradigm" of science (empirical, theoretical, computational, and now data-driven) and asserted that "everything about science is changing because of the impact of information technology and the data deluge." See "Data Science," Wikipedia, last modified October 27, 2018, https://en.wikipedia.org/wiki/Data_science#cite_note-TansleyTolle2009-4.

21. James G. Neal, "Raised by Wolves: Integrating the New Generation of Feral Professionals into the Academic Library," Columbia University Academic Commons, 2006, https://doi.org/10.7916/D8X06550.

BIBLIOGRAPHY

Alpaydin, Ethem. *Introduction to Machine Learning.* Cambridge, MA: MIT Press, 2014.

———. *Machine Learning: The New AI.* MIT Press Essential Knowledge Series. Cambridge, MA: MIT Press, 2016.

Barrat, James. *Our Final Invention: Artificial Intelligence and the End of the Human Era.* New York: Thomas Dunne Books, 2013.

Bengio, Yoshua. "Machines Who Learn." *Scientific American,* June 2016.

Bostrom, Nick. *Superintelligence: Paths, Dangers, Strategies.* Oxford: Oxford University Press, 2014.

Brynjolfsson, Erik, and Tom Mitchell. "What Can Machine Learning Do? Workforce Implications." *Science* 358, no. 6370 (December 22, 2017): 1530–34. https://doi.org/10.1126/science.aap8062.

Davis, Ernest, and Gary Marcus. "Commonsense Reasoning and Commonsense Knowledge in Artificial Intelligence." *Communications of the ACM* 58, no. 9 (September 2015): 92–103. https://doi.org/10.1145/2701413.

Deng, Boer. "The Robot's Dilemma: Working Out How to Build Ethical Robots Is One of the Thorniest Challenges in Artificial Intelligence." *Nature* 523 (July 2, 2015): 25–26.

Dennett, Daniel C. *Consciousness Explained.* New York: Back Bay Books, 1991.

Dormehl, Kuke. *Thinking Machines: The Quest for Artificial Intelligence and Where It's Taking Us Next.* New York: Penguin, 2017.

Ford, Martin. *Rise of the Robots: Technology and the Threat of a Jobless Future.* New York: Basic Books, 2015.

Ford, Paul. "Our Fear of Artificial Intelligence." *MIT Technology Review,* February 11, 2015.

Hacking, Ian. *The Emergence of Probability: A Philosophical Study of Early Ideas about Probability, Induction, and Statistical Inference.* 2nd ed. Cambridge: Cambridge University Press, 2006.

Haugeland, John. *Artificial Intelligence: The Very Idea.* Cambridge, MA: MIT Press, 1985.

Hebb, Donald O. *Organization of Behavior: A Neuropsychological Theory.* New York: John Wiley and Sons, 1949.

Hinton, Geoffrey E. "How Neural Networks Learn from Experience." *Scientific American,* September 1992, 145–51.

Horvitz, Eric, and Deirdre Mulligan. "Data, Privacy, and the Greater Good." *Science* 349, no. 6245 (July 17, 2015): 253–55. https://doi.org/10.1126/science.aac4520.

Jordan, M. I., and Tom Mitchell. "Machine Learning: Trends, Perspectives, and Prospects." *Science* 349, no. 6245 (July 17, 2015): 255–60. https://doi.org/10.1126/science.aaa8415.

Kaplan, Jerry. *Humans Need Not Apply: A Guide to Wealth and Work in the Age of Artificial Intelligence.* New Haven, CT: Yale University Press, 2015.

Knight, Will. "Can This Man Make AI More Human?" *MIT Technology Review,* December 17, 2015. www.technologyreview.com/s/544606/can-this-man-make-ai-more-human/.

Lewis, David. *Reimagining the Academic Library.* Lanham, MD: Rowman & Littlefield, 2016.

Lohr, Steve. "The Origins of 'Big Data': An Etymological Detective Story." *New York Times,* February 1, 2013. https://bits.blogs.nytimes.com/2013/02/01/the-origins-of-big-data-an-etymological-detective-story/.

McAfee, Andrew, and Erik Brynjolfsson. *Machine, Platform, Crowd: Harnessing Our Digital Future.* New York: W. W. Norton, 2017.

Mitchell, Tom. *Machine Learning.* New York: McGraw Hill, 1997.

Nguyen, Tien T., Pik-Mail Hui, F. Maxwell Harper, Loren Terveen, and Joseph A. Konstan. *Exploring the Filter Bubble: The Effect of Using Recommender Systems on Content Diversity.* Seoul: IW3C2, 2014. https://doi.org/10.1145/2566486.2568012.

Nilsson, Nils J. *The Quest for Artificial Intelligence: A History of Ideas and Achievements.* New York: Cambridge University Press, 2010.

NYU Center for Mind, Brain and Consciousness. "Does AI Need More Innate Machinery? A Debate between Gary Marcus and Yann LeCun Moderated by David Chalmers." YouTube, October 20, 2017. https://youtu.be/vdWPQ6iAkT4.

O'Neil, Cathy. "How Algorithms Rule Our Working Lives." Guardian, September 1, 2016. www.theguardian.com/science/2016/sep/01/how-algorithms-rule-our-working-lives.

———. *Weapons of Math Destruction: How Big Data Increases Inequality and Threatens Democracy.* New York: Crown, 2016.

Pinker, Steven. *How the Mind Works.* New York: W. W. Norton, 1997.

Polanyi, Michael. *The Tacit Dimension.* Rev. ed. Chicago: University of Chicago Press, 2009.

Raine, Lee, and Janna Anderson. "Code-Dependent: Pros and Cons of the Algorithmic Age." Pew Research Center, February 2017. www.pewinternet.org/2017/02/08/code-dependent-pros-and-cons-of-the-algorithm-age.

Rumelhart, David E., Geoffrey E. Hinton, and Ronald J. Williams. "Learning Representations by Back-Propagating Error." *Nature* 323 (1986): 533–36. https://doi.org/10.1038/323533a0.

Shalev-Shwartz, Shai, and Shai Ben-David. *Understanding Machine Learning: From Theory to Algorithms.* Cambridge: Cambridge University Press, 2014.

Tegmark, Max. *Life 3.0: Being Human in the Age of Artificial Intelligence.* New York: Alfred A. Knopf, 2017.

Turing, A. M. "Computing Machinery and Intelligence." *Mind: A Quarterly Review of Psychology and Philosophy* 59, no. 236 (October 1950): 433–60.

Watt, Jeremy, Reza Borhani, and Aggelos Katsaggelos. *Machine Learning Refined.* Cambridge: Cambridge University Press, 2016.

Witten, Ian, Eibe Frank, and Mark A. Hall. *Data Mining: Practical Machine Learning Tools and Techniques.* 3rd ed. New York: Elsevier, 2011.

Chapter Seventeen

Mobile Technology

Gordon F. Xu and Jin Xiu Guo

The most recognized definition of *mobile technology* is "technology used for cellular communication." Broadly speaking, we can define mobile technology as any technology that is portable and uses wireless connectivity to perform a variety of tasks via mobile devices, including cell phones, personal digital assistants (PDAs), tablets, e-readers, laptops, netbooks, and all Internet-capable handheld devices.

Cellular communication uses radio technology for communication and has its origins in the early part of the twentieth century. The transmission of speech by radio has a long history, and its concept and predecessors can be traced back to 1908.[1] In 1918, the German railroad system started to test wireless telephony on military trains between Berlin and Zossen.[2] In 1924, official trials started with telephone connection on trains between Berlin and Hamburg, and then a company was established to supply train telephony equipment. In 1926, telephone service in trains of the German National Railway was approved and offered to first-class travelers.[3] Radio telephony for military use was the main innovative technology in the Second World War, and handheld radio transceivers became available. Some armies had portable radios that could be carried in backpacks.[4] Some telephone providers started to offer mobile telephones for automobiles in the 1940s.

Compared to modern cellular networks allowing for persistent use of mobile phones for both voice and data communications, early devices were bulky and consumed a lot of power, and networks only supported a few simultaneous conversations. The Second World War advanced electronics technology for these portable devices. In the United States, Bell Labs started working on a system that used a single radio channel, and the user had to press a button to talk. Soon after, AT&T offered mobile telephone service that provided limited coverage areas and only a few available channels in urban areas. In 1947, a "highway" system using frequencies in the 35 to 44 MHz band began operating along the highway from Boston to New York. Slowly this spread to other cities, but the limitation on the number of channels held the system back.[5] It was not until 1956 that the Federal Communications Commission (FCC) committed to making more channels available for the public. In 1970, the FCC finally reserved a radio frequency window explicitly for cell phone use. In 1973, Motorola introduced the first cell phone to the public in New York City. It weighed 2.5 pounds and had a battery that only lasted for twenty minutes.[6]

Since those early days, cell phones have become smaller and smarter. The first smartphone, Simon, was released by International Business Machines Corporation (IBM) in 1993. Although as bulky and clumsy as all of its predecessors, Simon could access e-mails as well as send and receive phone calls. In 1996, Palm Computing released Pilot, the first generation of PDA, which was not a cell phone but actually a much smaller, hand-sized computer allowing users to save personal contacts in an address book, check e-mail, and use other applications, such as a calendar, calculator, notepad, and so on. It had the ability to easily "HotSync" with computers through a serial cable. Microsoft also joined the PDA market with the introduction of the Windows CE operating system and later with Pocket PC.

As new technologies like smaller processors; rechargeable, long-life batteries; and wireless networking became available, mobile devices became much more powerful and cheaper, making mobile technology accessible to more people than ever before. Today, a variety of smartphones are available on the market. The current market is dominated by Apple's iPhone (iOS) and Google's Android operating systems. The year 2010 witnessed a major revolution in tablet computing with the introduction of the Apple iPad. Compared to a laptop, the iPad offers superior performance in terms of its intuitive multitouch screen interface, quick start-up, lightweight design, offline review while in commute, excellent battery life, and so forth. Just a few months after iPad release, Steve Jobs predicted that tablets would eventually pass PCs. In that year, the sales ratio between PCs (desktops and laptops) and iPads was 60:1. After just five years of rapid expansion, Jobs's post-PC prophecy had been fulfilled in 2015.

The advances in mobile technology networks can be traced in successive generations, from the early "0G" services like Mobile Telephone Service (MTS), to first-generation (1G) analog cellular networks, to second-generation (2G) digital cellular networks, to third-generation (3G) mobile broadband data services, to the state-of-the-art fourth-generation (4G) native-IP networks. The "generation" terminology only became widely used when 3G was launched but is now used retroactively when referring to the earlier systems. Fifth generation (5G) mobile networks, based on the IEEE 802.11ac standard of broadband technology, are currently under development and an increasing number of companies are investing to prepare for it. These latest networks aim at higher capacity than the current 4G, allow a higher density of mobile broadband users, and support device-to-device, more reliable, and massive machine communications.[7] They also aim at lower latency and lower battery consumption than 4G equipment for better implementation of the Internet of Things.[8]

THE IMPACT OF MOBILE TECHNOLOGY ON THE IT INDUSTRY

Today, most teenagers and young adults never go anywhere without a mobile computing device. ComScore reported that 94 percent of eighteen- to twenty-four-year-olds in the United States possess smartphones and that an increasing percentage of mobile users are reading books, watching videos, handling transactions, conducting research online, and more.[9] It seems that no IT trend in the last twenty years has been as rapidly pervasive as mobile technology. The ability to access any content on any mobile device over any network in any location is becoming a reality. In recent years, overall IT spending has been steady or shrunk while the amount spent on mobility is increasing. According to Herbert's study, in 2011 and 2012, mobility budgets were 40 percent larger than in 2010. Organizations found that the number of employees with smartphones increased from less than 50 percent in 2010 to more than 70 percent by 2013.[10]

The current IT industry centers on the adoption of a new platform characterized by mobility, cloud computing, and social networking. Cloud computing involves providing software as services rather than as products over the web. Traditionally, software is purchased or licensed, installed, maintained, and updated by an institutional IT department. An institution typically invests 70 percent of time and resources in infrastructure and 30 percent in initiative. Cloud computing can help reverse this ratio because it can transfer responsibility for software updates and maintenance away from the IT department and free IT staff from a considerable amount of software support, as those assignments are automatically included as part of the service. Most teenagers and young adults prefer highly interactive, online, and real-time services, so intuitive design, dynamic interaction, portability, and social elements are among the most popular trends of web design. Many organizations integrated Web 2.0 technologies into their websites, including instant messaging, RSS, YouTube, Facebook, and the like. Enterprise mobility provides end users with more flexibility and freedom than desks and PCs. More employees do work outside the office with mobile devices, sharing and accessing data via cloud services. Except the social networking technologies mentioned above, other technologies like blogs, wikis, and document sharing are useful tools for collaboration. Social networking evolved massively in recent years and became the preferred way of interaction, sharing, and collaboration between people. An institutional IT department needs to keep up with the latest mobile computing evolutions. They should invest in innovative devices, operating systems, mobile apps, tools, and platforms to improve responsiveness, foster collaboration, enhance operational efficiency and employee productivity, and so on.

If we consider our first computing platform as mainframes and terminals and the second as the client-server model, today the cutting-edge technology is repositioning in "the third platform," which assembles mobility, big data, cloud computing, and social networking. IDC, the IT market research company, believes that the organizations should shift to "the third platform." IDC predicts that 60 percent of IT spending will be likely on cloud, social, mobility, and big data technologies by 2020, and the third-platform revenue will grow by 12 percent each year for the next seven years. By contrast, the second platform spending will only grow by about 1 percent per year.[11]

THE IMPACT OF MOBILE TECHNOLOGY ON LIBRARIES

According to an Association of College & Research Libraries survey, of those college students who own a mobile device, more than 66 percent use them for educational purposes, 59 percent search for information online, and 24 percent obtain library resources.[12] Nationwide, some people can access the Internet only via a mobile device and have no luxury of a choice of platform. In 2015, the Pew Research Center reported that 15 percent of the US population is considered to be "mobile dependent," with no alternative or limited online access other than a mobile device. Those mobile-dependent people are likely to be of lower socioeconomic status or nonwhite.[13] Mobile learning can be very promising when cost is a significant barrier for learning. It presents a great opportunity in rural areas, where infrastructural challenges hinder other education models, especially e-learning. Mobile technology is more affordable than the PCs and broadband connections that are necessary for e-learning. Higher-education institutions can deliver educational services to learners via the ubiquitous mobile devices. M-learning (mobile learning) based on mobile devices has become a very popular kind of e-learning.

To cope with users' needs for the ever-growing development of mobile technology, higher-education institutions and academic libraries are beginning to mobilize their teaching and learning services. Many educators strive to incorporate mobile technology into teaching and learning environments. In the era of the Internet, library websites are a gateway to library resources and services. An increasing number of users are visiting library websites via mobile devices. However, websites designed for desktop computers are too complicated for users to navigate and access information via their mobile devices. As an increasing number of patrons use mobile technology, libraries should consider strategies to support those technologies. For example, a library could provide a mobile website for its users through a mobile-friendly portal that offers an interface designed for small screens. Increasingly, library websites should take multidevice users into consideration and move toward mobile-first site designs, where the websites are fully functional on mobile devices but sophisticated enough to satisfy users on any platform. Responsive web design, in which the website is built to fit the confines of smartphone's screen, has become the recommended practice. In responsive web design, websites can automatically resize based on the screen size of a device, which optimizes the user experience, whether they are viewing a site on a desktop, tablet, or smartphone.

THE PRACTICES FOR EARLY ADOPTERS

According to Aumcore's 2017 mobile marketing statistics, there were more than 3.5 billion unique mobile Internet users by August 2017. About 95 percent of Americans had cell phones, and 77 percent owned a smartphone in 2017 (up from 35 percent in 2011). By 2017, there were about 8 million apps in the Google Play store, 2.2 million in the Apple App Store, 669,000 in the Microsoft Store, and 600,000 in the Amazon Appstore. Of all media time spent on mobile devices, 90 percent is spent in apps, and 10 percent is spent on the web. It is projected that in 2017, free apps will be downloaded 91 billion times (up from 57.33 billion in 2012), and paid apps will be downloaded 78 billion times (up from 2.89 billion in 2011).[14] In her book *Best Apps for Academics: A Guide to the Best Apps for Education and Research,* Hennig compiles a thorough list of apps organized by their library-related purposes, such as reading, productivity, research and reference, taking notes and writing, and so on. The entry for each app includes the developer, version, platform, description, audience, instructions for use, and so on.[15] For example, the book describes how a professor used Penultimate to take live notes on an iPad connected to a projector during a lecture and then saved the notes as a PDF to add to class resources after the lecture. This is an essential reference book for keeping academics up to date with the best mobile technologies.

The 2013 NMC Horizon Report Higher Education Edition predicted that tablet computing would enter mainstream use within one year,[16] the 2014 Library Edition expected mobile apps,[17] and the 2017 Higher Education Edition foresaw mobile learning.[18] Since it was introduced to the world, iPad has quickly become such a fixture of our modern life that it already blends into our culture. Cornell University explored the pedagogical, technical, and evaluative issues for the use of mobile technology in teaching natural sciences.[19] The British Educational Communications and Technology Agency reported on a pilot project identifying real value in the use of mobile devices for both teachers and students.[20] The University of Brighton implemented Student Messenger, enabling faculty to send SMS to the cell phones of first-year students to provide emotional and social peer support.[21] Texas A&M University found that the iPad is a useful, viable option for mobile management of electronic resources.[22] The University of Central Florida Library piloted a cataloger to work remotely and found that telecommuting was a feasible solution for bibliographic maintenance.[23] Boise State University incorporated iPads into programs to make library instruction mobile and scalable, with the goal of improving the curriculum, increasing student engagement, and improving related librarian training activities.[24]

A number of major publishers (including Penguin, Macmillan, HarperCollins, Hachette, and Simon & Schuster) have joined Apple's e-book platform to sell books and subscriptions to newspapers and magazines for iPads and other iOS devices. It is expected that more and more publishers will jump on board.[25] At the 2012

Digital Book World Conference, the British Library, together with its technology partner, earned the prestigious Publishing Innovation Award for their historical collection iPad app. This is a wonderful instance of the old and the new coming together in harmony. Those ancient books are kept in their original form, providing complete illustrations and font—even including the occasional damaged paper. You can move your fingers on the iPad screen and turn the pages of exquisite royal manuscripts that belonged to kings and queens, which you could never touch in real life.[26] The New York Public Library created an iPad app that brings its research collection into "the palms of the public's hand."[27] The University of Maryland and the International Children's Digital Library Foundation launched an iPad app that provides access to the world's largest freely available collection of online children's books.[28]

Many libraries reported using iPads to integrate information literacy into curriculum or English-as-a-new-language courses and to provide library instructions and reference services. Some libraries released apps for self-checkout, allowing patrons to acquire materials using their own devices, including iPads, rather than the libraries' kiosks. In collaborative, inquiry-based classroom instruction, iPads can foster student engagement and mastery of search techniques. Using iPads at the reference desk can facilitate more active learning by allowing students to search and navigate with the iPad rather than passively watching the librarian on the computer. Providing reference services outside of the library with iPads, or roving reference services, can address students' questions at the point of need. Today, mobile devices are much more powerful than large computers of a generation ago. We should take advantage of their benefits in higher education by planning how best to employ mobile devices in online and traditional learning.

We have touched on many examples of mobile technology in higher-education settings. However, we must continue to go where our users are—an increasingly digital world. We are on the edge of a digital revolution. The technology, standards, and user demands are there for us to move forward. We are bound only by our own creativity; thus we strongly believe that facilitating the connection between mobile users and libraries is essential for libraries' long-term relevancy and survival.

THE FUTURE TREND OF MOBILE TECHNOLOGY

Mobile technology has dramatically affected both libraries and users. The ubiquitous reach that mobile technology has brought provides many possibilities for learning.[29] Learning via mobile devices can be spontaneous, disruptive, and full of fun experiences. Users will be motivated to learn independently; meanwhile, scholars conduct their research and communicate with others in the network more efficiently. With various emerging user behaviors, how should librarians deal with these nuances and bring the best learning experience to patrons?

As mobile technology evolves, it will continue to transform higher education and library services. The future of mobile technology will focus on user interface, standardization, functionality and apps, content customization, infrastructure, data collection, and artificial intelligence.

User Interface and Standardization

The interface on mobile devices will be influential in user experience. People can browse content while the site automatically resizes to fit the screen size of the devices in their hands.[30] It is up to the individual to choose the responsive website or open the site with a free mobile app to view the contents. To ensure some features, standardized functionality across devices is in need. For instance, a direct link or icon to the sheet music is more convenient for a patron who wants to download music after listening to a demo online. The compatibility and consistency of library materials on mobile devices will affect user experience as well.[31] Some existing features, such as frequently reminding users of their current location in the site, breaking content into short paragraphs, and using recognizable multimedia icons for image, text, and audio,[32] should be kept for the consistency of the mobile site.

Content Customization

The mobile Internet increases the potential for online education. Mobile devices could be an excellent mechanism to provide online support for e-learning and other information momentums that require just-in-time interference with enhanced performance.[33] It is also crucial to offer platform-neutral mobile apps for users to maneuver the content and objects by supporting distinct features on mobile devices.[34] The optimal content helps users find information in a restricted time; therefore, website designers will optimize and deliver the content in an appropriate format[35] and make advanced search available on the mobile website.

Functionality and Apps

Will librarians perform their duties on mobile devices in the future? Given librarians' motivation to provide excellent customer service, the answer is affirmative.

Electronic-resources librarians more often have to resolve issues on mobile devices such as iPads when they are out for conferences or vacations. Some possible questions include usage statistics, troubleshooting of access issues, review of e-resource licenses, and EZproxy setup. Mobile apps might be a sound solution to execute these tasks, such as Microsoft Word and Excel, GoodReader, ILS apps, and other apps with functionalities of file management, password management, note taking, and so on.[36]

Mobile Infrastructure

Libraries will deliver services to users in a mobile cloud-computing model. The mobile infrastructure at the organizational level has to support such a trend. The aforementioned third platform—composed of mobile devices and applications, cloud services, explosive data growth, and a new generation of solutions—will become the new business technological environment.[37] How does an organization integrate this third platform into its existing IT infrastructure to ensure that mobile technology continuously enhances responsiveness and fosters collaboration? The popularity and convenience of mobile devices have created many business opportunities as well as risk. Security is another concern because mobile devices are more susceptible to malware, resulting in new forms of attack.[38] Organizations have to develop their long-term mobile strategic visions to guarantee that the adoption of mobile technology will meet tomorrow's needs.

Data Collection

Mobile technology has brought transformative change to field research. For instance, researchers utilize cameras, audio recording devices, GPS hardware on mobile devices, and downloadable software—such as random number generators for random sampling, geospatial tracking software for enumerator navigation, and encryption software for data security in the field—to collect data. In qualitative research, mobile apps translate responses into English during the data-entry process.[39] Furthermore, survey software can help scholars collect research data remotely and efficiently. In this regard, researchers can expand and share their knowledge of mobile mapping, data storage, data transfer, data security, device protection, and data access to ensure secure and consistent practices.[40] Therefore, librarians will respond to these demands by providing support for researchers to use emerging apps or facilitate partnerships across campuses or organizations. Health care is one evidence-based practice, and gathering clinical data is critical to studies in this field. For instance, health care professionals now use mobile apps like Fitbit (activity), Leaf (menstrual cycles), SmartTemp Thermometer (temperature), and iBGStar (blood glucose) to collect synchronized data. However, when choosing health apps, librarians need to be aware that apps are unregulated.[41]

Collecting this kind of mobile data will set libraries on a course to enter the era of big data. Librarians not only seek innovative ways to manage research data but also gain insights with big data analytics to support scholars throughout the research lifecycle.

Artificial Intelligence / Machine Learning

The implementation of artificial intelligence in libraries and the publishing industry will advance user interfaces, functionality, and content customization on mobile devices. A smart-library online catalog will enable users to find what they want efficiently. The smart catalog may contribute to the e-learning environment in higher education through machine learning, possibly answering reference questions in a timely fashion.

The application of machine learning will empower libraries to manage resources more economically and efficiently. For example, machine learning can help libraries optimize their workflows and search engines, which will also benefit end users. Libraries will become frequent users of cloud computing for digital contents and enterprise resource planning (ERP) systems and will continue to develop the scalable virtual storage for growing electronic contents.

THE FUTURE LIBRARY

Mobile technology has transformed the traditional IT infrastructure. Mobile devices and applications, cloud computing, and big data analytics provide the impetus for technological changes in the business world. These changes will also afford opportunities for the future library to improve operational effectiveness and deliver better products or services to a broader range of users. Therefore, the future library will fully embrace customer relationship management (CRM), big data analytics, and hybrid acquisition models to meet the needs of future patrons.

Customer Relationship Management

Mobile technology will enable more remote users to enjoy library resources and allow local patrons to utilize self-checkout and self-return services. The chat reference will become more dynamic and interactive. The future library needs a systematic method to manage the customer relationship and create positive user experiences. CRM systems enable libraries to capture information about customer interactions and integrate it with related functions and data points, which helps libraries automate their operational processes that identify, describe, and retain valuable customers.[42] Customer service data will support future library leaders in making evidence-based decisions about improving library programs and services. Academic libraries will have a consistent approach to recognizing valuable customers, such as faculty and scholars who have positive and in-depth interactions with libraries over the years, and acquiring remote learners who access educational resources periodically.

Analytics-Driven Collection Strategy

On the one hand, librarians will also utilize cloud computing and big data technology to innovate the content strategy for libraries, especially large research libraries. Leaders in these kinds of institutions will have to find a balance between collections of resources for general populations and unique local collections. The concept of owning all types of collections will become financially impossible and unnecessary in the future. Sharing resources and maximizing the benefits for users in the local and global communities will be the goal of collection strategy. Big data analytics will be an essential means of gaining insights by making big data meaningful and enabling library leaders to make evidence-based, strategic decisions.

Artificial intelligence, on the other hand, can optimize the online catalog through continuously improving algorithms to empower users to access licensed content and local digital collections both efficiently and economically. With the growing effort in digital humanities, cloud computing will offer a scalable infrastructure for research libraries to preserve these locally created collections in secure cloud storage and allow global users to access the content freely.

Hybrid Acquisition Models

Future library leaders will creatively adopt hybrid acquisition models to bring more content to end users in a cost-effective manner. Mobile technology and cloud computing have made such hybrid models realistic for libraries. The patron-driven acquisition model will permit users to access a massive pool of licensed e-contents, including e-books and videos, and only trigger the purchase when the criteria are met. The on-demand book acquisition model will still be employed to purchase physical materials for specific programs or services. After use, these items will be integrated into the collective for sharing in the network. To ensure that the content is quickly accessible to end users, resource acquisitions processes will have to be automated and streamlined. Cloud-based library systems will be integrated into the ERP systems of the parent organization, where transactional and usage data will become an indispensable source of big data at the organizational level. Big data analytics will allow library administrators to assess their operational effectiveness and make evidence-based decisions systemically and consistently. In the meantime, the resource management team will closely work with the library IT department to improve search engine optimization and scalable discoverability. The resource discovery team in academic libraries will also collaborate with the university IT department to implement and improve the mobile learning environment for students—especially those who only have the Internet connection through either satellite or broadband services for their mobile devices.

Future End Users

Mobile technology will make it easier for remote users to access library resources and services. Although it is unclear who the mobile users will be, we can predict that they will want the same experience that local patrons can get from visiting a physical branch. Therefore, the future library must consider synchronizing local activities and programs with those available online. The future library is not only a physical place for local users to discover knowledge and socialize with others in the community but also a virtual community to connect people with the same purpose. Additionally, academic libraries will develop online programs and services to support remote learners. For instance, these patrons can stream videos on mobile devices. Virtual library users will seek every opportunity to maximize their learning. This phenomenon will strategically shift library services and programs. When developing a service or program, both public and academic libraries have to consider the deliverables to in-person patrons as well as virtual users. CRM is an information system that manages the interactions between a library and its current and potential customers. The system uses data analytics to assist libraries in developing a sustainable relationship with local and remote users. Thereby, the analysis offers insights for librarians to build collections and design new services and programs suitable for different types of end users.

The impact of mobile technology on the future library is dramatic as well as disruptive. Just like other industries, the library community must understand the end users' needs and behavior, make strategic changes using evidence-based decisions, and then implement new approaches along with library stakeholders.

NOTES

1. "Wireless Phone Cases Dismissed," *San Francisco Call* 104, no. 37 (July 7, 1908), https://cdnc.ucr.edu/cgi-bin/cdnc?a=d&d=SFC19080707.2.68.
2. "Von 1900 bis 1999," Deutsches Telefon Museum, n.d., www.deutsches-telefon-museum.eu/1900.htm.
3. "Öffentlicher beweglicher landfunk" ["Public countrywide mobile radio"], ÖbL, n.d., www.oebl.de/A-Netz/Rest/Zugfunk/Zug1926.html.
4. L. H. Anderson, "The First Walkie-Talkie Radio," Repeater Builder, June 25, 2005, www.repeater-builder.com/motorola/pdfs/scr300.pdf.
5. W. R. Young, "Advanced Mobile Phone Service: Introduction, Background, and Objectives," *Bell System Technical Journal* 58 (1): 1–14.
6. A. W. Gleason, *Mobile Technologies for Every Library*, Medical Library Association Books (Lanham, MD: Rowman & Littlefield, 2015).
7. A. Osseiran et al., "Scenarios for 5G Mobile and Wireless Communications: The Vision of the METIS Project," *IEEE Communications Magazine* 52, no. 5 (2014): 26–35.
8. J. Best, "The Race to 5G: Inside the Fight for the Future of Mobile as We Know It," *TechRepublic*, December 15, 2014, www.techrepublic.com/article/does-the-world-really-need-5g.
9. "U.S. Cross-Platform Future in Focus," comScore, March 30, 2016, www.comscore.com/Insights/Presentations-and-Whitepapers/2016/2016-US-Cross-Platform-Future-in-Focus.
10. L. Herbert, "The Forrester Wave: Enterprise Mobility Services, Q1 2013," Forrester, February 15, 2013, www.infosys.com/mobility/features-opinions/Documents/enterprise-mobility-services-leader.pdf.
11. B. Cole and D. Essex, "Third Platform of IT Goes Mainstream at IDC Directions," TechTarget, March 14, 2013, http://searchmanufacturingerp.techtarget.com/news/2240179619/Third-platform-of-IT-goes-mainstream-at-IDC-Directions-2013.
12. ACRL Research Planning and Review Committee, "2012 Top Ten Trends in Academic Libraries: A Review of the Trends and Issues Affecting Academic Libraries in Higher Education," *College & Research Libraries News* 73, no. 6 (2012): 311–20.
13. A. Smith, "U.S. Smartphone Use in 2015," Pew Research Center, April 1, 2015, www.pewinternet.org/2015/04/01/us-smartphone-use-in-2015/.
14. M. J. Fritschle, "Mobile Marketing Statistics to Help You Plan for 2018," *Aum* (blog), October 6, 2017, www.aumcore.com/blog/2017/10/06/mobile-marketing-statistics

-for-2018/?lipi=urn%3Ali%3Apage%3Ad_flagship3_pulse_read%3BRDWhLeY%2FTAGf6h%2FlIpLYnQ%3D%3D#.

15. N. Hennig, *Apps for Librarians: Using the Best Mobile Technology to Educate, Create, and Engage* (Santa Barbara, CA: Libraries Unlimited, 2014).

16. L. Johnson et al., *NMC Horizon Report: 2013 Higher Education Edition* (Austin, TX: New Media Consortium, 2013).

17. L. Johnson, S. Adams Becker, V. Estrada, and A. Freeman, *NMC Horizon Report: 2014 Library Edition* (Austin, TX: New Media Consortium, 2014).

18. S. Adams Becker et al., *NMC Horizon Report: 2017 Higher Education Edition* (Austin, TX: New Media Consortium, 2017).

19. R. Rieger and G. Gay, "Using Mobile Computing to Enhance Field Study" (paper presented at the Second International Conference on Computer Support for Collaborative Learning, Toronto, Canada, 1997).

20. D. Perry, *Handheld Computers (PDAs) in Schools*, Beta ICT Research report, March 2003, http://dera.ioe.ac.uk/1644/7/becta_2003_handhelds_report_Redacted.pdf.

21. D. Harley, S. Winn, S. Pemberton, and P. Wilcox, "Using Texting to Support Students' Transition to University," *Innovations in Education and Teaching International* 44, no. 3 (July 19, 2007): 229–41, https://doi.org/10.1080/14703 290701486506.

22. E. Hartnett and A. Price, "iPotential: Mobile Electronic Resource Management on an iPad," *Library Collections, Acquisitions & Technical Services* 35, no. 4 (2011): 118–28, https://doi.org/10.1016/j.lcats.2011.06.001.

23. S. K. Jaskowski, L. M. Sobey, and L. J. Sutton. "Cataloging Coast to Coast," *Technical Services Quarterly* 19, no. 2 (January 2, 2002): 43–52, https://doi.org/10.1300/J124v19n02_04.

24. C. Moore, J. Black, B. Glackin, M. Ruppel, and E. Watson, "Integrating Information Literacy, the POGIL Method, and iPads into a Foundational Studies Program," *Journal of Academic Librarianship* 41, no. 2 (January 30, 2014): 155–69, https://doi.org/10.1016/j.acalib.2014.12.006.

25. D. Tonkery, "The iPad and Its Possible Impact on Publishers and Libraries," *Searcher* 18, no. 8 (January 10, 2010): 39–42.

26. G. Price, "The British Library 19th Century Historical Collection App Wins Prestigious Publishing Innovation Award," INFOdocket, February 2, 2012, www.infodocket.com/2012/01/24/the-british-library-19th-century-historical-collection-app-wins-publishing-innovation-award/.

27. Felicia R. Lee, "New York Public Library Introduces iPad Apps," *New York Times*, May 20, 2011, www.nytimes.com/2011/05/20/arts/design/new-york-public-library-introduces-ipad-apps.html.

28. J. Duke, "International Children's Digital Library and University of Maryland Launch Children's Library iPad Application," *Advanced Technology Libraries* 39, no. 5 (2010): 6.

29. R. Toteja and S. Kumar, "Usefulness of M-Devices in Education: A Survey," *Procedia—Social and Behavioral Sciences* 67 (2013): 538–44.
30. N. Carlson, A. Sonsteby, and J. DeJonghe, "A Mobile-First Library Site Redesign: How Designing for Mobile Provides a Better User Experience for All," in Mobile Technology and Academic Libraries: Innovative Services for Research and Learning, ed. Robin Canuel and Chad Crichton (Chicago: American Library Association, 2017), 35–53.
31. S. Chaveesuk, S. Vongjaturapat, and N. Chotikakamthorn, "Analysis of Factors Influencing the Mobile Technology Acceptance for Library Information Services: Conceptual Model," in *Proceedings of the 2013 International Conference on Information Technology and Electrical Engineering* (Piscataway, NJ: ICITEE, 2013), 18, https://doi.org/10.1109/ICITEED.2013.6676204.
32. O. Famakinwa, P. Barker, P. Schaik, and J. Onibokun, *Exploring the Use of Mobile Technology for Delivering Electronic Support* (Cyprus: University of Cyprus Press, 2016).
33. Ibid.
34. Ibid.
35. Ibid.
36. Hartnett and Price, "iPotential."
37. L. Hurbean and D. Fotache, "Mobile Technology: Binding Social and Cloud into a New Enterprise Applications Platform," *Informatica Economică* 17, no. 2 (2013): 73–83.
38. Ibid.
39. W. Johnston, "Mobile Technology Support for Field Research," in *Mobile Technology and Academic Libraries: Innovative Services for Research and Learning*, ed. R. Canuel and C. Crichton (Chicago: Association of College and Research Libraries, 2017), 123–33, www.researchgate.net/publication/317129708_Mobile_Technology_Support_for_Field_Research.
40. Ibid.
41. C. Schubert, M. Lane, and S. Versen, *Consumer Health: Public and Academic Libraries Partnering for Community Events about Mobile Health Resources* (Harrisonburg, VA: JMU Scholarly Commons, 2016).
42. "CRM 101: What Is CRM?," Salesforce, n.d., www.salesforce.com/crm/what-is-crm/.

About the Contributors

KELLI BABCOCK has been the digital initiatives librarian with the University of Toronto Libraries since 2013. She has served as president for the Archives Association of Ontario and on the Documentation Interest Group for the Islandora community. Kelli is currently focusing her research on exploring technology that can efficiently enable access to digital special collections.

JULIA BAUDER is the social studies and data services librarian at the Grinnell College Libraries, where she has worked since 2008. She received her MLIS degree from Wayne State University in 2007. Prior to becoming a librarian, she worked as a freelance writer and editor of reference books.

MATTHEW CONNOLLY is an application developer in the Web Development Group of Cornell University Library's Information Technology Department. He writes code for a variety of internal- and external-facing library projects, including the library catalog, search interface, and discovery systems. He's also a core contributor to the nascent FOLIO project code base. Connolly is a longtime member of the library's Usability Working Group and lends technical support to experimental technology projects. He has written or coauthored several articles, chapters, and books on library technology, most recently *User Privacy: A Practical Guide for Librarians*.

ALAN DARNELL is the director of Scholars Portal, a service of the Ontario Council of University Libraries, founded in 2003. In this role, he has been responsible for implementing collaborative technology solutions for the twenty-one academic libraries in the province, including digital collection and preservation services. He holds a master's degree from the Faculty of Information at the University of Toronto and is currently on research leave studying the applications of machine learning to library and archives.

About the Contributors

MARK DEHMLOW is the director of library information technology for the Hesburgh Libraries at the University of Notre Dame. He is responsible for providing leadership, vision, and oversight for the strategic and functional directions of the library IT program, including stewardship for the budget and personnel. As director for most of the Hesburgh Libraries' core technical infrastructure and services, he collaborates with key library and university stakeholders and partners to plan and implement technology solutions that contribute to a transformative academic research library. With a background in web application development and library technology integration, he has written and presented on software development, open source, organizational change, cloud computing, and technology management. Mark holds BAs in English literature and mathematics from the University of Maine and an MS in library and information science from the University of Illinois. He can be reached at mark.dehmlow@nd.edu.

RACHEL DI CRESCE worked at the University of Toronto as digital project librarian. She previously has worked at McGill University in the Digital Initiatives Department and at the Burlington Public Library setting up their digital collections platform. At the University of Toronto, Rachel worked on a grant-funded project to integrate IIIF with new exhibit tools for manuscript and digital humanities scholars. She is currently a cochair of both the IIIF Manuscript and IIIF Outreach groups and has continued her research into expanding IIIF support at the library as well as new methods to increase the usability and sustainability of digital collections.

KATE DOHE is the manager of the Digital Programs & Initiatives Department at the University of Maryland (UMD) Libraries. Her department facilitates the creation, acquisition, discovery, and preservation of digital assets in support of the mission of the UMD Libraries. Kate's team oversees day-to-day activities related to digital repository management, digital preservation activities, research data services, and electronic publishing. Prior to joining UMD, she was the digital services librarian at Georgetown University and the digital librarian for an academic textbook publisher in California. Over the course of her career, she has created and managed digital repositories on multiple platforms with an eye to scalable, transparent, and sustainable operations in support of the research mission of the institution. She earned her MLISc from the University of Hawaii and also holds a BSEd in speech and theater from Missouri State University.

DAVID DURDEN is a data services librarian for Digital Programs and Initiatives at the University of Maryland Libraries, where he works at the intersection of research data management and library data services. He holds an MLIS in archives and digital curation from the University of Maryland and an MA in musicology from Brandeis University. He supports data management through application support, consultative services, and workshops.

ELLEN ENGSETH is curator of the Immigration History Research Center Archives and head of the Migration and Social Services Collections at the University of Minnesota Libraries. She earned her master of library and information science and master of arts in history from the University of Wisconsin–Milwaukee (UWM). She is active and holds leadership positions in the Society of American Archivists. Additionally, as adjunct faculty with the iSchool at UWM, she teaches an occasional study abroad course.

JIN XIU GUO is the winner of the Georgia Library Association Team Award, where Jin as the project manager led the team to merge two state university libraries through consolidating two Ex Libris Voyager systems. Jin has been providing leadership in acquisitions, collections and resource management, digitization, institutional repository, library technology, preservation, and collection assessment at academic libraries for more than ten years. Jin holds a master of library and information science from McGill University and a master of science in information systems from Kennesaw State University. Jin is currently the director of collections and resource management at Stony Brook University Libraries.

DANIEL JOHNSON is the English and digital humanities librarian at the University of Notre Dame. He teaches literary research and digital humanities workshops, consults on both digital and "traditional" scholarship, and manages the British, American, and broader Anglophone literature collections at the Hesburgh Library. His research and teaching span time periods and digital methodologies, but he has special interest in eighteenth- and nineteenth-century literature, early microcomputing culture, and digital editions. Daniel holds an MA in English from Wake Forest University and a PhD in English from Princeton University. He can be reached at djohns27@nd.edu.

ELIZABETH JOAN KELLY is the digital programs coordinator at the Monroe Library at Loyola University New Orleans where she manages digital programs including digital collections and preservation, digital scholarship, scholarly communications, and library web services. Her research interests include digital library and archives assessment, particularly the reuse of digital library objects, as well

About the Contributors

as library pedagogy. Recent publications on these subjects include articles in the *Journal of Web Librarianship,* the *Journal of Contemporary Archival Studies, College & Undergraduate Libraries, Codex,* and *Archival Practice,* among others. Kelly is the cofounder of the Digital Library Federation Pedagogy Group (#DLFteach) and a member of the research team for the Institute of Museum and Library Services–funded project, "Developing a Framework for Measuring Reuse of Digital Objects."

JOSEPH KOIVISTO is a systems librarian at the University of Maryland, College Park, providing systems support for the seventeen member campuses of the University System of Maryland and Affiliated Institutions consortium. He earned his BA in English from the University of Scranton (2009) and his MSLIS from the Catholic University of America (2014). His work focuses on acquisitions workflows, institutional repositories, and authority creation.

CLIFF LANDIS is a digital initiatives librarian at the Atlanta University Center Robert W. Woodruff Library in Atlanta, Georgia. Cliff's research interests include information organization, digitization, linked data, archival technology, metadata, user-centered service, assessment, and the coevolution of humanity and technology. His website is http://clifflandis.net.

MONICA MACELI is an assistant professor at Pratt Institute School of Information, focusing on emerging technologies in the information and library science domain. She earned her PhD and MSIS from the College of Information Science and Technology (iSchool) at Drexel University. She has an industry background in web development and user experience, having held positions in e-commerce, online learning, and academic libraries. Her research areas of interest include end-user development, human-computer interaction, and information technology education.

LAUREN MAGNUSON is the head of collection management and technical services at California State University, San Marcos, and also works as the development coordinator for the Private Academic Library Network of Indiana. She is the editor of *Data Visualization: A Guide to Visual Storytelling for Libraries* (2016) and several articles on library technology integrations, automation, and open source application development. Lauren is a PHP and Python developer and shares code on GitHub at https://github.com/lpmagnuson.

AUSTIN OLNEY is a digital media specialist at the White Plains Public Library, teaching patrons to be digitally literate and providing them with the technology skills necessary for the modern world. Using the library's teen space as a backdrop, he presents students with a hands-on approach. Receiving his master's degree of science in education from SUNY Cortland in 2011, he gained a New York State Social Studies teaching certification and an A+ (Plus) Certification from CompTIA IT Industry & Association. Austin has experience teaching in a variety of educational institutions and enjoys applying advanced technology skills to actively engage students with diverse backgrounds and learning styles.

MARGUERITE RAGNOW is the curator of the James Ford Bell Library and a member of the graduate faculties of History, Early Modern Studies, and Medieval Studies at the University of Minnesota. She is the director of the Digital Research Workshop for the Mellon-funded Consortium for the Study of the Premodern World at Minnesota as well as a member of its board of regents. She is active in both the Rare Book and Manuscript Section of the Association for College and Research Libraries and the American Library Association, for which she currently holds a leadership position with the Map and Geospatial Information Round Table.

JEANETTE CLAIRE SEWELL is the database and metadata management coordinator at Rice University's Fondren Library. She is actively involved in using metadata to promote library resources in unique and engaging ways, creating everything from digital timelines and coloring books to Twitter bots and LibGuides. Jeanette also serves as the library science subject specialist at Fondren Library.

TODD SUOMELA is a digital pedagogy and scholarship specialist at Bucknell University. He works with faculty and students to incorporate technology into their research, teaching, and learning. Before moving to Bucknell, he worked as a CLIR/DLF postdoctoral fellow in data curation for the social sciences and humanities at the University of Alberta. He received a PhD in communication and information from the University of Tennessee in 2014 for research into science communication and citizen science. He completed an MIS from the University of Michigan in 2007. He is currently conducting research on web archives, research ethics, library management, and history of science and technology.

JESSICA WAGNER WEBSTER is the digital initiatives librarian at Baruch College, City University of New York (CUNY). She holds a master's in library science (archives concentration) as well as a master's in history from the University of Maryland. Her responsibilities include selecting materials for digitization, locating and accessioning born-digital collections, designing workflows to support processing, managing digital archives projects, and creating systems to ensure both access to and long-term preservation of digitized and born-digital materials. She also coleads the implementation team for Baruch's institutional repository. She has developed and taught a course on digital archives and society at Baruch College and has presented widely on a variety of topics. Her research focuses on trends in archival work and on documenting underdocumented populations.

JOSHUA A. WESTGARD is a systems librarian for Digital Programs and Initiatives at the University of Maryland Libraries, where he supports various digital repository systems and serves as an adjunct instructor in the iSchool. He holds an MLS in the curation and management of digital assets from the University of Maryland and a PhD in medieval European history from the University of North Carolina at Chapel Hill. He has published on the transmission and reception of the works of the Venerable Bede (ca. 673–735) and is a contributor to open source software development projects.

JUSTIN M. WHITE is the scholarly communications librarian at the University of Texas Rio Grande Valley. He has written and presented on academic piracy and the future of copyright as it pertains to scholarly communications. He also has a background in early modern labor history, focusing on the transformation of free and bound labor.

GORDON F. XU is the head of Library Systems at Northern Michigan University. Prior to moving to Northern he worked as a systems librarian at South Dakota State University and City University of New York over ten years. He is a highly motivated IT professional in adaptation, development, and implementation of library systems. He has published many research papers including a book on information systems. He was a highly commended award winner at the Emerald Literati Network Awards for Excellence 2012 for one of his papers. He holds a master of library and information studies degree from McGill University and a BSc and MSc in natural science from Zhengzhou University and the Chinese Academy of Sciences, respectively.

Index

A

access
    digital publishing and, 173–177
    digital repositories for, 153–154
    to digital repository materials, 159–160, 164
    with institutional repositories, 154
    as investment strategy, 176
    to preservation repository, 157, 159
    in web archiving, 45
access repositories, 155–156
accessibility
    of access repository materials, 156
    of personalized data, 102–103
    of web archives, 53
account credentials, 66–67
Adam Matthew Digital (AMD), 171–176
advertising
    IBeacons for library advertising, 22–23
    web browser plug-ins to block, 61–62
advocacy, 97–98
AGI (artificial general intelligence), 232
AI
    See artificial intelligence
ALA (American Library Association), 60
Albert, Kendra, 31–32
Allison-Cassin, Stacy, 13
"alt" tags, 102
always-on assistants, 23
Amazon
    Alexa-enabled Dot/Echo, 213

    Echo, library use of, 18, 23
    Echo, specialized script for, 215
    platform lock-in, web archiving and, 50
Amazon Web Services (AWS), 146–147, 231
Amber project
    independent snapshots of web pages, 31
    WordPress plug-in, 33
    work of, 30
AMD (Adam Matthew Digital), 173–176
American Library Association (ALA), 60
Ammon, Keith, 68
Amnesic Incognito Live System (Tails), 66
analytics
    analytics-driven collection strategy, 251
    Google Analytics, 143
    LTI integrations for, 207
    Matomo, 143–144
And Chill chat bot, 220
Andrews, Carl R., 199
AngularJS, 140
Annals of Mathematical Statistics, 90
ANNs (artificial neural networks), 228–231
anticircumvention laws, 38
API
    See application programming interface
Apple
    e-book platform, 246–247
    facial-recognition software, 60
    HomePod, library use of, 23
    iPhone, Siri of, 213

Index

Apple (cont.)
    platform lock-in, web archiving and, 50
    Siri, library use of, 23
Apple iPad
    apps, 247
    e-book platform, 246–247
    as fixture in modern life, 246
    introduction of, 242–243
application programming interface (API)
    bot interaction with for content delivery, 215
    for ML in library, 235
    See also IIIF Image API
applications (apps)
    data collection with mobile technology, 249–250
    for iPad, 247
    for mobile devices, 246
    mobile technology, future of, 248–249
    SeeCollections, 94
archival digital repositories
    access repositories, 155–156
    future directions for, 161–163
    preservation repositories, 156–159
archival management system, 157
Archive-It, 46, 47
Archivematica, 157
archives
    digital publishing through third-party vendors, 168–170
    linked open data in archives/special collections, 10–12
    tools for linked open data, 12–13
    See also web archiving
Archives and Special Collections Department, UMN Libraries
    digital delivery modes, platforms, products, 169–170
    digital publishing case study, 173–176
    technology for digital conversion projects, 170–173
ArchivesSpace, 160
archivists, 50–52

artificial general intelligence (AGI), 232
artificial intelligence (AI)
    augmented intelligence, 233
    data in machine learning, 231–232
    fears of AI apocalypse, 232–233
    as feature of life for ordinary people, 236
    in future library, 251
    ML definition in context of, 224
    ML in library, 233–235
    on mobile devices, 250
    modeling brain with ANNs, 228–230
    teaching machines using symbols, 224–225
    uncertainty/experience in teaching machines, 225–228
artificial neural networks (ANNs), 228–231
Ashton, Kevin, 18
assessment data, 89–90
Association of College & Research Libraries, 244–245
AT&T, 242
audiovisual materials, 191–192
augmented intelligence, 233
Aumcore, 245–246
Austin Public Library, 218
authors, 160–161
automated task
    bots, functionality of, 214–216
    bots for, 212
    bots in libraries, 216–218
AWS (Amazon Web Services), 146–147, 231

B

Babcock, Kelli, 181–193, 257
backups
    of preservation repository materials, 158
    for web archiving, 34, 35
Bagger, 157–158
BagIt, 157
Bahde, Anne, 94
bar chart, 75
Bauder, Julia, 75–86, 257
Bell Labs, 242

Berkeley Electronic Press, 141
Berkman Klein Center for Internet and Society, 30
Berners-Lee, Tim, 6, 48
Best Apps for Academics: A Guide to the Best Apps for Education and Research (Hennig), 246
Bibliographic Framework Initiative (BIBFRAME), 7–9
bibliographic metadata, 7–10
bibliographic records
    large-scale linked data in libraries, 7–8
    research in future with linked open data, 13
BiblioGraph.net extension, 10
Biblissima, 192
big data analytics, 251, 252
Boise State University, 246
Bond, Sarah E., 134
books
    e-books, production process for, 43–44
    JSTOR's Topic**graph** for search of, 81–83
    See also e-books
Bostrom, Nick, 232
botnets, 25
Botnik Studios, 220
bots
    characteristics of, 214–216
    for civic causes, 220
    conclusion about, 220–221
    definition of, 212
    history of, 213–214
    for internal library communication, 220
    in libraries, 216–218
    for library instruction/outreach, 218
    for library services/events, 220
    library use of, 211–212
    tool kit for, 219
"Bots and the Library: Exploring New Possibilities for Automation and Engagement" (Sewell), 211–221
BotSpot website, 213

Botwiki
    definition of bot, 212
    features of, 219
    on types of bots, 213
Bouquin, Daina, 98
brain, 228–230
Breaking the Book (Mandell), 128
A Brief History of Data Visualization (Friendly), 90
Briney, Kristin, 100
British Educational Communications and Technology Agency, 246
British Library, 191, 247
Brooklyn Public Library
    Digital Privacy Project, 69
    IV for public services data, 92, 93
browsing
    history, VPNs and, 63
    IV for visual search and browse, 94–96
Burkell, Jacquelyn, 61
business analytics, 92
"buttonology," 128

C

California, 108
Canvalytics, 205
Canvas LMS, 198, 205–206
Capek, Karel, 212
Carlson, Scott, 217
Carolina Digital Humanities Initiative (CDHI), 130
Carrot Document Clustering Workbench, 85
Carrot Project, 85
Carrot Search, 80
Case Map, in Ravel platform, 83–85
case study
    digital publishing, 173–176
    EBSCO Curriculum Builder at Louisiana State University, 201–203
    Ex Libris Leganto at University of New South Wales, 203–205
    LibGuides at Utah State University, 205–206

Index

Catal Hyük map, 90
CDHI (Carolina Digital Humanities Initiative), 130
cell phones, 241–243
   See also smartphones
cellular communication, 241–243
chat bots
   description of, 212–213
   development of, 214
   for internal library communication, 220
   for libraries, benefits of, 216
Cheap Bots Done Quick, 219
checksum, 157, 158
Chesapeake Project, 32
"Chronicling America" newspaper archive, 126
citations
   data citation initiative, 145
   Ravel Law visualizations of court cases, 83–85
   reference rot and, 31–32
   reference rot prevention strategies, 36
"Cite It!" bookmarklet, 203, 204
civic causes, 220
CKAN, 146
cloud computing
   adoption of in libraries, xi
   analytics-driven collection strategy, 251
   in future library, 251
   hosted data environments, 146–147
   hybrid acquisition model in future library, 251–252
   impact of mobile technology, 243–244
   mobile infrastructure, future of, 249
   scalability for ML tasks with, 231
clustering, 228
CMS
   See content management system
CMS LTI tool, Springshare, 206
Coalition for Networked Information and Data Science Training for Librarians, 100
Codecademy, 219

coding languages, 215
Colaboratory, Google, 130
Cold War International History Project, 94, 95
collaboration
   for digital humanities, 127–128, 133–134
   at UMN Libraries, 170
   for web archiving, 52
collaborative websites, 213, 214
Collection Analyzer, 131, 132
Collection Discovery, 131, 132
collection metadata, 47
collection policy, 46
collections
   analytics-driven collection strategy, 251
   digital collections/digital humanities platform, 131–133
   digital publishing through third-party vendors, 167–170
   IV for visual search and browse, 94–96
   See also special collections
Collections U of T, 189
College & Research Libraries News, 124
College of Charleston, 94
comment threads
   dynamic content, as challenge for web archiving, 49–50
   web as venue for new media objects, 44
communication
   bots for internal library communication, 220
   through vision, 91
   See also scholarly communication
community
   future community of IIIF-enabled institutions, 192–193
   web archives, access to, 53
compression, 157
Compton, Kate, 219
computers
   IP address as unique identifier, 19
   VR headset requirements, 115
ComScore, 243

Conner, Matt, 94, 96
Connexion, 216
Connolly, Matthew, 17–27, 257
consciousness, 223–224
content customization, 248
content drift, 30
content management system (CMS)
    IIIF and, 190
    link preservation, 33
    web archiving and, 37
ContentDM, 141
context, link rot and, 31
Convocate project, 132
cookies, 62
cooperation, 50–51
    See also collaboration
copyright
    access repository materials and, 156
    Leganto and, 204–205
    vendors links to e-resources and, 38
Cornell University
    Fedora, development of, 138–139
    IIIF use by, 191
    on mobile technology for teaching, 246
Corporation for National Research initiative, 138–139
costs
    of digital publishing, 175–176
    LTI applications for lower course materials costs, 206–207
course materials
    EBSCO Curriculum Builder at Louisiana State University, 201–203
    Ex Libris Leganto at University of New South Wales, 203–205
    LibGuides at Utah State University, 205–206
    LTI use cases for libraries, 198–200
court cases, 83–85
Cramer, Tom, 190
Creative Commons Rights Expression Language, 8
credentials, 199

Crontab, 215
CurateND platform, 133
curatorial expertise, 168
customer relationship management (CRM), 250–251, 252

D

Dalhousie University Libraries, 96–97
dark archive, 157
Darnell, Alan, 223–236, 257
data
    aggregation, privacy threats with IoT, 26
    as experience for machine learning, 225–228
    Internet of Things, libraries and, 17–27
    link rot, reference rot, link resolvers, 29–38
    linked open data in libraries, 3–14
    in machine learning, 231–232
    privacy protection for account credentials/data, 66–67
    publishing by digital repositories, 147
    web archives, engaging libraries with, 43–54
    See also linked open data
Data (data journal), 147
data analytics
    IoT and, 27
    recognition of, 90–91
Data API, 146
data collection
    digital humanities in libraries, 127–128
    mobile technology and, 249–250
"Data for Discovery" (Bauder), 75–86
data journalists, 92
data journals, 147
data repositories, 144–146
data science, 235
Data Science and Visualization Institute of Librarians course, 100
"Data Visualization Camp Instructional Materials (2017)" (University of Wisconsin–Milwaukee), 100

Index

data visualizations
  early, 75
  Gale Topic Finder, 77–80
  JSTOR's Topic**graph**, 81–83
  Ravel Law visualizations, 83–85
  tools for creation of, 85–86
  visualized discovery interfaces, 76–77
  See also information visualization
Data Visualizations and Infographics (Mauldin), 100
data wrangling, 127
databases, 3–6
Dataverse, 145–147
DBpedia, 7
DEC (Digital Exhibits and Collections), 131, 132
Deep Blue Data at the University of Michigan, 145
DeepMind's AlphaGo, 231
Dehmlow, Mark, 123–134, 258
Delmas-Glass, Emmanuelle, 192
Dempsey, Lorcan, 168
Designing Bots: Creating Conversational Experiences (Shevat), 219
DH
  See digital humanities
D.H. Hill Library makerspace, 24
Di Cresce, Rachel, 181–193, 258
digital archival content, 155–156
digital collections repositories, 137–138
Digital Commons, 141, 143
digital conversion
  See digitization
digital exhibit platforms, 131–133
Digital Exhibits and Collections (DEC), 131, 132
"Digital Exhibits to Digital Humanities: Expanding the Digital Libraries Portfolio" (Johnson & Dehmlow), 123–134
digital humanities (DH)
  description of, 124

digital access repositories for scholars in, 155–156
digital exhibit platforms/tool kits, 128–130
future of, 133–134
IV, use of, 92
in libraries, 126–128
platform, developing, 131–133
tracing digital library to, 124–125
digital images
  IIIF, early adopters of, 190–191
  IIIF, future trends for, 191–192
  IIIF, how it works, 184–188
  in IIIF definition, 182–183
  IIIF use cases, 188–190
"'Digital' Is Not the Opposite of 'Humanities'" (Bond, Long, & Underwood), 134
digital libraries
  digital humanities in libraries, 126–128
  evolution of, 124–125
  future of digital humanities and, 133–134
  large-scale, adoption of in libraries, xi
  overview of, 123–124
Digital Privacy Project, 69
Digital Public Library of America, 9
digital publishing
  case study, 173–176
  conclusion about, 176–177
  of special collections, 167–168
  technology for, 170–173
  through third party vendors, 168–170
digital repositories
  archival digital repositories, 155–159
  conclusion about, 148, 163–165
  current trends/future directions, 142–148
  early adopters of, 141–142
  functions of, 153–154
  future directions for, 159–163
  IIIF, how it works, 184–188
  IIIF, impact on, 188–190

Index

IIIF and, 182
IIIF for digital images, 182–183
IIIF use cases, 188
institutional repositories, 154
investments in, 181
repository systems, 138–141
types of, 137–138
"Digital Repositories: A Systems Perspective" (Westgard, Dohe, Durden, & Koivisto), 137–148
"Digital Repositories" (Webster), 153–165
Digital Repository at the University of Maryland (DRUM), 145
digital repository vendors, 12–13
digital rights management (DRM), 33
digital scholarship
 centers, 125
 use of IV, 92
Digital Tools for Manuscript Study project, 189
digitization
 digital publishing, 176–177
 by libraries, 127
 technology for, 170–173
direct manipulation interfaces, 76
disambiguation, 8, 14
disciplinary problems, 51–52
discovery
 digital repositories, integration with, 159–160
 digital repositories, trends in, 142–144
 See also visualized discovery interfaces
discussion boards, 44
distribution channel, 43–44
document level metadata, 47
Dohe, Kate, 137–148, 258
Domain Name System (DNS), 64–65
DoNotPay bot, 220
DPLA Bot, 217
Dragoman Renaissance Research Platform, 7
DRM (digital rights management), 33
DRUM (Digital Repository at the University of Maryland), 145

Dryad, 147–148
DSpace
 code base, simplification of, 141
 for dedicated data repositories, 145
 features of, 139–140
 with Google Analytics, 143
 IIIF and, 190
 linked data capabilities of, 12
Dublin Core
 Metadata Terms, 8
 search engine optimization and, 144
DuckDuckGo, 63
DuraSpace, 138
Durden, David, 137–148, 258–259
Dyn, 25
dynamic content, 49–50
dynamic queries, 76

E

EAC-CPF (Encoded Archival Context-Corporate Bodies, Persons and Families), 12
early adopters
 of digital repositories, 141–142
 of IIIF, 190–191
 of mobile technology, 245–247
 of privacy-protection technology tools, 67–69
e-books
 Apple's e-book platform, 246–247
 EBSCO Curriculum Builder and, 202
 production process for, 43–44
EBSCO Curriculum Builder
 Leganto vs., 204
 at Louisiana State University, 201–203, 207
 personalization with LTI, 199
EBSCO Discovery Service
 EBSCO Curriculum Builder and, 201
 personalization with LTI, 199
economic consequences, of ML advances, 233
EDM (Europeana Data Model), 9

Index

education
    about VR, 110
    IV as library service, 96
    IV education for librarians, 101
    mobile learning, 245
    privacy education in libraries, 70
    with VR, 111
    See also training
EDUCAUSE, 207
EFF
    See Electronic Frontier Foundation
Ege, Otto F., 192
electronic devices
    Internet-connected, growth of, 19–21
    IoT, use of in libraries, 21–24
Electronic Frontier Foundation (EFF)
    browser-based privacy-protection tools of, 62
    privacy-protection policies/tools, 60
    VPN choice, information on, 64
electronic library, 125
Electronic Product Code (EPC), 19
ELIZA, 213
e-mail chains, 44
embeddedness
    EBSCO Curriculum Builder at Louisiana State University, 201–203
    Ex Libris Leganto at University of New South Wales, 203–205
    LibGuides at Utah State University, 205–206
    with LTI, 197
    LTI, conclusion about, 206–207
    LTI use cases for libraries, 198–200
"Embracing Embeddedness with Learning Tools Interoperability (LTI)" (Magnuson), 197–207
Encoded Archival Context-Corporate Bodies, Persons and Families (EAC-CPF), 12
encryption
    privacy protection for account credentials/data, 66–67
    by VPN, 63

"Engaging Libraries with Web Archives" (Suomela), 43–54
Engseth, Ellen, 167–177, 259
environment, library, 23–24
Environmental Data & Governance Initiative, 32–33
environmental sensors, 24
EPC (Electronic Product Code), 19
EPrints, 140
Epstein, Helen-Ann Brown, 98
equipment
    for digital conversion project, 172
    VR, knowledge about, 114–115
equivalence connections, 5
e-resources, 38
ethics, 54
European Union, 60
Europeana Collections, 9
Europeana Data Model (EDM), 9
"Everything Is Online: Libraries and the Internet of Things" (Connolly), 17–27
exit node, 68
experience, 225–228
exploratory interface, 11
"exposure therapy," 112
Extensible Markup Language (XML), 6

F

Facebook
    bots for internal library communication, 220
    chat bots, 214
    Oculus VR, purchase of, 109
    platform lock-in, web archiving and, 50
    virtual reality, future of, 116
factual statements, 4
faculty
    collaboration with librarians for digital humanities, 127–128
    collaboration with librarians with LTI, 198
    Leganto at University of New South Wales, 203–205

Index

LibGuides at Utah State University, 205–206
Fagerheim, Britt, 205
Federal Communications Commission (FCC), 242
Fedora
    code base, simplification of, 141
    development of, 138–139
    IIIF use cases, 188, 189
    linked data capabilities, 12–13
    RDF for linked open data, 142
Fedora Object XML (FOXML), 138
Fenner, Martin, 147
Few, Stephen, 102
Fifth generation (5G) mobile networks, 243
"Fighting Linkrot" (Nielson), 29
file fixity, 158
file formats
    for access repository material, 155
    format diversity as challenge for web archiving, 49
    metadata for archival repositories and, 162
    for preservation repository materials, 157, 158
file size
    of access repository materials, 156
    of preservation repository materials, 157
FilmFinder, 76
filter bubbles, 232
firmware update, 25–26
fixity checks, 158
Florida Library Association Marketing Committee, 97–98
Fondren Bot, 217
Fondren Library at Rice University, 217
format migration, 49
formats
    See file formats
Fortier, Alexandre, 61
FOXML (Fedora Object XML), 138
Frank, Emily
    on access to library materials, 198

EBSCO Curriculum Builder at Louisiana State University, 201–202, 207
FreeflyVR, 113
French Renaissance Paleography project, 188, 189
Friendly, Michael J., 90, 91
Front Porch Center for Innovation and Wellbeing, 218
Fulcrum, 133
funding, 169
future
    of digital humanities, 133–134
    IoT-connected library of future, 26–27
    of IV/libraries, 100–103
    of ML in library, 233–235
    of mobile technology, 247–250
"The Future of Data Analysis" (Tukey), 90

G

Gale, 76, 126
Gale Topic Finder, 77–80
General Data Protection Regulation (GDPR), 60
generations, of mobile technology networks, 243
Glitch, 219
Goel, Vindu, 116
Good Old-Fashioned Artificial Intelligence (GOFAI), 224
Goodreads, 220
Google
    Colaboratory platform, 130
    hosted data environments, 146–147
    OK Google, 23
    platform lock-in, web archiving and, 50
    search engine optimization and, 144
Google Analytics, 143
Google Cardboard, 114–115
Google Cloud Platform, 231, 235
Google Daydream, 114–115
Google Fusion Tables, 99
Google Home, 23, 213
Google Knowledge Graph, 3
Google Open Gallery, 131–132

Index

Google Scholar, 125, 144
Google Sheets, 99, 219
government information, 32–33

H

hackers, 25
hardware, for VR, 114–115
Harper, Stephen, 51
Harry Potter and the Deathly Hallows (Rowling), 4–5
Harvard Law Review, 32
Harvard University's Institute for Quantitative Social Science, 145–146
harvesting, 45
headset
    for VR, 108
    VR, knowledge for purchase of, 114
    VR, logistics of incorporating, 113
health apps, 250
health considerations, 113–114
Health Sciences Library at the University of North Carolina at Chapel Hill, 96
Hennig, N., 246
Hensley, Merinda Kaye, 128
Herbert, L., 243
Heritrix web crawler, 46, 48
Hesburgh Libraries, Notre Dame, 126, 131–133
Higgins, Devin
    on digital humanities tools, 128–129
    on text mining, 133–134
home automation
    description of, 18
    IoT devices, 19–20
    library use of IoT components for, 23–24
Honeycomb platform, 131–133
hosted data environments, 146–147
hosted solutions, 141
"How to Make a Twitter Bot with Google Spreadsheets" (Whalen), 215
Hsuanwei, Michelle Chen, 101
HTC Vive, 115
HTTPS Everywhere browser plug-in, 62
hybrid acquisition model, 251–252
hyperlinks, 30

I

IA
    See Internet Archive
iBeacons
    for library navigation, 26–27
    for library navigation/advertising, 22–23
    use of by stores, 18
IBM
    Simon (smartphone), 242
    Watson, 231
IDC, 244
If This Then That (IFTTT) online service
    bots for library instruction, 218
    for input from IoT devices, 18
    for IoT integration, 20–21
IIIF Image API
    function of, 184
    functionalities of, 191
    image returned by, 185, 186
    publication of, 190
IIIF viewer
    future community of IIIF-enabled institutions, 193
    library websites with, 189
    search and discovery through, 190
IIPC (International Internet Preservation Consortium), 44–45, 46
Image API
    See IIIF Image API
image recognition
    with ANNs, 230–231
    with Google Cloud Platform, 235
    ML in library, 234
images
    See digital images
imitation game, 225
IMLS
    See Institute of Museum and Library Services

Index

Immigration History Research Center Archives (IHRCA)
　digital publishing case study, 173–176
　purpose/work of, 170
　technology for project, 171, 172
"Impact of International Image Interoperability Framework (IIIF) on Digital Repositories" (Babcock & Di Cresce), 181–193
IMS Global Learning Consortium, 197
Incognito mode, 63
indexing, 144, 154
infographics
　information visualization and, 90
　for library advocacy, 97–98
information technology, 108
information visualization (IV)
　applications for, 91–92
　conclusion about, 103–104
　function of, 89–90
　future for IV/libraries, 100–103
　history of, 90–91
　for library advocacy, 97–98
　as library service, 96–97
　for library usage/public service data, 92–94
　for metadata/collections, 94
　tools for, 98–99
　tutorials on, 100
　vision, communication through, 91
　for visual search and browse, 94–96
　See also data visualizations
infrastructure, 48
innovation, 108–110
inside-out model
　costs reduction with, 176
　description of, 168
　sharing of digital materials in, 170
Institute of Museum and Library Services (IMLS)
　funding for privacy-protection projects, 69, 70
　privacy-protection policies/tools, 60

institutional challenges, for web archiving, 50–52
institutional repositories (IR)
　benefits of, 154
　current trends/future directions, 142–144
　DSpace, 139–140
　early adopters of, 141–142
　EPrints, 140
　function of, 137
　future directions for, 160–161
　research data, trends in, 144–146
　web archiving and, 37
intelligence
　artificial general intelligence, 232
　augmented intelligence, 233
　as part of consciousness, 223
　Turing test for AI, 225
interface
　of access repository, 156
　of DSpace, 139–140
　on mobile devices, future of, 248
International Children's Digital Library Foundation, 247
International Image Interoperability Framework (IIIF)
　definition of, 182–183
　early adopters of, 190–191
　future community of IIIF-enabled institutions, 192–193
　future trends for, 191–192
　how it works, 184–188
　impact on digital special collection repositories, 188–190
　need for, 181–182
　use cases, 188
International Internet Preservation Consortium (IIPC), 44–45, 46
International Standard Name Identifier International Agency, 8
International Standardization Organization (ISO) standards, 162
Internet
　bots developed for, 213–214

273

Internet (cont.)
  mobile technology, impact on libraries, 244–245
  mobile technology, practices for early adopters, 245–247
  user privacy protection, 59
Internet Archive (IA)
  large-scale web archiving efforts of, 48
  reference rot prevention, 36
  as tool for link rot, 33, 34
  Wayback Machine, 47
  web archiving work of, 35
Internet of Things (IoT)
  IOT-connected library of future, 26–27
  overview of, 17–18
  security concerns/privacy implications, 24–26
  technology of, 18–21
  uses of in libraries, 21–24
interoperability
  bots, 211–221
  IIIF, impact on digital repositories, 181–193
  with Learning Tools Interoperability, 197–207
  machine learning for libraries, 223–236
  mobile technology, 241–253
inventory control, 21–22
IoT
  See Internet of Things
IP address, 63, 64–65
IR
  See institutional repositories
Islandora
  Fedora and, 12–13
  IIIF and, 188, 189, 190
  for user interface on top of Fedora repository, 139
IT industry, 243–244
IV
  See information visualization

J

James Ford Bell Library (Bell Library)
  digital publishing case study, 173–176
  purpose/work of, 170
  technology for project, 172
JavaScript, 215
JavaScript Object Notation for Linked Data (JSON-LD), 6
JavaScript Object Notation (JSON) file
  for bots, 215
  manifest in form of, 186
  view of, 187
Jefferson, Charissa, 96
Jewish Heritage Project Navigator, 11
Jin Xiu Guo, 241–253, 259
Jobs, Steve, 243
Johnson, Daniel, 123–134, 259
Jones, Gwyneth, 23
journals
  institutional repositories, upload to, 160–161
  web as distribution channel for, 43–44
JSTOR, 76, 81–83

K

Kahle, Brewster, 30–31
Kain, Erik, 109
Kamada, Hitoshi, 124
Kelly, Elizabeth Joan, 89–104, 259–260
Kilton Library of Lebanon, New Hampshire, 67–68
Kingsborough Community College Library, 94
Koivisto, Joseph, 137–148, 260
Kyoto University Rare Materials Digital Archive, 191

L

Lampert, Cory, 10–11
Landis, Cliff, 3–14, 260
large-scale linked data, 7–10
latent Dirichlet allocation (LDA), 82–83
Lavin, Matthew J., 127

Index

learning
- LTI for learning analytics, 199–200
- meaning of, 223
- with mobile technology, future of, 247–250
- uncertainty/experience in teaching machines, 225–228
- *See also* machine learning

learning analytics, 199–200

learning management systems (LMS)
- EBSCO Curriculum Builder at Louisiana State University, 201–203
- Ex Libris Leganto at University of New South Wales, 203–205
- LibGuides at Utah State University, 205–206
- link preservation and, 36–37
- LTI, conclusion about, 206–207
- LTI for external tools for, 197
- LTI use cases for libraries, 198–200

Learning Tools Interoperability (LTI)
- benefits of, 206–207
- EBSCO Curriculum Builder at Louisiana State University, 201–203
- function of, 197
- Leganto at University of New South Wales, 203–205
- LibGuides at Utah State University, 205–206
- technical architecture of, 200–201
- use cases, 198–200

legal issues
- legal citations, 34
- legal decisions, reference rot and, 31–32
- Ravel Law visualizations of cases, 83–85
- references, Chesapeake Project for preservation of, 32

Leganto, Ex Libris, 203–205

Legrady, George, 94

Lessig, Lawrence, 31–32

Lewis, David, 233–234

LexisNexis
- Ravel Law, purchase of, 83
- Ravel Law visualizations, 76–77

LFI (Library Freedom Institute), 69, 70

LFP
- *See* Library Freedom Project

LibGuides, 205–206

librarians
- digital humanities in libraries, 126–128
- information visualization, functions of, 89–90
- IV and, future of, 100–103
- IV as library service, 96–97
- machine learning in library and, 233–234
- ML systems, interaction with, 234–235
- privacy education for, 70
- privacy-protection technology tools, early adopters of, 69
- privacy-protection tools, role in, 59–60
- as users of privacy-protection technology tools, 71
- VR, educating people about, 110
- VR, logistics of incorporating, 113–115
- web, views of, 43–44
- web archiving and, 37–38
- web archiving, institutional challenges of, 50–52
- web archiving, technical challenges for, 48–50

libraries
- bots in, 211–221
- bots in, conclusion about, 220–221
- digital humanities and, 124–125
- digital humanities, future of, 133–134
- digital humanities in, 126–128
- digital libraries field, changes in, 124
- digital publishing case study, 173–176
- digital publishing through third-party vendors, 167–170
- Internet of Things, use of, 18
- IoT, security/privacy concerns, 24–26
- IoT, use of in, 21–24
- IoT integration tools, 20–21
- IoT-connected library of future, 26–27
- IV and, future of, 100–103

Index

libraries (cont.)
    IV as library service, 96–97
    IV for advocacy, 97–98
    IV for metadata/collections, 94
    IV for usage/public service data, 92–94
    IV for visual search and browse, 94–96
    large-scale linked data in, 7–10
    link rot/web archiving and, 32–33
    LTI use cases for, 198–200
    machine learning in, 233–235
    media transformation with web and, 43–44
    mobile technology, future library and, 250–253
    mobile technology, future of, 247–250
    mobile technology, impact of, 244–245
    privacy-protection technology tools and, 60–61, 69–71
    reference rot prevention and, 36–37
    Tor in, program for, 67–68
    virtual reality, demand for, 107–108
    virtual reality in, 108–110
    virtual reality in future and, 116–117
    visualized interfaces, tools for creation of, 85–86
    VR, logistics of incorporating, 113–115
    VR in, possibilities for, 110–113
    web archiving and, 37–38
    web archiving, ethical issues, 54
    web archiving, institutional challenges of, 50–52
"Libraries and Information Visualization: Application and Value" (Kelly), 89–104
library and information science (LIS) programs, 101
Library Coalition, 133
Library Freedom Institute (LFI), 69, 70
Library Freedom Project (LFP)
    privacy-protection policies/tools, 60, 69
    resources of, 71
    Tor in libraries program, 67–68
library instruction, bots for, 218

Library of Congress
    archive of tweets, 48
    BIBFRAME from, 7–9
    "Chronicling America" newspaper archive, 126
    Labs website, LC for Robots page, 217–218
    MODS, 138
    Twitter archive at, 53
library service, IV as, 96–97
library usage data, 92–94
library users
    See users
licensing, 173–174
Liebert, June, 31, 34
Liebler, Raizel, 31, 34
lifelogging, 101, 103
lighting, 23–24
linear model, 226–227
link resolvers, 30
link rot
    conclusion about, 37–38
    definition of, 30
    in early days of web, 29–30
    libraries and, 32–33
    link resolvers for, 30
    prevention, future of, 36–37
    scope of problem, 30–32
    solutions for, 33–35
"Link Rot, Reference Rot, and Link Resolvers," 29–38
Linked Jazz Network Visualization Tool, 11
Linked Jazz project, 11
linked open data
    in digital repositories, 142
    extra-special collections, 10–12
    large-scale linked data in libraries, 7–10
    overview of, 3–7
    research in future, 13–14
    tools for, 12–13
"Linked Open Data in Libraries" (Landis), 3–14

Index

LIS (library and information science) programs, 101
LMS
  See learning management systems
local history, VR for, 113
location-aware devices, 26–27
Lonog, Hoyt, 134
Los Angeles Times, 217
lossless compression, 157
Louisiana State University (LSU), 201–203, 207
LTI
  See Learning Tools Interoperability
LTI launch, 200
LTI tool consumer (TC), 200
LTI tool provider (TP), 200
LUNA Imaging Inc., 172
Lynch, Clifford
  on OA journals, 33
  speech by, 31
  on web archiving, 51–52

M

Maceli, Monica, 59–71, 260
Machine Learning for Language Toolkit (MALLET), 85
"Machine Learning for Libraries" (Darnell), 223–236
machine learning (ML)
  ANN, pattern recognition, 230–231
  augmented intelligence, 233
  concerns about AI, 232–233
  conclusion about, 236
  data in, 231–232
  description of, 223–224
  librarian interaction with ML systems, 234–235
  in libraries, future of, 250
  in library, as third technology wave, 233–234
  neural networks, modeling brain with, 228–230
  teaching machines using symbols, 224–225
  uncertainty/experience in, 225–228
machine translation
  with Google Cloud Platform, 235
  in library, 234
Macrina, Alison, 68
macros, 216
magazines, 44
Magnuson, Lauren
  on IIIF, 193
  information about, 260
  on LTI, 197–207
maintenance, of linked open data, 6
makerspace
  bots for library instruction in, 218
  IoT-specific workshops at library, 24
  library as novel technology space, 70
  VR in library and, 111–112
malicious content, 217
MALLET (Machine Learning for Language Toolkit), 85
malware, 60
Manakin framework, 140
Mandell, Laura, 128
manifest, 187–188, 189
MAP (Metadata Application Profile), 9
MARC records, 175
MarcEdit, 216
Margulies, 34
Mary Washington University, 130
master files, 172, 173
Matomo, 143–144
Mauldin, Sarah K. C., 100
"Maximizing Assets and Access through Digital Publishing: Opportunities and Implications for Special Collections" (Engseth & Ragnow), 167–177
McAndrew, Chuck, 68
McCartney, Paul, 112
Mellon Foundation, 133
Memento links
  function of, 34–35

Index

Memento links (cont.)
  reference rot prevention, 36
  of web resources, 37
Mentor Public Library of Ohio, 216
Merge VR, 114–115
metadata
  for access repository material, 155
  for archival repositories, 161–162
  for digital repositories, 159, 164
  digital repositories, trends in, 142–144
  information visualization for, 94
  for large-scale linked data in libraries, 7–10
  for linked open data, 5–6
  for preservation repository materials, 157
  research in future with linked open data, 13–14
  web archiving considerations, 47
Metadata Application Profile (MAP), 9
Metadata Object Description Schema (MODS), 138
Microsoft
  in PDA market, 242
  platform lock-in, web archiving and, 50
  virtual assistant for Cortana, 213
Mindmeister, 99
Mirador viewer
  IIIF use cases, 188, 189
  images in, 183
Mirai botnet, 25
misinformation, 217
Mitchell, Tom M., 224
ML
  See machine learning
mobile infrastructure, 249
mobile learning, 245
mobile technology
  definition of, 241
  early adopters of, 245–247
  future library with, 250–253
  future trend of, 247–250
  history of development of, 241–243
  impact on IT industry, 243–244
  impact on libraries, 244–245
  networks, generations of, 243
  "Mobile Technology" (Xu & Jin), 241–253
  mobile users, 252–253
  mobile-dependent people, 245
MODS (Metadata Object Description Schema), 138
Moodle, 198, 201, 204
Morgan, Eric Lease, 134
Morrone, Melissa, 69
Motorola, 242
Murray Hill Middle School Library, Maryland, 23

N

Nadella, Satya, 214
named entity recognition, 85–86
Named Entity Recognizer (NER), 85–86
National Archives and Records Administration (NARA), 162, 171
National Digital Stewardship Alliance (NDSA), 146
National Library of France, 191
National Library of Israel, 191
National Library of Norway, 191
National Science Foundation (NSF), 144–145
Natural Language Processing (NLP), 85
natural-language processing, 234
navigation, 26–27
NDSA (National Digital Stewardship Alliance), 146
Neal, James, 235
needs assessment
  for privacy-protection technology tools, 61
  for web archiving program, 45–46
Neil, Alison, 203–204
NER (Named Entity Recognizer), 85–86
networks, security tools for, 63–66
neural networks, 228–230
New York Public Library, 214, 247

New York Times
    on Facebook and VR, 116
    Google Cardboard and, 114
    NYT Politics Bot, 217
New York University (NYU), 69
news, preservation systems for, 31
news organizations, 36
newspapers, 44, 126
Nielson, Jakob, 29
NLP (Natural Language Processing), 85
NMC Horizon Report: 2013 Higher Education Edition (Johnson et al.), 246
NMC Horizon Report: 2014 Library Edition (Johnson, Becker, Estrada, & Freeman), 246
North Carolina State University Libraries
    data visualization workshops, 100
    IoT-specific workshop at, 24
Notre Dame Center for Civil and Human Rights, 132
Notre Dame's Hesburgh Libraries, 126, 131–133
NSF (National Science Foundation), 144–145
"NYC Digital Safety: Privacy & Security" initiative, 69
NYPL Postcard Bot, 217

O

OAIS (Open Archival Information System), 162
OAuth, 200
Oculus Rift, 115
Oculus VR, 109
OERs
    See open educational resources
Olney, Austin, 107–117, 260–261
Omeka
    Honeycomb platform and, 131
    IIIF use cases, 189
    Omeka S, 12
omnidirectional content, 112, 116

Online Computer Library Center (OCLC)
    BiblioGraph.net extension, 10
    ContentDM, 141
open access, 154
open access (OA) journals, 33
Open Archival Information System (OAIS), 162
Open Archives Initiative Protocol for Metadata Harvesting (OAI-PMH), 160
open data
    See linked open data
open educational resources (OERs)
    adoption of, LTI and, 202–203
    from institutional repositories, 154
    LTI applications for lower costs, 206–207
Open Graph, 9–10
open licensing, 6
open source
    digital repositories, early adopters of, 141
    repository systems, 138–140
OpenAI movement, 235
OpenML movement, 235
outreach, 176, 218
outsourcing, 45–46
OWL (Web Ontology Language) vocabulary, 5
ownership
    access repository materials and, 156
    of data, 232
Oxford University, 191

P

Palm Computing, 242
Pandorabots, 219
partnerships
    archival repositories and, 163
    digital publishing case study, 173–174
    See also collaboration
password managers, 66
patch crawl, 47
pattern recognition, 230–231

Index

Pattuelli, Cristina, 11
paywall, 173–174
PC Part Picker, 115
PDA, 242
Perma.cc
    reference rot prevention, 36
    as tool for link rot, 33, 34
    web archiving work of, 35
personal assistants
    bots for library instruction, 218
    development of, 213
personalization
    accessibility issues, 102–103
    with LTI, 199, 207
    privacy issues, 103
Pew Research Center, 217, 245
Philips, 20
pie chart, 75
Piktochart, 99
planetary scanning systems, 172
platform lock-in, 50
platforms
    AMD partnerships with, 172–173
    bots, interaction with, 215
    for data repositories, 145–146
    digital humanities/digital exhibit platforms, tools for, 128–130
    for digital publishing, 169, 170
    Honeycomb platform, 131–133
    IIIF interoperability and, 189–190
    platform lock-in, web archiving and, 50
    See also digital repositories
Playfair, William, 75
PlayStation VR, 115
plug-ins, 61–63
Posner, Miriam, 130
POWRR (Preserving Digital Objects with Restricted Resources), 53
predictive analytics, 102
Presentation API
    audiovisual materials and, 191–192
    function of, 184
    manifest, 186
    publication of, 190
preservation
    data repositories for, 145
    digital repositories for, 153–154
    link rot, solutions for, 33–35
    link rot/web archiving and, 32–33
    reference rot/link rot and, 31
    in web archiving, 45
preservation copies
    of digital file, 153–154
    uncompressed/lossless compression, 157
preservation repositories
    function of, 153–154
    future directions for, 161
    key features of, 156–159
Preserving Digital Objects with Restricted Resources (POWRR), 53
printers, 24
privacy
    always-on assistants and, 23
    information visualization and, 103
    IoT's implications for, 24–26
Privacy Badger, 62
privacy-protection technology tools
    for account credentials/data, 66–67
    IMLS support for early adopters, 69
    librarian's role in explaining, 59–60
    libraries of future of, 69–71
    libraries' role in, 60–61
    security while traversing networks, 63–66
    Tor in libraries, 67–68
    for web browsing/browser safety, 61–63
"Privacy-Protection Technology Tools: Libraries and Librarians as Users, Contributors, and Advocates" (Maceli), 59–71
probability, 225–228
processing power, 115
professional development, 101
programming languages, 200
Project Counter, 143

Index

Proteus VR Labs, 113
public service data, 92–94
publishers
    on Apple's e-book platform, 246–247
    web archiving, collaboration for, 52
    See also vendors
publishing
    digital content through third-party vendors, 168–170
    by digital repositories, 147
    See also digital publishing
Python, 130, 215

Q

quality control, 47

R

radio telephony, 241–242
Ragnow, Marguerite, 167–177, 261
RAMP (Repository Analytics and Metrics Portal), 143
rapid capture, 171–172
Ravel Law
    visual interface of, 76–77
    visualizations of court cases, 83–85
RDA (Resource Description and Access), 8
RDF (Resource Description Framework), 6, 142
RealAudio, 49
Reclaim Hosting, 130
recommender systems, 232
redundant backups, 158
reference rot
    conclusion about, 37–38
    with content drift/link rot, 30
    legal implications for, 31–32
    prevention, future of, 36–37
    in scholarly communication, 31
    solutions for, 33–35
RelFinder, 7
Renaissance Computing Institute, 96
repositories/access
    digital libraries portfolio, 123–134

digital publishing, 167–177
digital repositories, 153–165
digital repositories, systems perspective, 137–148
Repository Analytics and Metrics Portal (RAMP), 143
repository systems
    DSpace, 139–140
    EPrints, 140
    Fedora 4, 138–139
    hosted solutions, 141
research
    data, trends in, 144–146
    IIIF's impact on, 192–193
    scholarly output, digital library and, 125
    virtual research ecosystems, 147–148
research data repositories, 138, 144–146
"Research Help" tool, 205, 206
research journal, 43–44
Research Libraries Group (RLG), 162
researchers
    digital access repositories and, 155–156
    web archives access for, 53
    web archiving, collaboration for, 52
"Resilience and Engagement in an Era of Uncertainty" (Lynch), 31
Resistbot, 220
resource description, 7–10
Resource Description and Access (RDA), 8
Resource Description Framework (RDF), 6, 142
resource discovery, 13–14
responsibility, for web archiving, 50–51
responsive web design, 245
RFID tags
    in future library collections, 27
    for Internet of Things, 18–21
    IoT, library use of, 21–24
    for libraries, benefits of, 21–22
Rhodes, John S., 29–30, 38
Rhodes, Sarah, 32
RightsStatements.org, 9
risks, 113

Index

RLG (Research Libraries Group), 162
Robert Morris College, 216
robot, 212
robot.txt files, 52
Rosenfeld, Jennifer, 94, 96
routing, 65
Rowling, J. K., 4–5
Russell, John E., 128

S

safety recommendations, 113–114
SAGE Publishing, 171
"sameAs" predicate, 5
Samsung Gear VR, 114–115
Samvera, 12–13, 139
Sanchez, Anthony, 130
Santa Rosa Junior College, 202
scans, 171–172
Schema.org, 9–10
scholarly communication
    in evolution of digital library, 125
    institutional repositories for, 142, 154
    institutional repositories, future directions for, 160–161
    libraries as publishers of, 133
    reference rot in, 31
School of Electronics and Computer Science at the University of Southampton, 140
scope, 46
Scott, Dan, 13
search
    Gale Topic Finder, 77–80
    IV for visual search and browse, 94–96
    JSTOR's Topic**graph**, 81–83
    with linked open data, 13–14
    Ravel Law visualizations of court cases, 83–85
    visual search tools, future of, 101–102
    in web archiving process, 46
search engine optimization (SEO), 144
Seattle Central Library, 92, 93, 94
security
    IoT and, 24–26
    of mobile devices, 249
    of preservation repository, 157
Sedol, Lee, 231
SeeCollections (web application), 94
seed, 46, 47
selection, 45
self-checkout systems, 21–22
SELIDA project, 20
semantic search, 4
SEO (search engine optimization), 144
services
    data for discovery, 75–86
    information visualization, libraries and, 89–104
    privacy-protection technology tools, 59–71
    virtual reality, 107–117
Sewell, Jeanette Claire, 211–221, 261
shelf organization, 22
Shevat, Amir, 219
Shneiderman, Ben, 76
Simon (smartphone), 242
Siri, 23, 213
Sirico, 34
Sisk, Matthew, 134
Slack, 214, 220
"smart" light bulbs, 20
smartphones
    history of, 242–243
    impact on IT industry, 243–244
    IoT, library use of, 22, 23
    personal assistants/apps for, 213
    practices for early adopters, 245–246
SMO (social media optimization), 144
SNAC (Social Networks and Archival Context) Cooperative, 11–12
social media
    bots, misinformation spread by, 217
    bots for, 213–214
    dynamic content, as challenge for web archiving, 49

preservation of materials, 36
VR and, 109
web as venue for new media
    objects, 44
social media optimization (SMO), 144
social networking
    data, ownership of, 232
    impact of mobile technology on, 244
    institutional repositories and, 161
    VR in future and, 116
Social Networks and Archival Context
    (SNAC) Cooperative, 11–12
software
    for archival repositories, 161
    bots and, 215
    for data repositories, 145–146
    for digital publishing, 170
    for digital repositories, 159, 163
    IoT integration and, 20–21
    IoT security concerns and, 25–26
    for link rot, 33–35
    privacy-protection tools, 59
    that supports digital libraries, 123
    for web archiving, 45–46, 52
Southwick, Silvia, 10–11
SPARQL (PARQL Protocol and RDF Query
    Language), 6
special collections
    digital publishing case study, 173–176
    digital publishing, conclusion about,
        176–177
    digital publishing through third-party
        vendors, 168–170
    IIIF and, 182, 188–190
    inside-out model and, 168
    investments in, 181
    library collaboration with faculty for,
        127–128
    linked open data in, 10–12
    opportunities for sharing, 167
    tools for linked open data, 12–13
speech-to-text tools, 234
Spotlight, 131, 132

Springshare LibGuides, 205–206
staffing issues, 174–175
Stager, Gary, 111
standards
    IIIF, 181–193
    as technical challenge for web archiving,
        48–49
Stanford University
    IIIF initiated by, 190–191
    Named Entity Recognizer, 85–86
statistics
    as experience for machine learning,
        225–228
    institutional repository, usage statistics
        for, 142–144
    IV for library usage/public service data,
        92–94
STEM, 192
stereoscope, 108–109
storage
    for archival repositories, 161
    for digital assets, 173
    for digital publishing, 170
    for digital repositories, 164
    preservation repositories for, 156–159
Storymap JS, 99
Student Messenger, 246
students
    LTI applications for lower course
        materials costs, 206–207
    mobile technology use by, 244–245
subject-area repositories, 137
Suomela, Todd, 43–54, 261
Superintelligence: Paths, Dangers, Strategies
    (Bostrom), 232
supervised learning, 227
symbols, 224–225

T

Tableau, 99
tablets
    Apple iPad, 242–243
    direct manipulation, 76

tablets (cont.)
  IoT devices and, 20, 24
  mainstream use of, 246
Tails, 66
TDR (Trusted Digital Repository), 162–163, 164
teacher noise, 232
teachers
  See faculty
technical architecture, of LTI, 200–201
technical infrastructure, 45–46
technologists, 52
technology
  for digital publishing, 169–173, 177
  of Internet of Things, 18–21
  libraries and innovation, 108–110
  LTI technical architecture, 200–201
  predictions/outcomes, xi–xii
  waves of technology in libraries, 233–234
temporal context information, 34–35
Tensorflow, 235
Texas A&M University, 246
text clustering, 85
text encoding, 127–128
text mining, xi
textbooks, 206–207
therapy, 112
third platform
  future of, 249
  switch to, 244
third-party vendors
  digital publishing case study, 173–176
  digital publishing through, conclusion about, 176–177
  publishing digital content through, 167–170
3-D printing
  IIIF and, 192
  IV as library service, 96–97
  of VR headset, 115
three-part statements, 4
TimeMapper, 99

tools
  bot tool kit, 219
  for digital humanities, 128–130
  for fixity checks, 158
  Honeycomb platform, 131–133
  for information visualization, 98–99
  for IoT integration, 20–21
  for IoT use in libraries, 21–24
  link rot, solutions for, 33–35
  for linked open data, 12–13
  privacy-protection technology tools, 59–71
  for visualized interfaces, 85–86
Top Technologies Every Librarian Needs to Know (Varnum), xi–xii
Topic Finder, Gale, 77–80
Topic**graph**, JSTOR, 81–83
Tor
  anonymity network, 65
  in libraries, program for, 67–68
  for network security, 65–66
  relays, library privacy protection contributions, 71
  relays, routing traffic through, 65
T-PEN, 188
TRAC (Trustworthy Repositories Audit & Certification: Criteria and Checklist), 162
Tracery library, 219
tracking, 70
training
  digital-privacy training in libraries, 69
  for IV tools, 98, 100
  of library staff in VR, 114
  for LTI tools, 206
  See also education
triples
  description of, 4–5
  standards for expressing, 6
Trump administration, 32–33
Trusted Digital Repository (TDR), 162–163, 164

Index

Trustworthy Repositories Audit & Certification: Criteria and Checklist (TRAC), 162
Tufte, Edward, 91
Tukey, John, 90
Turing, Alan, 225
Turing test, 225
tutorials, 100
Twitter
    API rate limit, 215
    archive at Library of Congress, 48, 53
    bot tools for, 219
    bots on, 214, 217

U

UBlock Origin, 62
uncertainty, 225–228
Underwood, Ted, 134
Uniform Resource Identifier (URI)
    IIIF functions and, 184
    link rot, prevention of, 14
    Linked Jazz Network Visualization Tool, 11
    linked open data in triple databases, 5
    reference rot in scholarly communication, 31
Uniform Resource Locator (URL)
    link rot/reference rot and, 30–32
    LTI for access to library materials, 198
    permanent, for link rot prevention, 34
    reference rot prevention, 36
    in web archiving process, 46
United States, data protection laws in, 60
University of Arizona Libraries, 130
University of Brighton, 246
University of California, Davis, 94, 96
University of California, Los Angeles, 130
University of Central Florida Library, 246
University of Houston, 96
University of Illinois at Urbana–Champaign Library, 8
University of Maryland, 247
University of Massachusetts, 85
University of Michigan Library and Press, 133
University of Minnesota (UMN) Libraries
    digital delivery modes, platforms, products, 169–170
    digital publishing case study, 173–176
    technology for digital conversion projects, 170–173
University of Nebraska–Lincoln, 216
University of Nevada, Las Vegas (UNLV), 10–11
University of New South Wales, 203–205
University of North Carolina, 130
University of North Carolina at Chapel Hill, 94, 96
University of Patras Library, Greece, 20
University of Toronto Libraries (UTL)
    IIIF, how it works, 184–188
    IIIF early adopters, 190–191
    IIIF projects, 182
    IIIF use cases, 188
    impact of IIIF on digital special collection repositories, 188–190
University of Toronto Scarborough, 7
University of Virginia, 138
University of Wisconsin–Milwaukee, 100
unsupervised learning, 228
upload
    of digital repository materials, 159
    of publications into institutional repository, 160–161
URI
    See Uniform Resource Identifier
URL
    See Uniform Resource Locator
US Supreme Court, 34
usage statistics, 142–144
use cases
    IIIF, 188–190
    LTI, 197, 198–200
user interface
    See interface

Index

users
    customer relationship management in future libraries, 250–251
    data, ownership of, 232
    future library end users, 252–253
    LTI technical architecture and, 200
    personalization with LTI, 199
    privacy, information visualization and, 103
    privacy protection for, libraries and, 70–71
    privacy protection, lack of, 59
    VR, risks/health considerations, 113–114
    VR in library and, 110–113
Utah State University, 205–206

V

Vandegrift, Micah, 124
Varian, Hal, 91–92
vendors
    collaboration for digital repositories, 163
    digital publishing case study, 173–176
    digital publishing through, conclusion about, 176–177
    publishing digital content through third-party vendors, 167–170
VeraCrypt, 66
Viral Texts Project, 126
virtual conferencing rooms, 116
Virtual International Authority File (VIAF), 8
virtual library
    in evolution of digital library, 125
    users, 252
virtual private network (VPN), 63–65, 71
"Virtual Reality: Out of This World" (Olney), 107–117
virtual reality (VR)
    demand for, 107–108
    description of, 108
    development of, 108–109
    future of in libraries, 116–117
    in libraries, logistics of incorporating, 113–115
    in libraries, possibilities for, 110–113
    libraries and innovation, 108–110
virtual research ecosystems, 147–148
virtual spaces, 111
Viscoll, 189
vision
    accessibility of IV, 102–103
    communication through, 91
The Visual Display of Quantitative Information (Tufte), 91
visual perception, 91
visual search tools, 101–102
visualization
    history of, 90–91
    Linked Jazz Network Visualization Tool, 11
    tools for creating, 7
    See also data visualizations; information visualization
visualized discovery interfaces
    development of, 76–77
    Gale Topic Finder, 77–80
    JSTOR's Topic**graph**, 81–83
    precursors to, 75–76
    Ravel Law visualizations, 83–85
    tools for creation of, 85–86
vocabularies
    of BiblioGraph.net, 10
    external relationship vocabularies, 11
    for resource description, 8
    of URIs, 5
voice-activated personal assistants, 213, 218
voice-recognition technology, 26
Voyant Tools, 85, 99
VPN (virtual private network), 63–65, 71
VR
    See virtual reality
VR viewers, 114–115

W

waiver, 113–114
WARC (Web ARChive) file format, 46–47
Watters, Audrey, 33

Waugh, Mike
  on access to library materials, 198
  EBSCO Curriculum Builder at Louisiana State University, 201–202, 207
web address, 5
web advertising, 50
Web ARChive (WARC) file format, 46–47
web archives
  accessibility of, 53
  conclusion about, 53–54
  definition of, 44–45
  institutional challenges for, 50–52
  starting/operating, 45–47
  technical challenges for librarians, 48–50
  web, librarian views of, 43–44
web archiving
  automated, 36
  conclusion about, 37–38
  decentralized, link rot and, 30
  definition of, 44–45
  link rot, libraries and, 32–33
  link rot, solutions for, 33–35
  reference rot prevention, 36–37
web browser, 61–63
web crawler
  limited number of, 48
  standards and, 49
  web archiving process, 46–47
Web Ontology Language (OWL) vocabulary, 5
web seeds, 48, 53
websites
  full-service, Reclaim Hosting for, 130
  mobile technology and, 245
  responsive websites for mobile technology, 248
"Websites That Heal" (Rhodes), 29–30, 38
Webster, Jessica Wagner, 153–165, 261–262
Westgard, Joshua A., 137–148, 262
Whalen, Zach, 215, 219
"What Is Digital Humanities and What's It Doing in the Library?" (Vandegrift), 124

Wheatstone, Charles, 108–109
White, Justin M., 29–38, 262
Whitehouse.gov, 32
Wikidata, 3–4
Wikipedia
  bots, use of, 212
  link rot and, 32
  LTI application, 197
  Wikidata, linked open data, 3–4
Wilson Center, 94, 95
Wingfield, Nick, 116
Woodson Research Center Special Collections and Archives, 217
WordPress, 33
workflow automation tools, 20–21
workshops, on information visualization, 100
World War II, 241–242
World Wide Web
  views of from librarian perspective, 43–44
  in web archiving definition, 44–45
  See also Internet
WorldCat, 10

X

XML (Extensible Markup Language), 6
Xu, Gordon F., 241–253, 262

Y

Yale Centre for British Art, 192
Yale University, 127
Yewno, 77

Z

Zapier, 20–21
Zittrain, Jonathan, 31–32
Zuckerberg, Mark, 109

027 N

New top technologies every librarian needs to know

NEW BOOK